ENGLISH CISTERCIAN MONASTERIES AND THEIR PATRONS IN THE TWELFTH CENTURY

english
cistercian
monasteries
and their patrons
in the twelfth century

B E N N E T T D. H I L L

U N I V E R S I T Y   O F   I L L I N O I S   P R E S S

U R B A N A   C H I C A G O   L O N D O N

1968

Frontispiece: Fountains Abbey. Photographed by Sydney W. Newbery.

foR my fatheR anò motheR

What is man that . . . you have made
him a little less than the angels?

Psalm 8

preface

The history of the Cistercian Order in England is a very great subject, a subject that has attracted the interest of students not only of ecclesiastical history, but of economic, constitutional, and social change as well. For yet another consideration of this problem, I take inspiration from Macaulay's observation that "on all great subjects, much remains to be said." One reason for this study is that the relationship between Cistercian monasteries and their patrons has previously gone unobserved. The connection between religious houses and their benefactors is important as one factor in the reciprocal dependence of religious and lay interests in the Middle Ages, or, more broadly, in the relations of Church and State. Secondly, the Congregation of Savigny which was united with the Cistercian Order in 1148, and which had an impact on the White Monks as significant as it was serious, has been almost entirely ignored by students of monastic history. And, thirdly, it is now a commonplace to medievalists that in the age of the Gregorian Reform movement, the objectives of the monks were by no means identical with those of the papal Gregorians at Rome. Nevertheless, as is illustrated by the lives and activities of the English Cistercians, the monks made a heavy contribution to the success, at least the moral success, of the program of the Curial Gregorian reformers.

This little book is intended as a study of certain aspects of the Cistercian Order in the first century of its history in England. Although the book's central theme is a constitutional problem, in a broader sense it is concerned with the economic and political influences which shaped the spiritual bases of a monastic institute. The research which composes it was begun under the supervision of Professor Joseph R. Strayer of Princeton University, to whom I cannot begin to express my gratitude. His direction, his encouragement, and the understanding which has ennobled his wisdom place me eternally in his debt. Like most academic writers, I am able to go only a few steps beyond where others have led me, and I would be much at a loss if I were required to weigh exactly what other students have contributed to my work. Yet I must express my large debt to the writings of Dom David Knowles, formerly of Cambridge University, especially to his classic achievement, *The Monastic Order in England.* It is from this rich quarry that so many of us have gathered our little heap of stones. In the summer of 1962 Father Knowles was good enough to talk to me at length about this project, and I, *quondam novitius,* can especially appreciate his point of view. He provided me with some valuable information and gave me an introduction to Dr. Christopher Holdsworth of the University of London, who directed me to several interesting materials. Mr. R. W. Southern of All Souls College, Oxford, discussed several aspects of this book with me and steered me away from several dangerous suppositions and outright errors.

The idea from which this book developed was originally suggested to me by Professor Norman Cantor in a graduate seminar at Princeton University. I appreciate his advice and his continued interest in my work. Professor Ralph Giesey of the University of Iowa read the entire manuscript and gave me many valuable suggestions. I would also like to express my gratitude to the staff of the Reading Room of the British Museum for their courteous and very generous assistance; to Mlle. Marie-Thérèse d'Alverny of the Salle des Manuscrits in the Bibliothèque National whose knowledge of the source materials of Norman and Breton history saved me a great deal of time; to Mlle. Simone Pontoniée at the Institute de Recherche et d'Histoire des Textes in Paris who helped me to locate several manuscripts of the Congregation of Savigny; to Dom Anselm Strittmatter of St. Anselm's Abbey, Washington, D.C., and the Institute for Advanced

Study at Princeton for many bibliographical suggestions; and to Professor Peter V. Marinelli of the University of Toronto who made graceful stylistic recommendations. The Princeton Graduate School awarded me a Travelling Fellowship in 1962, and the University of Illinois Graduate Research Board at several critical moments generously supported my research. I am much indebted to Mr. Eugene Crook for his intelligent and conscientious assistance in helping me to prepare this book for publication and to Mrs. Sandra Boucher of the University of Illinois Press for her care and skill in editing. Any errors or shortcomings in this book are, of course, entirely my own.

Finally, I want to express my gratitude to my friend Donald W. Pfaff for his support, interest, and understanding.

ABBREVIATIONS FREQUENTLY CITED

Acta Sanctorum L. d'Achéry and J. Mabillon, eds., *Acta Sanctorum Ordinis S. Benedicti*, 9 vols. (Paris, 1668–1701).

A.H.R. *American Historical Review.*

Calendar of Documents J. H. Round, ed., *Calendar of Documents Preserved in France 918–1206*, vol. I (London, 1899).

D.N.B. *Dictionary of National Biography.*

E.H.D. D. C. Douglas, ed., *English Historical Documents*, vol. II (London, 1953).

E.H.R. *English Historical Review.*

E.Y.C. William Farrer, ed., *Early Yorkshire Charters*, vols. I, II, III (Edinburgh, 1914–23).

Histoire de Savigny A. Laveille, ed., *Histoire de la Congregation de Savigny par Dom Claude Auvry*, 3 vols., Société de l'histoire de Normandie, no. 30 (Rouen and Paris, 1896–99).

H.F. M. Bouquet, ed., *Recueil des historiens des Gaules et de la France*, vols. XII, XV, XXIII (Paris, 1840–1904).

M.O. Dom M. D. Knowles, *The Monastic Order in England* (corrected ed., Cambridge, 1950).

Monasticon W. Dugdale, ed., *Monasticon Anglicanum*, 6 vols., esp. vol. V (new ed., London, 1846).

Monuments Ph. Guignard, ed., *Les Monuments primitifs de la règle cistercienne* (Dijon, 1878).

P.L. J. P. Migne ed., *Patrologiae Latinae cursus completus*, vols. LXXV, CLXXI, CLXXXI, CLXXXII, CLXXXV, CLXXVIII, CXCV, CCIV (Paris, 1844–64).

P.U. W. Holtzmann, ed., *Papsturkunden in England*, in Abhandler Akademie der Wissenschaften in Göttingen, Philologisch-Historische Klasse, vol. I (1930–31), vol. II (1935), vol. III (1952).

Statuta	Dom J. M. Canivez, ed., *Statuta Capitulorum Generalium Ordinis Cisterciensis 1116–1220*, vol. I (Louvain, 1933).
T.R.H.S.	*Transactions of the Royal Historical Society.*
V.C.H.	*Victoria County Histories.*

contents

✠

introduction

the foundation of cîteaux

- Liberty is by no means an invitation to indifference or to irresponsible power; nor is it the promise of unlimited well-being without a counterpart of toil and effort. It supposes application, perpetual effort, strict government of self, sacrifice in contingencies, civic and private virtues. It is therefore more difficult to live as a free man than to live as a slave, and that is why men so often renounce their freedom; for freedom is in its way an invitation to a life of courage, and sometimes of heroism, as the freedom of the Christian is an invitation to a life of sainthood.

Georges Lefebvre

Monasticism is, of course, a product of the East; and from the East came the fundamental ideas of Western monasticism. The monk is, first of all, a man who seeks God. He is a man who believes that he has been called by God to seek Him, and that because he was begun to seek God, he has already begun to find Him. Prayer, the means by which the monk seeks God, is the center and sole purpose of his life. The basic principle of early Christian monasticism lay in the intense desire of the individual for complete self-surrender to God combined at the same time with a yearning

1

for the isolation wherein to seek Him. Some Christians of the apostolic Church, intent on the exact following of the gospel teachings, first in the East, Africa, and Asia Minor, and then in the West, saw no alternative to the corruptions of city life except a total renunciation of the material things of this world. Therefore, the monastic vocation in its primitive form was the quest of God through the pursuit of moral and spiritual perfection of the individual soul in the desert. The early Christian monk and theologian John Cassian (360–435) expressed this goal as "the world forgetting by the world forgot. Every monk who looks for the perfect way aims at uninterrupted prayerfulness."[1] Pope Gregory the Great (590–604), whose understanding and interpretation of the monastic life is certainly typical of the Church Fathers, is emphatic. By definition, the nature of the monastic life, he maintained, required total separation from the world. The monastery is an isolated port where the monk devotes himself in quiet security to the praise of God and to contemplation in a life of prayer and mortification.[2] The monastic vocation, as Thomas Merton has expressed it, "is distinguished even from other religious vocations by the fact that he [the monk] is essentially and exclusively dedicated to seeking God, rather than seeking souls for God."[3] Almost from the time of the death of Christ the monastic way has been one approach to the Christian life, one aspect of the Christian idea of reform. Monasticism was an institution which the

[1] "The Conferences of Cassian" in O. Chadwick, ed., *Western Asceticism* (Philadelphia, 1958), p. 214. See also E. Pichery, ed., *Jean Cassien: Conferences*, I (Paris, 1955), 78–108; H. B. Workman, *The Evolution of the Monastic Ideal* (rev. ed., Boston, 1962), pp. 121–122; Dom H. Van Zeller, *The Benedictine Idea* (Springfield, Ill., 1959), pp. 3–4; Dom M. D. Knowles, *The Monastic Order in England* (corrected ed., Cambridge, 1950), pp. 11–12, 683; G. Ladner, *The Idea of Reform* (Cambridge, Mass., 1959), pp. 319–340, for a remarkably learned treatment of this idea in the early Church; T. Merton, *The Waters of Silence* (London, 1950), pp. 4–5, and the same author's *The Silent Life* (New York, 1957), pp. vii–viii.
[2] *Sancti Gregorii Magni Vita*, by Paul the Deacon, in J. P. Migne, *Patrologia Latinae cursus completus* (Paris, 1844–64), LXXV, col. 43.
[3] Merton, *The Silent Life*, p. viii.

West imported from the East and sought to mold and adapt to its own intellectual and physical climate.

In order to understand the origins of the Cistercian Order we should remember that the Cistercian ideal grew out of, in fact was a reaction to, what have felicitously been called the Benedictine centuries. For over five hundred years, from about 550 to 1050, almost all organized religious life in northwestern Europe, from Sicily to Scotland and from Spain to Saxony, meant monasticism and, to a very great extent, Benedictine monasticism. For the source of so pervasive an influence, attractive to so many diverse peoples, we are led back to a small volume, in size so disproportionate to its effect, *The Rule of St. Benedict.* This book laid equal stress on a trinity of prayer, work, and study; and it was stamped with the characteristics (those of its Roman author) of practicality, adaptability, simplicity, and moderation. But St. Benedict had not foreseen the tremendous expansion of his idea, its relation to the coming feudal order, and the accumulation by some monasteries of great wealth. The result was, by the ninth century, the demand for reform.

The significant monastic reform movements which originated in Gaul between 800 and 1000 — those of Benedict of Aniane (d. 821) in the ninth century and Cluny in the tenth century — had very similar objects; in fact the Cluniac movement may be said to have developed from that of Benedict of Aniane. Both stressed the cultivation of a personal spiritual life, essentially through greater emphasis on the liturgical activity of the choir, with a corresponding reduction of manual labor. Both had as an essential aim independence of permanent lay control. And, both of these movements promoted the dignity of the Church and raised the moral standards of the religious vocation higher than they had been since the days of the apostolic Church.[4] But St. Benedict of Aniane

4 The most comprehensive treatment of the reforms associated with St. Benedict of Aniane is that of Dom Philibert Schmitz, *Histoire de l'ordre de Saint-Benoît,* tome I (rev. ed., Maredsous, Belgium, 1948), 102–116, esp. 110–116; see also L. J. Lekai, *The White Monks* (Okauchee, Wisc., 1953), pp. 8–10, and Watkin Williams, "St. Benedict of Aniane," *The Downside Review,* LIV (1936), 357–374. The best recent appreciation

had depended for the application of his reforms on the support of the Holy Roman Emperor, and with the disintegration of the Carolingian dynasty, his work collapsed. Likewise, while Cluny became famous for her artistic and liturgical splendors, and although she exerted a strongly revitalizing influence on the monastic life and eventually on the spiritual life of the entire Church in the eleventh century, there can be no doubt that her enormous wealth and political power within the feudal order were in gross contravention of the spirit and letter of the *Rule of St. Benedict.*

As the monastic institution originated in Italy, so too new reforming measures began there, this time in the northern part of the peninsula, and shortly before the year 1000. At first individuals or small groups left organized society or long-established monasteries to live under conditions of extreme simplicity or in small groups under no real authority. These new ascetic impulses inaugurated a spiritual revival which differed from previous reforms in two significant ways: they expressed a desire to return to an eremitical (as opposed to coenobitic) penitential life, and they consciously emphasized the very austere ascetic vision of the Desert Fathers of the East.[5] By the middle of the eleventh century these new currents had gained the nature of a widespread spiritual movement in the area between Rome and the Alps. In the last quarter of that century all of Western Europe, except for the territories under the control of the dukes of Normandy, was under weak secular governments. The times, therefore, were propitious, and the various monastic movements were also movements of independence from secular control. Given the well-known revolutionary pretensions of

of the piety and fervor that developed from these movements is Dom Jean Leclercq, F. Vandenbroucke, and L. Bouyer, *La Spiritualité du moyen âge* (Paris, 1960), pp. 100–107, esp. 102–105, and pp. 136–141.
[5] Very few aspects of this eleventh-century monastic development have been studied. See Gioacchino Volpe, *Movimenti religiosi e sette ereticali nella societa medievale italiana* (Florence, 1926); O. J. Blum, *St. Peter Damien: His Teachings on the Spiritual Life* (Washington, D. C., 1947); for the activities of some pre-Gregorian reformers, see the fundamental A. Fliche, *La Réforme grégorienne* (Louvain, 1924–27), I, 24–25, 445–446.

Pope Gregory VII (1073–85) about the "freedom of the Church," these monastic impulses had the full support of the papacy.[6] At the same time, within the monasteries the desire was being expressed for a more austere form of religious life than was currently available in the rich abbeys of Gaul. Against this background of political instability and ecclesiastical ambitions, the Cistercian Order had its beginnings.

• In 1098 twenty monks followed the Abbot Robert from the rich monastery of Molesmes in Burgundy into the forest of Cîteaux. The name Cîteaux itself suggests the nature of the original site where the famous monastery was to begin: in its older form, *Cisteaux* or *Cistercium* seems to be derived from *Cisternae*, which DuCange explains as a marsh with stagnant pools, or *cistels*, or *citeals* or *cisteauls* — Old French words meaning marsh rushes.[7] The monks who settled there intended to establish a house in poverty and seclusion governed by a strict interpretation of the *Rule of St. Benedict*.[8] For a short time all went well. But the third abbot of Cîteaux, the Englishman Stephen Harding (d. 1134), was soon faced with the old problems: the acquisition of great property and treasures, the presence of powerful benefactors, and the desire among some of the monks for a mitigation of the *Rule*. Stephen decreed that in every department of life the utmost simplicity should exist, and he insisted that the *Rule of St. Benedict* be observed *ad litteram*. In spite of opposition from many of his monks, and although the community experienced extreme hardships and poverty, the abbot held to his course.[9] He insisted on the observance of an Eastern-like

[6] Fliche, *La Réforme grégorienne*, I, 41–43.
[7] Charles du Fresne DuCange, ed., *Glossarium Mediae et Infimae Latinitatis* (Niort, 1883–87), II, 344.
[8] *Carta Caritatis* in Dom J. M. Canivez, ed., *Statuta Capitulorum Generalium Ordinis Cisterciensis 1116–1220*, I (Louvain, 1933), xxvii. "Nunc vero volumus illisque precipimus ut *regulam beati Benedicti per omnia observent* sicuti in novo monasterio observatur."
[9] The entire account of the departure from Molesmes and the early days at Cîteaux is given in the *Exordium Parvum*, which is printed in Ph. Guignard, ed., *Les Monuments primitifs de la règle cistercienne* (Dijon, 1878), pp. 79–84. See also W. A. Parker-Mason, "The Beginnings of the Cistercian Order," T.R.H.S., New Series, XIX (1905), 169–200.

asceticism in the regulations at Cîteaux. Because of meager harvests which brought the community close to starvation, a contagious disease which sharply reduced the number of the monks, and above all because of a serious lack of vocations, the collapse of the foundation seemed imminent when, in 1112, the young Bernard arrived with thirty of his relatives and friends. In 1115, with the foundation of Clairvaux, the growth of the Order began.

The rapid and astonishing expansion of the Cistercians and the influence which they exercised throughout most of the twelfth century on the public life of the Church and the spiritual life of individuals — an influence at first due largely to the personality and activity of Bernard of Clairvaux — these alone would give the Cistercians a significance possessed by no other contemporary religious body. The Cistercians, however, have a further importance for the history of their times and for the history of the religious orders because they possessed a written constitution of great originality. Their constitution was consulted and imitated from the beginning, and strongly influenced the organization of all later monastic and religious orders.[10]

10 I am relying heavily here on Knowles, *M.O.*, pp. 208–212. The essential documents for the early history of Cîteaux are printed in Guignard, *Monuments*. The only important work which is not included in this volume is the *Exordium Magnum*, a long hagiographical account of the early Cistercian years, written in the late twelfth century. It is printed in Migne, *P.L.*, vol. CLXXXV. The *Carta Caritatis* is also in Canivez, *Statuta*, vol. I. Because of the accessibility of this last-mentioned volume, I refer to it throughout, rather than to Guignard. There are several good secondary accounts of the beginnings of the Cistercian Order; the best probably remains that of Dom Ursmer Berlière, "Les Origines de Cîteaux et l'ordre benedictin du XII siècle," *Revue d'histoire ecclésiastique*, I (1900), 253–290. See also A. King, *Cîteaux and Her Elder Daughters* (London, 1954), and the learned and still valuable P. G. Müller, *Cîteaux unter dem Abte Alberich* (Berlin, 1909). For the origins of the Cistercian lay brothers, the freshest treatment remains James S. Donnelly, *The Decline of the Medieval Cistercian Laybrotherhood* (New York, 1949), pp. 1–15. As with so many enigmatic problems in monastic history, we are indebted to Knowles for his penetrating treatment of the diplomatics of the early Cistercian sources. See his "The Primitive Cistercian Documents," in *Great Historical Enterprises and Problems in Monastic History* (London, 1963), pp. 198–222, which carves a clear and reason-

The laws, practices, and ideals of the Cistercian Order are to be found in the four documents which together make up its constitutions:

1. *Exordium Cistercienses Coenobii*, also called the *Exordium Parvum*. This is an account of the withdrawal from Molesmes and of the first years at Cîteaux. It was written by St. Stephen Harding.

2. *Consuetudines*. This contains a list of the customs for the monks and lay-brothers. It probably dates from the rule of Alberic, second abbot of Cîteaux, 1099–1109.

3. *Carta Caritatis*. This document is also the work of Stephen Harding. It legislated on the interrelations of the various houses and the election of all officials of the monasteries.

4. *Instituta*. This is a collection of the definitions of the General Chapters of the Order as codified beginning in 1134 and reaffirmed with additions in 1154.

To keep the political entanglements of the feudal world out of their lives, the Cistercians placed themselves directly under the authority of the pope or his legate. (It may be noted that the papal legate in France at the time of the beginnings of the Order was Hugh, Archbishop of Lyons, who was an intransigent, ultra-Gregorian reformer.) [11] The Cistercians

able path through the jungle of learned literature on early Cistercian legislation and history. In the tone of this monograph, however, Professor Knowles departs considerably from the gracious charity and Benedictine humility which for so long now we have associated with his impeccable scholarship. Cf. Hayden V. White's review in *Speculum*, XLI, no. 1 (1966), 146–147. In a recent and useful little study of the constitutional development of the religious orders, Knowles has written that the Cistercians constituted "in a true sense, and for the first time in Europe, a religious Order. . . ." See David Knowles, *From Pachomius to Ignatius: A Study in the Constitutional History of the Religious Orders* (Oxford, 1966), p. 27.

[11] Hugh, Archbishop of Lyons, was an inflexible champion of papal rights and completely opposed to the papacy's compromising in any way with secular rulers over the issues of the Gregorian Reform program. As papal legate in Gaul he was a vigorous enemy of abuses and exerted a strong influence on Archbishop Anselm of Canterbury (1089–1109) in the latter's conflict with William Rufus (1087–1100) and Henry I (1100–35). See Fliche, *La Réforme grégorienne*, III, 311, 450–451; F. Lot and R. Fawtier, *Histoire des institutions françaises au moyen âge*, tome III: *Institutions ecclésiastiques* (Paris, 1962), pp. 89–90, 93; R. W. Southern, *Saint Anselm and His Biographer* (Cambridge, 1963), pp. 161, 175–176; N. F. Cantor, *Church, Kingship and Lay Investiture in England, 1089–1135* (Princeton, 1958), pp. 41, 60–61.

radically rejected all articles and symbols of luxury and wealth, be they domestic or artistic, economic or ecclesiastical. They renounced all civil possessions and the exploitation of "feudal" sources of wealth such as manorial bakeries, mills, fairs, and serfs; all church properties such as rents, tithes, and advowsons. They resolved to accept for their new monasteries only land far from habitation, to be worked and exploited solely for the uses of the community and principally by its own laborers. By these means, the first fathers of Cîteaux sought to escape from "feudal" economic conditions. Finally, the primary objective of the Cistercian legislation was the spiritual one of securing for the individual monk a means of salvation through a life of prayer. Because the three-part division of the monastic life of St. Benedict had suffered severe modification by the eleventh century and had become essentially centered around the liturgy, the Cistercians removed all additions to the *Opus Dei*, the work of the choir, except for the daily conventual or community mass. The time gained by the removal of many hours of elaborate ceremonial was to be devoted to a very sharply defined type of spiritual reading and to a great deal of manual labor. Absolute silence was prescribed, the full canonical year of novitiate before religious profession was re-enforced, and the ancient practice of accepting oblate children was forbidden.[12]

12 The practice of parents dedicating their children to God goes back very far in Old Testament history. Aside from the well-known offering of Abraham (Genesis 22), the young Samuel was consecrated to the service of the Temple (I Samuel 1), and St. John the Baptist seems to have been offered in the same way (Luke 1:63–80). Just as in antiquity the rights of fathers over their children were virtually absolute, so the Christians of the early Church considered it natural to offer their children to monasteries. In Western Europe by St. Benedict's time, it was a common practice for parents to bind one or several of their young children permanently to the religious life. The term "oblate," then, was applied in the early Middle Ages to the children dedicated to a monastery for life by their parents and placed there to be brought up. Two famous monks who, as they tell us themselves, had been given to monasteries as oblates are the Venerable Bede and Ordericus Vitalis. This ancient discipline was modified by canon law, and the Council of Trent insisted that a valid profession of religious vows could be made only at the completion of the sixteenth year. See Dom P. Delatte, *Com-*

8

Almost all modern research on the medieval religious orders has been highly compartmentalized. Historians have discussed the various orders' contributions to agriculture, or to economic development, or to the growth of royal administration, or to the development of parliament. These studies, very valuable though they are for economic, social, or political history, have usually been very subjective and have considered the monastery's or the order's work without reference to the spiritual bases of the institute,[13] which are, after all, the main reasons for its existence. As good products of the twentieth century, historians have been strongly influenced by Marx, and modern scholarship in monastic history has, to a very great extent, reflected his economic interpretation. (The exceptions to this tendency have been the achievements of such prolific scholars as Dom Kassius Hallinger in Germany, Dom Jean Leclercq in Luxembourg, and Dom David Knowles in England, who are themselves monks, and whose works have been characterized by a more moral, or what might be called the personal-devotional interpretation.)

mentary on the Holy Rule of St. Benedict, trans. Dom Justin McCann (London, 1921), pp. 406–412; Dom H. Van Zeller, The Holy Rule (New York, 1958), pp. 384–386; F. L. Cross, The Oxford Dictionary of the Christian Church (rev. ed., London, 1958), p. 972; see for the present law T. L. Bouscaren, S.J., and A. C. Ellis, S.J., Canon Law: A Text and Commentary (rev. ed., Milwaukee, 1953), pp. 272–273, which has been modified by the Second Vatican Council.

13 The technical canonical term "institute" (as distinguished from the more general "institution") as it is used throughout these pages is applied in the sense defined in Roman canon law, canon 488, 1°, that is, a society approved by legitimate ecclesiastical authority, the members of which strive after evangelical perfection according to the laws proper to their society, by profession of public vows, either perpetual or temporary, the latter to be renewed after fixed intervals of time. An "order" is an institute in which solemn vows are taken; a "congregation" is an institute in which simple vows are taken; a "monastic congregation" is a union of a number of independent monasteries. Solemn vows are considered final, that is for life. Simple vows depend on the nature of the religious institute; they may be vows which are renewed at periodic intervals in the life of the religious, or they may begin a further period of probation before the profession of solemn vows. See Bouscaren and Ellis, Canon Law, pp. 231–232.

Perhaps an economic interpretation is largely valid, because while man may live from every word that proceeds from the mouth of God, he still requires his daily bread. But the exclusive emphasis on an economic interpretation disregards the basic idea, the essence of monasticism. The present work is conceived primarily as a study in monastic and constitutional history. It is a study of certain aspects of the Cistercian Order in England in the first century of its history. It is an assessment of the form and practice of the Cistercian life in the twelfth century made on the basis of the Cistercians' own constitutions.

It must be repeated that the monk is a man who seeks God. ("But his delight is in the law of the Lord, and in his law he meditates day and night." Ps. 1:2.) This objective has been true for all times and places in which Christian men have sought to order their lives on some pattern based on the *Rule of St. Benedict*. The student, like the monk, can lose sight of this fact only at the peril of gravely misconstruing the purpose and function of the institution. The monk's purpose in life is otherworldly. He lives in the world, but he must not be a part of the world. If the ordinary lay Christian can never be completely at home in this world, so much the more is this true of the monk who attempts to live the Christian life extraordinarily. Here is the beginning of the conflict, for the objectives of this world are always opposed to those of men whose lives are directed exclusively to God. While the monk lives a life devoted to God, at the same time the religious constitution or rule by which he professes to live must be flexible enough to come to terms with the world in which he lives, without at the same time bringing the world into the cloister. The laws which are enacted to govern any particular society or organization, religious as well as secular, must be suited not only to the needs of that society but to the larger environment in which it exists. A constitution, even a paper one or an imaginary one, has no significance apart from actual practice.

The Cistercian constitutions drawn up in the early twelfth

century, although they reflect a profound idealism and symbolize the faith of the age, cannot be called a realistic attempt to legislate for the conditions of the time. The intent of the Cistercian statutes was to establish and maintain the Order's total separation from the world. This was so revolutionary an objective, involving the complete divorce of the monastic life from the life of secular society, that it was an impossible aim. The observance of the law and the effective functioning of the institute [14] were drastically vitiated, from the start, by the extreme demands of the law. Western society had for five hundred years depended on the services of the monks, and Western society and Western monasticism were so closely interdependent in so many different ways that the monks simply were in no position to be able to sever all connections. At the same time, the effect of the Cistercian insistence on so much manual labor was that the White Monks were to acquire wealth, and, in an age characterized by so much economic dynamism, this wealth came to them very rapidly. The emphasis on total renunciation was rapidly to demonstrate that absolute poverty as an ideal defeated itself. The only way for an individual or a religious institute to be poor in spirit is for him or it to be poor in fact.

Cistercian liturgical austerity and the insistence on the observance *ad litteram* of the *Rule of St. Benedict* in every aspect of the conventual life appeared at first to be fresh new ideas. But each was quickly misconstrued. As early as the 1120's St. Bernard was hurling his famous attacks at Cluny's wealth, luxuries, and artistic beauty.[15] Literal observance within less than ten years had become pharisaism, and material simplicity, puritanism. The characteristics of pharisaism and puritanism were not traits unique to the Cistercians, but quickly came to typify them. Any institution which begins its existence from a legally inflexible and rigidly dogmatic position starts from a defensive and virtually indefensi-

14 Again, the term "institute" as it is used here and throughout is meant in the strict canonical sense. See note 13 above.
15 The best treatment of this affair is Dom M. D. Knowles, *Cistercians and Cluniacs* (London, 1955).

ble position. The downward path to practical reality which it will take is usually very steep.

From the time of their beginnings, the Cistercians were strong defenders of papal authority and opposed to monastic or any other type of privileged ecclesiastical exemption from lawfully established jurisdiction. According to St. Bernard, just as the bishop ought not to disobey his archbishop, so the abbot ought not to disobey his bishop. He even compared the ecclesiastical hierarchy to the hierarchy of the celestial legions to demonstrate that it would be criminal for the pope to alter with his power of dispensation a long-established usage.[16] The Cistercians were, then, in a sense the first of the militantly religious orders which, like the Dominicans in the thirteenth century and the Jesuits in the sixteenth, sought to bring the Christian world under the authority of the Roman pontiff. But such a responsibility for the Cistercians was itself detrimental to the preservation of the intentions of the first fathers of Cîteaux. The Cistercians became the auxiliaries of Rome: to a very great extent they represented the Gregorian Reform movement, and Cistercian abbots in several capacities actively advanced the program of the reforming papacy. The rapid consequence was that the Cistercian ideal became materialized in the hands of the pope to be used for his purposes. The papacy appeared to recognize and encourage the Cistercian expression of the Christian life, but in reality it stooped to conquer and after rendering homage drew into its service the very ideal which it had claimed to be its superior.

An underlying assumption of the present study is that the ideal or expression of the monastic life stated in the Cistercian constitutions was completely unsuited to the conditions of the twelfth century. There was an inherent conflict between the practical realities of English life in the twelfth century and the ideal of the monastic life as set forth in the Cistercian constitutions. What may have been possible in the simpler, less sophisticated world of the sixth, eighth, or

[16] E. Vacandard, *Vie de S. Bernard* (5th ed., Paris, 1927), I, 450.

even tenth centuries was completely out of tune with the twelfth. From the time of the monks' arrival in England, the conditions surrounding the establishment of their monasteries placed a strain on the constitutions. Within fifty years of their settlement, the nature of their feudal and financial obligations, their absorption of a peculiar religious institute into the Order, the responsibilities laid on the monks by the papacy as agents of the Gregorian Reform movement, these problems — to say nothing of the Order's complex economic dealings and its phenomenal growth in numbers — placed an intolerable strain on the Cistercian constitutions. This is not, however, to draw a conclusion which may appear to be the result of such a line of reasoning. The implication may seem to be that all monasticism, or any religious ideal, once it is institutionalized, is in the last analysis self-defeating. But this is not true. As long as they enable the individual to seek a goal outside himself, as long as they elevate his ideals, change his patterns of thought and course of behavior, as long as they enable the individual to know himself, no matter to what small degree, then the ideal and the institution which expresses it have "succeeded." [17]

If a saint is a man whose heroism is a reflection of the fortitude of God, the intention of the Cistercian legislation was a life of such heroism, of such strength that all who lived it would have been compelled to become saints. But saints are usually not made by human laws, and for that reason the Cistercian constitutions, being immoderately and unreasonably demanding for the climate of Western Europe, were almost from the beginning a legislative failure. There was something too fundamentally Eastern about the Cistercian constitutions for the Western social and spiritual atmosphere for which they were designed. Even before the death of St.

[17] See the sensitive and sympathetic studies of Cistercian spirituality by Dom Jean Leclercq: "Les Meditations d'un moine du XII siècle," *Revue Mabillon*, XXXIV (1944) pp. 1–10; "St. Bernard et la théologie monastique du XII siècle," *Analecta Sacri Ordinis Cisterciensis*, vol. IX (Rome, 1953); and "St. Bernard et le XII monastique," in M. Viller, ed., *Dictionnaire de spiritualité*, vol. IV (Paris, 1958).

Bernard, the Order of Cîteaux had departed far from its first principles, although throughout the century it continued, in Ophelia's words, "to preach the steep and thorny way to heaven." In fact, it recked not its own rede. The vocation to a life of courage, sometimes of heroism, had become sidetracked in the comfortable paths of power.

chapteR one

the english cisteRcians
and the nobility
in stephen's Reign

England, bound in with the triumphant sea,
Whose rocky shore beats back the envious siege
Of wat'ry Neptune, is now bound in with shame,
With inky blots and rotten parchment bonds.
That England that was wont to conquer others
Hath made a shameful conquest of itself.

Richard II

The Cistercian Order in England owed its establishment and its development to the support of the feudal nobility, and the history of the White Monks in England is inseparable from that of the nobility. The achievements of English civilization, as those of any civilization in the Middle Ages, were the result of the corporate nature of society — the communal prayer of the monks, the fighting life of the nobility, and the toiling efforts of the peasants. These three classes, clearly defined, tightly unified, and strongly interdependent — because each provided and performed for the other important social services — composed the social structure of the land. Thus it was that in the time of feudal ascendancy, in fact during the period when the English nobility

15

gained a greater degree of power than it ever had before or after in the twelfth century, the Cistercians underwent their remarkable expansion. The growth of the Cistercian Order in England should properly be seen against the background of the political and social history of the times.

The anarchy of the reign of King Stephen (1135–54) was a period of feudal reaction, a time when the Anglo-Norman baronage sought, under the haze of disorder which hung over the land, to recover rights or possessions which they claimed had belonged to their ancestors, or which were once associated with the title of earl. Once they were in a position to do so, these earls tried to exercise the political powers which had accompanied the title of earl generations before, especially since King Stephen's position was not such that he could have checked very many barons, and certainly not the greatest of them, for any length of time.

Late in November, 1135, Henry, Duke of Normandy, King of England (1100–35), and the youngest son of William the Conqueror, after a strenuous day's hunting in the forest of Lyon, dined immoderately on lampreys, an eel-like fish forbidden by his doctors. A week later he was dead.[1] His heart was removed and preserved at the monastery of St. Mary des Pres near Rouen, and the other remains were transported across the channel to be buried at the abbey of Reading.[2] With his passing England quickly descended into grave feudal disorder, becoming, as one contemporary put it, "a home of forwardness, a haunt of strife, a training ground of disorder and a teacher of every kind of rebellion." [3]

The twenty years of anarchy which began in 1135 were the result of several fundamental and interrelated difficulties. Any successor of Henry I would have been faced with a situation which would have taxed the strongest of English medieval kings. Apart from his financial exactions, the harsh

[1] R. Howlett, ed., Richard of Hexham, *Historia*, in *Chronicles of the Reigns of Stephen, Henry II, and Richard I*, III (Rolls Series, no. 82, London, 1886), 139–141.
[2] J. A. Giles, ed., *William of Malmesbury, Chronicles of the Kings of England* (London, 1847), p. 490.
[3] K. R. Potter, ed., *Gesta Stephani* (London, 1953), p. 1.

character of Henry's government would have invited a baronial reaction.[4] By the end of his reign the higher baronage no longer held the power in local administration which it had held under the Conqueror, and to a very great extent the government of the country had passed from lords with strong local interests to men who were essentially the king's ministers and friends. Moreover, in numerous instances Henry had acted outside of feudal law, interfered with the laws of succession, and confiscated the estates of his vassals, on one pretext or another. Under his successor, the great lords revolted against the idea that their lands were merely tenements held at the king's pleasure.[5] Thirdly, the almost spontaneous outburst of feudal disorder following the death of the master who had known how to control the nobility was aggravated by a disputed succession.

The traditional explanations of the civil war under Stephen, Count of Mortain and Boulogne and a nephew of Henry I, such as his personal weakness and his reckless concessions, "depend more on the frequency with which they have been repeated than on any compelling evidence to support them." [6] In the brief line of three Norman kings who had preceded him, there was nothing unprecedented in a disputed succession; but the disputed successions of William Rufus (1087–1100) and of Henry I had not resulted in prolonged anarchy. In Stephen's case, as Prestwich so aptly put it, "it would be more accurate to hold that the civil war caused the disputed succession than that the disputed succession caused the civil war." [7]

In 1120 the only surviving legitimate son of Henry I, William, had drowned when the White Ship sank in the channel. The king, wishing to avoid a civil war and the probability of

[4] G. O. Sayles, *Medieval Foundations of England* (rev. ed., London, 1958), pp. 295–300.
[5] F. M. Stenton, *The First Century of English Feudalism 1066–1166* (rev. ed., Oxford, 1961), p. 221; R. H. C. Davis, "What Happened in Stephen's Reign," *History*, XLIX (1964), 6–7.
[6] J. O. Prestwich, "War and Finance in the Anglo-Norman State," *T.R.H.S.*, 5th Series, IV (1945), 37.
[7] *Ibid.*

a disputed succession, had compelled his great barons to recognize his daughter Matilda as his rightful heir.[8] The widow of Henry V, Holy Roman Emperor (1106–25), Matilda had been married to Geoffrey Plantagenet, Count of Anjou, who could well have supplied the strength so badly needed until his young son, the future Henry II, came of age. But Theobald, Count of Blois and Champagne, and his brother Stephen, Count of Mortain, who were grandsons of William I through their mother, Adela, laid claim to the English throne in 1135 on the ground that they were the only surviving male descendants of the Conqueror old enough to rule. According to feudal custom their right as heirs male was superior to that of Matilda, but inferior to that of her infant son, Henry Plantagenet. The situation was even more complicated. On the one hand, the great men of the kingdom had sworn allegiance to Matilda as her father's heir, although many had declared prophetically that they would break their plighted oaths;[9] on the other hand, many argued that the English crown was elective and that the oaths forced upon them by Henry I were not binding. What the English barons actually wanted was security in their tenements and an increase in their private power, which is to say, as much independence from the central authority as possible. Wise men may have acknowledged that the country needed the strong hand of a male ruler, but few felt that that hand should be in the iron glove of Geoffrey Plantagenet. Confusion reigned. The barons of Normandy recognized Theobald of Blois while Geoffrey invaded the duchy to protect his wife's interests.[10]

8 Giles, *William of Malmesbury*, p. 481.
9 *Ibid.*, p. 483.
10 The standard study of the disputed succession and its attendant anarchy has long been J. H. Round, *Geoffrey de Mandeville* (London, 1892). Round's views have lately been attacked by R. H. C. Davis in "What Happened in Stephen's Reign," and the same author's "Geoffrey de Mandeville Reconsidered," *E.H.R.*, LXXIX, (1964), 299–307. Davis suggests that Geoffrey de Mandeville and Ranulf de Gernons are less the villains of the piece than Stephen. For Stephen, by arresting them and confiscating parts of their estates, violated his own feudal and coronation oaths, and thus provoked the barons' revolts. There is truth in

The situation in England was resolved temporarily by the quick action of Count Stephen of Mortain. He was probably at Boulogne when he heard of Henry's death and, quickly crossing to England, he won recognition from a part of the baronage. Through the influence of his younger brother Henry, the powerful Bishop of Winchester (1129–71), Stephen was crowned king by the Archbishop of Canterbury.[11] It is significant that a small number of the lay nobility, only three bishops, and none of the great abbots were present at his coronation.[12]

At Neuberg in Normandy, a council of nobles hearing of Stephen's coronation elected him their duke. Many held fiefs in both Normandy and England, and they probably preferred to serve under one lord. Stephen's elder brother, Count Theobald, indignant at the loss of what he considered his rightful inheritance, soon left the duchy. As Stephen was preoccupied in England, Normandy was left without leadership, and Stephen's enemies were to make what private gains they could there.[13]

Stephen was in possession of the English throne, and, in the absence of an active pretender, the barons for the most

this argument, but Stephen violated his contracts precisely because the power of the barons had become too dangerous for the crown. His arrest of these two earls was not made on any specific evidence of their treason, but nervous concern over the danger of too powerful subjects. Contrary to Round, I would suggest that Ranulf de Gernons is a much better example than Geoffrey de Mandeville of what Round calls "the feudal and anarchic spirit that stamps the reign of Stephen." Both Round's and Davis' arguments emphasize a vicious circle of power threatening power. Round's interpretation of Stephen's reign remains basically sound; Davis has further documented it. I regret that I was unable to incorporate the researches of R. H. C. Davis, *King Stephen, 1135–1154* (Berkeley, 1967), which appeared after my book had already gone to press.

[11] Giles, *William of Malmesbury*, pp. 482–483. Stephen himself had been the first baron, after the Archbishop of Canterbury, to take the oath of loyalty to Matilda.

[12] Potter, *Gesta Stephani*, pp. 3–4.

[13] T. Forester, ed., *Ordericus Vitalis' Ecclesiastical History of England and Normandy*, IV (London, 1856), 155. S. Painter, *William Marshall* (Baltimore, 1933), pp. 2–3, maintains that "Theobald immediately resigned his claim," but Painter cites no reference for this statement.

part had little choice but to acquiesce in the *fait accompli*. Stephen had moved so quickly and decisively after his uncle's death that he was able to take control of the country "in the twinkling of an eye." [14] Nevertheless, many lords maintained that Matilda's cause should not have been so easily forsaken.[15]

All this emphasizes the fact that Stephen's position was far from secure. His position in feudal custom posed the inherent weakness to his claim to the English throne. Stephen had sworn an oath of fealty to Matilda in 1127. His violation of this oath and seizure of the English crown eight years later appeared to public opinion, as represented by the chroniclers, as the gravest sin in feudal society — treacherous disloyalty. The judgment of God was only to be expected to fall on the perjurer, and this philosophy of history was to be a serious political factor throughout his reign.[16] Although he had some staunch adherents, most of the great barons remained aloof with the undoubted intention of selling him their support in return for lands and privileges. In the first years of his reign, however, Stephen acted firmly, and his cause appeared to prosper. When the king wore his crown at his Easter court in 1136, most of the important men of England assembled and swore obedience to him. Shortly thereafter, the very influential Robert, Earl of Gloucester, one of the many sons of Henry I born on the wrong side of the sheets,[17] made his submission. In these early months, Stephen did not show weakness in yielding to baronial demands or foolishness in dealing with their threats. He did not strip himself of power and revenues by keeping his general promises on danegeld, deforestation, and the freedom of

14 D. C. Douglas, ed., Henry of Huntingdon, *History of the English*, in *English Historical Documents*, II (London, 1953), 306.
15 *Ibid*.
16 Isabel Megaw, "The Ecclesiastical Policy of Stephen, 1135–1139: A Reinterpretation," in H. A. Cronne, T. W. Moody, and D. B. Quinn, eds., *Essays in British and Irish History in Honour of James Eadie Todd* (London, 1949), pp. 26–27.
17 Henry I begot more bastards than any other English king: nine sons and eleven daughters. See Douglas, *E.H.D.*, II, Table 4, p. 985.

ecclesiastical elections.[18] He refused the territorial demands of Richard Fitzgilbert and crushed the revolt of Baldwin de Redvers.[19] He understood the vital importance of private fortresses and forced the surrender of the castles of Norwich, Bampton, Exeter, Bedford, and Bamborough.[20] Nor again did he neglect the dangers on the borders of Wales, Scotland, and Normandy. For example, in February, 1136, he led a large army north and obtained from King David of Scotland the surrender of several castles. A year later, in March, 1137, he landed in Normandy and made vigorous attempts to destroy the forces of Geoffrey of Anjou who had made heavy inroads there.[21]

Again, the strength of Stephen's position was more apparent than real. Stephen had secured the throne through an act of disloyalty to his cousin Matilda, and some of the higher baronage, preferring a male ruler and disliking Matilda's arrogant and domineering personality, had acquiesced for the moment in this treachery. The Anglo-Norman barons did so with the undoubted intention of using Stephen's weak position to force him to recognize their claims to tenements as hereditary. But as Stephen's position deteriorated, he behaved in the same way towards his barons as he had done towards Matilda. Henry I had interfered with the rules of inheritance by forfeitures, escheats, exchanges, and by charging excessively high reliefs. He had rewarded his servants and favorites — without reducing the royal demesne — by giving them the lands of other people. Stephen, in a much weaker legal position, followed this dangerous precedent with the result that the proliferation of confiscations and claims ensured the continuance of the civil war. In every shire there were families with rival hereditary claims to the same honour, and in the wars they automatically joined opposing camps. The events of 1138 were to prove the folly of Stephen's policy.

[18] Douglas, Henry of Huntingdon, *History of the English*, p. 285; Round, *Geoffrey de Mandeville*, pp. 377–378.
[19] Potter, *Gesta Stephani*, pp. 12–24.
[20] *Ibid.*, pp. 19–32.
[21] Howlett, Richard of Hexham, *Historia*, pp. 145–147; Forester, *Ordericus Vitalis*, IV, 155–178.

In that year Robert of Gloucester was in Normandy plotting with Matilda. In various parts of England and Normandy individual barons rose in revolt, and Stephen's attempts to put them down had no lasting effect because when one rebel was crushed several more appeared. The arrival in England in September, 1139, of Matilda and Earl Robert accelerated the chaotic conditions. From his fortresses of Bristol and Gloucester, Earl Robert ravaged the lands of those who remained loyal to Stephen, and this policy was soon adopted by other partisans of Matilda, operating from their lands. The retaliations of the king and his followers, far from having even any temporary effect, only served to exacerbate conditions.[22]

Finance is the one other factor which contemporaries emphasized and which helps to explain the degeneration of Stephen's fortunes. Stephen's political and military strength was closely related to the large treasury left by his predecessor. But not even Henry's riches, supplemented by the traditional sources of royal revenue, together with the wealth which accrued to the crown by the death of the Archbishop of Canterbury, William de Corbeil (21 November 1136), could sustain for very long the rate of expanditure required by the campaigns of the first three years of the reign. Stephen spent rapidly, and as the monetary basis of his strength declined, his military and royal position weakened. The decline and exhaustion of his reserves helps to explain the mounting confidence of his opponents and the ability of a coalition of magnates and mercenaries to begin undisguised warfare.[23]

The appearance of the Empress Matilda, therefore, inaugurated twenty years of violence, rebellion, and disorder. The first decade, 1138–48, seems to have witnessed a situation as follows. There were two claimants to the throne in England, each of whom was accepted and generally obeyed in a small group of shires. The empress, or rather her half brother, the

22 Potter, *Gesta Stephani*, pp. 58–92; Giles, *William of Malmesbury*, pp. 490–513; R. H. C. Davis, "What Happened in Stephen's Reign," pp. 9–11.
23 Prestwich, "War and Finance," pp. 40–43.

Earl of Gloucester, who acted for her, held sway over a belt of territory in the west which varied widely, but of which the nucleus was formed by Somerset, Gloucestershire, the modern Monmouthshire, Herefordshire, and sometimes Worcestershire. Stephen controlled an area which was roughly bounded on the south and west by Hampshire and the Cotswolds, on the north and northeast by the Welland, the fens in the lower part of the Ouse and the River Waveney. Except at the time of his captivity at the Battle of Lincoln in 1141, Stephen's jurisdiction was established within these limits. Toward the end of his reign, he secured Worcestershire and gained the support of an important element in Yorkshire, and gradually mastered the castles of his enemies in Wiltshire and Dorset. It is difficult to be more precise because until the very end of the reign the territories of the rival factions interlaced and overlapped.[24]

It is also difficult to bring the various objectives pursued by different barons at different times under any general definition. Each individual was motivated by a particular set of circumstances which he proceeded to use to his own best advantage. There can be no doubt, however, that throughout the reign of Stephen there were three main objectives which all the greater barons sought: the control of castles, a position in which they could exercise the royal power in the shires, and the dignity of an earldom.[25]

In times of external threat or internal confusion, castles were of extreme importance. They served as a protection for a baron's own lands and as a convenient basis for plundering his neighbor's. If he could fill a district with his own fortresses and exclude those of the king and other lords, his control of the region was secure. The well-known series of charters alternately issued by King Stephen and Matilda to Geoffrey de Mandeville show a strategic group of fortresses being constructed and held in the southeast.[26] The example

[24] H. W. C. Davis, "The Anarchy of Stephen's Reign," *E.H.R.*, XVIII (1903), 631–632.
[25] Stenton, *First Century*, pp. 223–224.
[26] Round, *Geoffrey de Mandeville*, pp. 81–122, 136–162, 163–200.

of the notorious Earl of Essex's fortress construction, which Round described and all later students have slavishly repeated, is typical but not the best example of castle building. The same process was going on in other parts of England. A treaty between the earls of Chester and Leicester, written in the language of two sovereign powers, demonstrates better than any other known document the intentions of the great barons, their assumed right to make war at their own pleasure, and the military importance of the private castles of central England. The two earls here do admit the existence of an authority higher than themselves, but it is not the authority of a king but of a liege lord, and they define by careful agreement the conditions under which they will serve him.[27]

The late Sidney Painter's study of the castle sites of this region shows that the Earl of Leicester and his cousin the Earl of Warwick each had a solid group of castles around his chief seat. Leicester held Groby, Hinkley, Lilbourne, Mountsorrel, and Whitwick. His cousin of Warwick controlled Beausale, Brailes, Brandon, Gilmorton, Schockerstone, and Tanworth. Hugh Bigod, Earl of Norfolk, held Bungley, Framlingham, Walton, and probably Ipswich. William de Aumale, Earl of York, obtained Scarborough from Stephen and built another in the West Riding of Yorkshire.[28]

Yet, the castle building activities of these earls, and even those of Geoffrey de Mandeville, shrink in significance before those of the powerful Palatine Earl of Chester. The career of Geoffrey de Mandeville illustrates the way the barons of Stephen's reign sold their support to the two contending factions during the anarchy, but the actual power which the Earl of Essex achieved, even at the height of his success, only approximates the vast territory Earl Ranulf of Chester controlled for much of Stephen's reign. The unknown author of the *Gesta Stephani* states that the Earl of

[27] Printed in Stenton, *First Century*, pp. 250–253.
[28] S. Painter, "English Castles in the Early Middle Ages," *Speculum*, (1955), 225–226.

Chester controlled a third of England,[29] which, if his family connections are taken into account, is almost true. It was Earl Ranulf's ambition to link by a chain of fortresses his estates in Chester and his lands in Lincoln and thus to bestride England from sea to sea. Thus he built Tickhill Castle, Belvoir Castle, Torksey, Grimsby, Newcastle-under-Lyme, Rathley, Mansfield, Stoneleigh, Nottingham, and Stafford.[30] In 1140 Ranulf seized Lincoln Castle, and for the next twelve years it was his continual object to maintain control of both the castle and the city. In this effort he was consistently opposed by King Stephen. But in 1141 Stephen suffered the disastrous defeat of his career at the battle before Lincoln.[31] In 1144 the king again failed to take the castle, but in 1146 he managed to capture the earl and to extort the castle's surrender. Three years later, in 1149, Stephen's position forced him to concede the castle and the city to the Earl of Chester with the curious reservation that Ranulf might hold them until the king secured for him the recovery of his inheritance and his castles in Normandy. Stephen was never able to achieve so much, and thus the earl remained in possession of the city and castle of Lincoln until his death in 1153.[32]

What was the significance of these castles? The chief obstacle to the authority of the English crown was the military power of the baronage, and the principal element of that power was the mass of fortresses controlled by the barons.

Throughout the reign of Stephen the other main object of the greater barons was to obtain positions in which they could exercise the royal power in the shires where they had territorial influence. The barons of Stephen's reign looked

29 Potter, *Gesta Stephani*, p. 121.
30 J. H. Round, "King Stephen and the Earl of Chester," *E.H.R.*, X (1895), 87–91.
31 Potter, *Gesta Stephani*, pp. 71–77; Douglas, Henry of Huntingdon, *History of the English*, pp. 306–308.
32 R. H. C. Davis, "King Stephen and the Earl of Chester Revised," *E.H.R.*, LXXV (1960), 658–660. Together with his vast estates Ranulf de Gernons, Earl of Chester, inherited the enormous relief of £1000 and nursed a grudge against the crown for the loss of the honour of Carlisle, which Henry I, increasingly anxious about the earl's concentration of territory, had confiscated.

back with ambitious nostalgia and yearned for the large delegation of royal power that had been exercised by the great baronial sheriffs of the Conqueror's time. As Stenton has suggested, it was through the acquisition of such administrative offices that the barons made their greatest encroachments on the civil authority of the crown.[33] While it is impossible to estimate the extent to which individual members of the higher baronage acquired sheriffdoms and county justiciarships, certainly the number of English earldoms increased from six in 1135 to twenty-two in 1154.[34] In the eleventh century this dignity had carried the right to preside over the shire court, and thus to maintain order and to dispense justice; to command the fyrd, and to execute royal commands. Its political importance had gradually declined after the Conqueror's time, and certainly by the end of the reign of Henry I an earldom gave its holder little more than a title and the social position which it implied. "When all allowance has been made for the vague possibility of reviving ancient official powers under a weak monarchy, the social distinction carried by an earldom remains its one essential advantage. Neither Stephen nor the empress was really weakening the royal power when they purchased support by the grant of earldoms."[35] Still, the men who became earls were the same barons who made serious inroads on the royal power through the construction or private control of castles, and this means or implies that they possessed hegemony over the territories these castles were designed to control.

Who were the men who attained this position under Stephen? The king restored to Simon de Senlis the earldoms of Northampton and Huntingdon which Henry I had taken from Simon's father. At the same time, in 1138, Stephen made Gilbert de Clare the earl of Pembroke. (This Gilbert de Clare married the sister of Waleran, Earl of Worcester, and Robert, Earl of Leicester. See chart following p. 30.) In

[33] Stenton, *First Century*, pp. 230–231.
[34] G. W. White, "King Stephen's Earldoms," *T.R.H.S.*, 4th Series, XIII (1930), 51–82.
[35] Stenton, *First Century*, p. 234.

1138 William d'Aumale was made earl of York, Baldwin de Redvers became earl of Devon, and Waleran, Count of Meulan, was given the earldom of Worcester. The nephew and namesake of Gilbert de Clare I, Gilbert de Clare II, who through his mother was the nephew of the Palatine Earl of Chester, was made, in 1141, earl of Hertford. Finally, in the same year, 1141, Hugh Bigod was made earl of Norfolk. William d'Aubigny gained the earldom of Sussex, and Hugh, called "the Poor," the younger brother of Robert, Earl of Leicester, and Waleran, Earl of Worcester, was created earl of Bedford.[36]

These earls who sought to increase their power through the construction of fortresses were also the greatest bene-factors of the Cistercian Order in England. It was in this same period, from 1135 to 1155, that the White Monks spread across the length and breadth of England, and indeed across Europe. English conditions were not peculiar. The same state of feudal disorder which prevailed on the continent for much of the twelfth century, where the private castle and the local feud were not forbidden, provided the political and psychological backdrop for the expansion of the most in-fluential religious order of the century.

The rapidity with which the Cistercian Order increased the number of its monks and multiplied the number of its foundations is very striking. Between 1135 and 1155, Cistercian houses in England grew from five to forty, and if we include the thirteen English abbeys of the Congregation of Savigny which were absorbed into Cîteaux in 1147, the figure rises to fifty-three; and from the original thirteen monks who came to Waverley in 1128, the figure had risen by 1160 to about six thousand, exclusive of their lay-brothers.[37]

Many modern historians have noted the fact — which, in-deed, did not escape the attention of the contemporary Wil-liam of Newburgh — that by far the greatest part of this monastic expansion occurred during the anarchy of Stephen's

[36] G. W. White, "King Stephen's Earldoms."
[37] Knowles, *M.O.*, pp. 246–247; see also his Appendix XI, pp. 707–708, in the same volume.

reign. The Augustinian canon, William, from his excellent vantage-point in Yorkshire, suggests that more religious houses were established in Stephen's short reign than had been founded in the previous hundred years.[38] For the ninety-odd years between the death of the Confessor and the accession of Henry II, mainly years of strong royal government, this generalization is well-founded. Significantly, the reign of Stephen, a period of weak monarchial control, witnessed the great advances of ecclesiastical interests. Sixty years ago Frank Stenton suggested that a period of feudal anarchy was not necessarily inimical to the ultimate interests of the Church; and that in eleventh-century Normandy the disorders of William I's minority coincided with the foundation of new monasteries in every diocese of the Norman church.[39] Likewise, in twelfth-century England, the anarchy was a period of unparalleled activity in the foundation of religious houses. There can be no doubt that monasticism loses none of its appeal in a time of political chaos and personal insecurity, that, in fact, its beginnings were dependent upon such conditions. This may help to explain the great resurgence of monasticism, especially Cistercian monasticism, in the United States after World War II.

Students of English medieval history have put forth various explanations. Poole attributes the great growth of the White Monks to their puritanical spirit, arguing that this element gave the movement its special appeal in England because "puritanism was always latent in the English character." [40]

38 R. Howlett ed., William of Newburgh, *Historia Rerum Anglicarum*, in *Chronicles of the Reigns of Stephen, Henry II, and Richard I*, vol. I (Rolls Series, no. 82, London, 1884). "Quid autem sentiendum est de his et aliis locis religiosis, quae in diebus regis Stephani copiosius exstrui vel florere coeperunt, nisi quod castra Dei sunt haec, in quibus, contra spiritualia nequitiae, Regis Christi excubant milites et exercentur tirones? . . . Denique multo plura sub brevitate temporis, quo Stephanus regnavit, vel potius nomen regis obtinuit, quam centum retro annis servorum et ancillarum Dei monasteria initium in Anglia sumpsisse noscuntur."
39 F. M. Stenton, *William the Conqueror* (London, 1908), p. 38.
40 A. L. Poole, *From Domesday Book to Magna Carta* (Oxford, 1951), p. 187.

Sayles traces the rapid multiplication of the Cistercian abbeys entirely to the influence of St. Bernard.[41] Knowles maintains that the chief cause of the Cistercian development in the twelfth century was the renaissance of the spiritual life and the centralization of ecclesiastical discipline after the Gregorian reform movement.[42] All students of monastic history have held that the warring barons who founded and endowed the monasteries wished to atone for their misdeeds by acts of piety.[43]

All these suggestions provide, given the religious climate of twelfth-century Europe, a partial solution to the problem. Yet they do not, it seems to me, raise certain essential political and social questions: Who were the men who founded and endowed Cistercian abbeys? What position did they hold in English society? Could there have have been a connection between baronial opposition to King Stephen and the barons' large and numerous grants to the White Monks? For England this subject has been neglected, although a monastery's survival, growth, and entire history depended very much on the conditions surrounding its foundation.

First of all, the complex network of Cistercian monasteries which spread across England in the twelfth century could not have been woven without the aid of the military nobility. Consequently, in seeking to understand its length and pattern, it is necessary to see it against the background of feudal institutions and feudal geography. As H. M. Colvin has demonstrated in his outstanding study of the Premonstratensian canons, feudal history is closely connected with geneal-

41 Sayles, *Medieval Foundations*, p. 360.
42 Knowles, *M.O.*, pp. 191–227.
43 See for example A. M. Cooke, "The Settlement of the Cistercians in England," *E.H.R.*, VIII (1893), 640–643; H. M. Colvin, *The White Canons in England* (Oxford, 1951), pp. 27–28; E. M. Thompson, *The Carthusian Order in England* (London, 1930), pp. 49–54; J. F. O'Sullivan, *Cistercian Settlements in Wales and Monmouthshire, 1140–1540* (New York, 1947), p. 3; J. B. Mahn, *L'Ordre cistercien et son gouvernement* (2nd ed., Paris, 1951), pp. 35–39; F. M. Powicke, ed., *The Life of Ailred Rievaulx by Walter Daniel* (London, 1950), pp. lix–lxvi, and J. C. Dickinson, *Origins of the Austin Canons* (London, 1950).

ogy.[44] In fact, wherever we turn in the politics of Stephen's reign — feudal or ecclesiastical — the issues seem to dissolve into family history.

As a class, those who founded and endowed the first generation of Cistercian monasteries, in the period 1130–55, were almost all barons[45] of the highest rank, that is to say, the great tenants-in-chief of the crown.[46] Lords of this class were considered to be the military backbone of the crown. The strength and power of the king consisted in the contingents of knights which each tenant-in-chief owed for military service, together with his ability to draw on their services when he needed them; and the success of the entire feudal military system depended upon the maintenance of stability in the tenure of lands which produced knights for the army.[47] Most of the barons who founded Cistercian monasteries had, or obtained from King Stephen, the title and dignity of earl. Many of those barons who were not earls had distinguished themselves in the royal service, either military or governmental.

The Basset family, or example, had come over with the Conqueror, and one of its members served Henry I as royal justiciar. Richard Basset, who founded the monasteries of Bruern and Combe,[48] succeeded to his father's circuit and under King Stephen held the office of joint sheriff in eleven counties.[49] Walter Espec established the abbey of Rievaulx, which became the most famous Cistercian house in medieval England; his foundation and endowment of Wardon Abbey started that monastery on the road to her later wealth.[50]

44 Colvin, *White Canons*, p. 33.
45 The legal definition of the term "baron" was well treated by S. Painter, *Studies in the History of the English Feudal Barony*, Johns Hopkins Studies, Series 61, no. 3 (Baltimore, 1943), p. 15; see also I. J. Sanders, *Feudal Military Service in England, Study of Constitutional and Military Power of the 'Barones' in Medieval England* (London, 1956), pp. 2–3, which is more significant, however, for the thirteenth century.
46 See Appendix herein.
47 Sanders, *Feudal Military Service*, pp. 3–4.
48 W. Dugdale, ed., *Monasticon Anglicanum* (new ed., London, 1846), V, 497, 582.
49 *D.N.B.*, III, 374, 386.
50 J. C. Atkinson, ed., *Cartularium Abbathiae de Rievalle*, Surtees So-

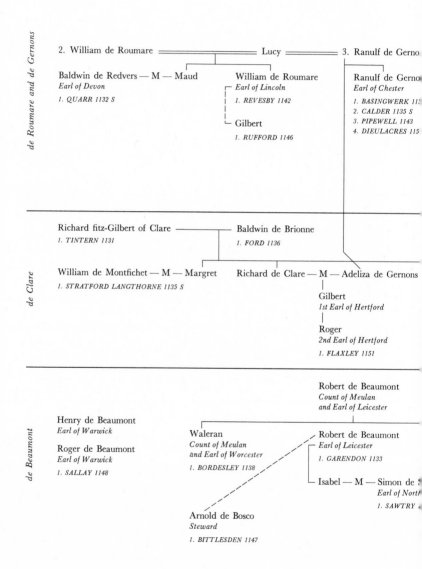

de Roumare and de Gernons

2. William de Roumare ══════════ Lucy ══════════ 3. Ranulf de Gerno

Baldwin de Redvers — M — Maud
Earl of Devon
1. QUARR 1132 S

William de Roumare
Earl of Lincoln
1. REVESBY 1142

Gilbert
1. RUFFORD 1146

Ranulf de Gerno
Earl of Chester
1. BASINGWERK 11
2. CALDER 1135 S
3. PIPEWELL 1143
4. DIEULACRES 115

de Clare

Richard fitz-Gilbert of Clare ——————— Baldwin de Brionne
1. TINTERN 1131   *1. FORD 1136*

William de Montfichet — M — Margret   Richard de Clare — M — Adeliza de Gernons
1. STRATFORD LANGTHORNE 1135 S

Gilbert
1st Earl of Hertford

Roger
2nd Earl of Hertford
1. FLAXLEY 1151

de Beaumont

Robert de Beaumont
Count of Meulan
and Earl of Leicester

Henry de Beaumont
Earl of Warwick

Roger de Beaumont
Earl of Warwick
1. SALLAY 1148

Waleran
Count of Meulan
and Earl of Worcester
1. BORDESLEY 1138

Robert de Beaumont
Earl of Leicester
1. GARENDON 1133

Isabel — M — Simon de S
Earl of North
1. SAWTRY

Arnold de Bosco
Steward
1. BITTLESDEN 1147

S: Congregation of Savigny
Broken lines indicate Knights holding fiefs of these lords.

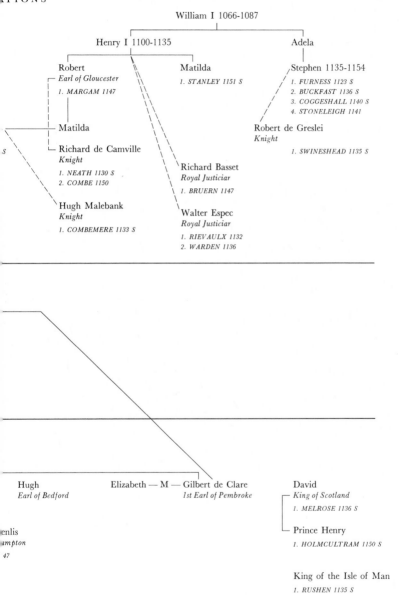

William I 1066-1087

Henry I 1100-1135 — Adela

Robert
Earl of Gloucester
1. MARGAM 1147

Matilda
1. STANLEY 1151 S

Stephen 1135-1154
1. FURNESS 1123 S
2. BUCKFAST 1136 S
3. COGGESHALL 1140 S
4. STONELEIGH 1141

Matilda

Robert de Greslei
Knight

Richard de Camville
Knight
1. NEATH 1130 S
2. COMBE 1150

1. SWINESHEAD 1135 S

Richard Basset
Royal Justiciar
1. BRUERN 1147

Hugh Malebank
Knight
1. COMBEMERE 1133 S

Walter Espec
Royal Justiciar
1. RIEVAULX 1132
2. WARDEN 1136

Hugh
Earl of Bedford

Elizabeth — M — Gilbert de Clare
1st Earl of Pembroke

David
King of Scotland
1. MELROSE 1136 S

enlis
ampton
47

Prince Henry
1. HOLMCULTRAM 1150 S

King of the Isle of Man
1. RUSHEN 1135 S

Espec had also served as a royal justice, and his paternal inheritance, which made up one of the largest accumulations of fiefs in Domesday Book, was increased by Henry I with new honours.[51] William de Chesney or Cheyney, who founded the monastery of Sibton,[52] was hereditary sheriff of Norfolk and Suffolk. He seems to have been connected with the Chesney family of Oxfordshire, but the precise relationship is uncertain.[53]

The genealogy of the English nobility in the first half of the twelfth century illustrates the fact that a high percentage of Cistercian monasteries owed their existence to family relations. The feudal barons who founded and endowed the abbeys were related to each other. Inasmuch as the entire Anglo-Norman baronage was closely interrelated, this fact may seem too obvious to require explanation. Yet it must be remembered because it helps to explain the establishment of Cistercian houses. In a society in which secular governments and local life depended so largely upon personal and family relationships, it would only follow that when the foundation or support of a monastery was first considered in the castle, feudal or family connections determined the choice of one order rather than another. Round has shown how the possession by Count Stephen of Blois of great estates on both sides of the channel led to the introduction of the

ciety, LXXXIII (Durham, 1889) pp. 263–264; Dugdale, *Monasticon*, V, 274.

[51] I. J. Sanders, *English Baronies: A Study of Their Origin and Descent* (Oxford, 1960), pp. 52, 133, 148.

[52] Dugdale, *Monasticon*, V, 369.

[53] The Chesney family of Oxfordshire produced Robert de Chesney, Bishop of Lincoln (1148–66), who was the uncle of Gilbert Foliot, Bishop of London (1163–87). This family is of interest because it shows the relationship between the feudal nobility and the higher ecclesiastics, and the Norman background from which so many of the prelates of the English Church came. For the Chesneys of Norfolk and Suffolk see L. F. Salzman, "Sussex Domesday Tenants. IV. The Family of Chesney or Cheyney," *Sussex Archaeological Collections*, LXV (1924), 20–53. For the Chesney family of Oxfordshire see H. E. Salter, ed., *Cartulary of the Abbey of Eynsham*, Oxford Historical Society, XLIX (Oxford, 1907), 411–423. See also Dom M. D. Knowles, *The Episcopal Colleagues of Archbishop Thomas Becket* (Cambridge, 1951), pp. 15–16.

Congregation of Savigny into England.[54] The early history of the Cistercian houses provides evidence of the same kind. It was because Ranulf de Gernons was the earl of Chester and his brother William de Roumare was the earl of Lincoln and between them they controlled a large part of England that the large number of Cistercian abbeys in the central parts of the country were established. Both monastic history and feudal history are inseparable from genealogy, and it is only through an awareness of baronial genealogy that we can understand the process of colonization of one monastery from another.

When Stephen was crowned king there were six earldoms in England: Chester, Buckingham, Gloucester, Leicester, Surrey, and Warwick. Three of these six belonged to a single, and powerful, family group. Leicester was the twin brother of Waleran, Count of Meulan and later (in 1138) Earl of Worcester; the Earl of Surrey was their stepbrother, and the Earl of Warwick, their first cousin.[55]

The English fortunes of the earls of Leicester were established by Hugh de Grentmesnil, a powerful lord of central Normandy who fought with Duke William at Hastings. His territorial rewards made him by far the greatest landholder in Leicestershire, while he held considerable estates in Warwickshire, Northamptonshire, Nottinghamshire, and Hertfordshire as well. Hugh died in 1093 and was succeeded in his English fiefs by his son Ivo. Ivo went off on the First Crusade, to finance which he mortgaged his lands to Robert, Count of Meulan. When the Earl of Leicester died in the Holy Land, the Count of Meulan ignored the claims of Ivo's son and united the Grentmesnil estates with his own.

This Robert, Count of Meulan, had come over in 1066 as plain Robert de Beaumont and, apparently, had distinguished himself at Hastings. He received large grants in Warwickshire, and small holdings in Leicestershire and

54 J. H. Round, "The Abbeys of Coggeshall and Stratford Langthorne," *Transactions of the Essex Archeological Society*, New Series, vol. V (1894–95).
55 G. W. White, "King Stephen's Earldoms," p. 51; see also Douglas, *E.H.D.*, II, Table 12, p. 993.

Northampton. In 1081 he inherited from his mother's family the comte of Meulan and succeeded also to the greater part of his father's lands in Normandy. Robert stood high in the favor of William Rufus (1089–1100), and was a trusted advisor of Henry I,[56] which helps to explain his acquisition of the Grentmesnil lands in 1101, including the earldom of Leicester.

It was the combination of these two groups of lands, of the Grentmesnils and the Beaumonts respectively, that constituted the bulk of the territorial entity which during the twelfth century came to be looked upon as the honour of the earls of Leicester. When Robert de Beaumont, Count of Meulan and Earl of Leicester, died in 1118, he divided his vast possessions between his twin sons, Robert, called "le Bossu," inherited all the English lands, together with the dignity of the earldom of Leicester; his brother Waleran succeeded to the family's Norman estates and some lands in Dorset. Soon after their father's death, his widow married William de Warenne, second earl of Surrey.[57]

The members of this powerful family were great patrons of the Cistercians. Robert "le Bossu," Earl of Leicester, founded the monastery of Garendon in 1133 and gave the town of Stockton for its support. The earl's sister, Margaret, Dowager Countess of Winchester, endowed the house with the town of Henley; her son and thus Leicester's nephew, Robert de Quensey, Earl of Winchester, gave the new monastery considerable lands in Belgrave, Thorpe, and Halthern. The possessions of Garendon Abbey were enlarged by the town of Badsley Endsor in the County of Warwick. This was the gift of Robert, Earl of Warwick, cousin of the Earl of Leicester.[58] It is significant that the first house colonized with

56 Levi Fox, "The Honour and Earldom of Leicester: Origin and Descent, 1066–1339," *E.H.R.*, LIX (1939), 386–387.
57 *Ibid.*, pp. 387–389; G. W. White, "The Career of Waleran, Count of Meulan and Earl of Worcester," *T.R.H.S.*, 4th Series, XVII (1934), 1. For the fortunes of the earldom of Leicester during the anarchy, see also H. W. C. Davis, "Some Documents of the Anarchy," in *Essays in History Presented to Reginald Lane Poole* (Oxford, 1927), pp. 172–176.
58 Dugdale, *Monasticon*, V, 328.

monks from Garendon was Bittlesden,[59] founded in 1147 by Arnold de Bosco, the steward of the Earl of Leicester. In the same year, 1147, the abbey of Sawtry[60] was begun in Huntingdonshire by Simon, Earl of Northampton, son-in-law of Earl Robert of Leicester. The Cistercian monastery of Bordesley in Worcestershire was also connected with the de Beaumont family — it was founded in 1138 by the earl's twin brother, Waleran, Count of Meulan.[61]

If the estates of the earls of Leicester and Worcester were large, the combined lands of the earls of Chester and Lincoln were enormous, undoubtedly the greatest territorial concentration between the Conquest and the death of Henry II. Ranulf de Gernons, Earl of Chester, was born in 1105, the son of Countess Lucy by her third husband, Ranulf de Meschin, hereditary vicomte of Bayeux and lord of the honour of Carlisle. (Lucy had first married Ivo de Taillebois, but no issue survived this union. The offspring of her second marriage to Robert Fitzgilbert de Roumare was a son, Robert de Roumare, who became earl of Lincoln and for a time royal justiciar in the shire.) When Richard d'Avranches, Earl of Chester, the cousin of Ranulf de Meschin, drowned in the sinking of the White Ship, King Henry I bestowed the earldom on Ranulf.[62]

The honour of Chester as the first Ranulf held it was enormous. Aside from the palatine county itself, it comprised tenements in twenty-two counties, of which the most significant strategically were the earl's Lincolnshire fiefs and a series of estates around the northern borders of Leicestershire and the southern edges of Nottingham and Derbyshire. Ranulf I had also controlled the dowry of his mother in Lincolnshire, her fief of Bolingbroke, and he held the wardship of William de Roumare's patrimony in Lincolnshire. It was this agglomeration of lands, with their twin centers in Chester and Lincoln and their line of communication across the Midlands, the nucleus of a most strategic position,

59 *Ibid.*, p. 364.   60 *Ibid.*, p. 522.   61 *Ibid.*, p. 407.
62 H. A. Cronne, "Ranulf de Gernons, Earl of Chester, 1129–1153," *T.R.H.S.*, 4th Series, XX (1937), 103–105.

which Ranulf de Gernons had inherited on the death of his father in 1129, and his brother had come into a little earlier.[63]

It was because the Earl of Chester controlled the single greatest concentration of lands in England during the twenty years of anarchy, and because he with his brother the Earl of Lincoln posed the single greatest threat to the power of King Stephen, that Ranulf de Gernons was the greatest single benefactor of the Cistercians in England. He himself founded in 1131 the abbey of Basingwerk;[64] both Combemere[65] (in the heart of Chester) and Calder[66] (in Cumberland) in the year 1135; Pipewell Abbey[67] in 1143; and Dieulacres in 1153.[68] His name heads the list of benefactors of Garendon Abbey,[69] and appears among those of Combe,[70] Louth Park,[71] Stoneleigh,[72] Revesby,[73] and Bordesley.[74] Thus, Earl Ranulf alone founded five Cistercian monasteries and helped to endow six others.

William de Roumare, Earl of Lincoln and Earl Ranulf's brother, likewise did a great deal to promote the cause of the White Monks. In 1142 the Earl of Lincoln founded the abbey of Revesby[75] near Horncastle in Lincolnshire. Four years later he established an abbot and the traditional twelve monks at Rufford[76] near Ollerton in Nottinghamshire. As his brother had, Earl William granted lands and rights to Garendon,[77] and was a benefactor of Kirkstall,[78] Vaudey,[79] and Swineshead.[80] Between them, therefore, the earls of Chester and Lincoln founded seven monasteries and endowed with estates and lands ten others. If a triangle be erected on the map of England with Chester, Lincoln, and Coventry as angles, we have inscribed an area in which seventeen monasteries were founded; if the bordering lands of the earls of Leicester and Worcester be added to these, the number of Cistercian foundations made by these two families in

---

[63] *Ibid.*, pp. 105–108; see also R. H. C. Davis, "King Stephen and the Earl of Chester Revised," pp. 654–660.
[64] Dugdale, *Monasticon*, V, 261.   [65] *Ibid.*, p. 321.   [66] *Ibid.*, p. 329.
[67] *Ibid.*, p. 431.   [68] *Ibid.*, p. 627.   [69] *Ibid.*, p. 328.   [70] *Ibid.*, p. 582.
[71] *Ibid.*, p. 413.   [72] *Ibid.*, p. 443.   [73] *Ibid.*, p. 453.   [74] *Ibid.*, p. 407.
[75] *Ibid.*, p. 454.   [76] *Ibid.*, pp. 517–518.   [77] *Ibid.*, p. 328.
[78] *Ibid.*, p. 530.   [79] *Ibid.*, p. 490.   [80] *Ibid.*, p. 336.

this area between 1130 and 1155 rises to twenty-five, or about one-half the total for all of England.

It is instructive to note, incidentally, that most Cistercian monasteries were not situated in Yorkshire. About half of them were located in the Midlands, and the rest were evenly distributed throughout the entire island. The great prestige of the abbeys of Fountains and Rievaulx, and the impact they had on the monasteries throughout the rest of England, the wealth of the Yorkshire houses and the survival of more evidence from the northern monasteries than from else-where — all these factors have contributed to the preservation of an idea which has no strong support in all the evidence.

The motives of the great Norman lords who founded and endowed religious houses in the decades immediately following the death of Henry I undoubtedly differed from those of the monastic patrons of the generation of Hastings. The men who settled in England in 1066 retained their loyalties to the family monasteries in the duchy of Normandy, and this helps to explain the gifts of English lands to Norman abbeys.[81] The great lords who founded and endowed the Cistercian abbeys owed their status as English landlords to the Norman Conquest. Their fathers and grandfathers had given lands on their English fiefs to Norman monasteries, but the magnates of Stephen's reign were probably beginning to regard themselves as English barons, and the foundation of monasteries on their lands is an indication of the way in which the Anglo-Norman nobility was beginning to settle down on English soil before the loss of Normandy obliged them to make a definite choice between France and England.

This does not explain why so many monasteries were founded during the anarchy of Stephen's reign. Is there some connection between the feudal disorder and the burst of religious foundations? Feudalism is essentially a political term. "It [feudalism] is a form of government in which political authority is monopolized by a small group of military

[81] Donald Matthew, *Norman Monasteries and Their English Possessions* (Oxford, 1962), p. 17.

36

leaders." [82] The period of the anarchy was a time of intensified feudalism, a time when the English barons sought to increase their personal political authority and private power, obviously at the expense of the crown's. This feudalism produced a civil war, which in turn contributed to the disputed succession. Because the English barons were loyal or treasonous to Stephen according to which course of action best promoted their interests at any given moment, and since, therefore, they changed sides frequently, it is impossible to state with any degree of exactness which barons supported the king and which aided Matilda. The closest we can come to the truth of the situation is that the great barons of Stephen's reign acted consistently on their own behalf and on no other's. As one contemporary summed up the behavior of the nobility during the entire reign: "the wealthy nobles of the land, rolling in affluence, care little to what iniquities the wretched sufferers [i.e., common people] are exposed; all their concern is for themselves and their adherents; and thus they store their castles and fortified towns with armed bands." [83] The only possible exception to this axiom was Robert, Earl of Gloucester, "the sole strength of the Angevin cause," who according to William of Malmesbury "alone or almost alone was never swayed from his loyalty by hope of gain or fear of

[82] J. R. Strayer, "Feudalism in Western Europe," in R. Coulborn, ed., *Feudalism in History* (Princeton, 1956), pp. 16–17. Every student of medieval history must eventually come to terms with the words "feudal" and "feudalism," even if they should be, according to Richardson and Sayles, "the most regrettable coinages ever put into circulation to debase the language of historians." See *The Governance of Medieval England from the Conquest to Magna Carta* (Edinburgh, 1963), pp. 30–33. Because the institution itself was constantly changing, the student may not be able to achieve a precise definition of feudalism applicable for all times and places, but he must develop one for the time and country with which he is dealing. In spite of its very impressive learning, Richardson and Sayles's lengthy attack on the English Establishment does not succeed in convincing one to reject the work of all the English and American scholars who have struggled with "the" problem of medieval history. Suggesting that the word be completely avoided, these authors do nothing to aid our understanding of feudalism but, rather, give us a treatment as confused as the confusion they are supposedly trying to dispel.
[83] T. Forester, ed. and trans., *Chronicle of Florence of Worcester* (London, 1854), p. 250.

loss." [84] These were the very same men who founded and endowed Cistercian abbeys, and they established monasteries because, as we shall see, they looked upon them as investments from which they might anticipate concrete material returns.

The connection between semi-independent lords and the expansion of the monasteries illustrates the pattern of the institutional relationship between the two groups in English society. When the great barons assisted the Cistercians with landed endowments, with privileges and with rights, and the monks accepted these gifts, there was established between the two institutions, the feudal and the monastic, a strong, close, and virtually indissoluble bond. The monasteries obviously depended on the barons for support. Without the lords the monasteries could not have been established, nor could they have prospered to the positions of considerable wealth and power which they rapidly did. On the other hand, the barons realized that the monasteries posed no threat to feudal power or ambition; indeed, the monasteries, by the very fact of their dependence on the nobles and by the fact of their close connection with the Holy See, implicitly supported the barons in their opposition to royal authority. The great lords exploited the monks by adding feudal, financial, and other strings to their "offerings." These original stipulations were such that the monasteries, by accepting them, became inextricably involved in the social structure of the land. As the endowments were made in perpetuity, so the obligations of the monks extended in *saecula saeculorum*.

The west and north of England were the strongholds of the semiautonomous barons of Stephen's reign, and it was in the west and north that the White Monks had their greatest impact. They brought to England austere ideals and a fervently emotional asceticism especially suited to the physical climate of those areas. The obligations of absolute poverty and perpetual silence, the prolonged periods of manual

84 Giles, *William of Malmesbury*, p. 527. William wrote his history for, and dedicated it to, Earl Robert of Gloucester. See the very laudatory preface, p. 480.

labor, and the decision to accept for habitation and cultivation only remote wastelands — all these ideals fitted in well with the atmosphere of the barren moors and bleak ridings of the west country and Yorkshire. This helps to explain why the Cistercian abbeys, although they were evenly distributed throughout the entire island, had their greatest influence in the north and west.

English conditions, however, were not peculiar. The expansion of the Order of Cîteaux in the German Empire and in the territories which were eventually to make up the Kingdom of France occurred under circumstances which offer striking parallels to the conditions in England. It was during periods of anarchy or civil war, periods when the central authority was weak and baronial power strong that the Cistercians made their greatest increases in the twelfth century. In the empire, "the weakening of the material foundations of the monarchy was, together with the strengthening of the electoral rights of the princes, a cardinal feature of the period 1106–1152," [85] the period of the introduction and the initial growth of the Cistercian Order in Germany. The Emperor Frederick Barbarossa (1152–87) sought to increase the imperial authority by strengthening the feudal basis of his government. His agreement of 1180 with his great barons gave them special privileges which raised them above the counts and lesser nobles; this move reduced the independence of the lesser nobles who now fell under the authority of the great princes of the empire. But the result was that as imperial power weakened in Frederick's last years and the early years of his successor, effective power was solidified in the hands of the German princes.[86] It was the princes, especially in those areas where the imperial influence was historically weak — in eastern Pomerania, in Mecklenburg, and in Silesia — who strongly supported the Cistercians.[87]

[85] G. Barraclough, *Origins of Modern Germany* (Oxford, 1952), pp. 159–160.

[86] *Ibid.*, pp. 189–190.

[87] J. W. Thompson, *Economic and Social History of the Middle Ages* (New York, 1928), pp. 611–619; see also H. Aubin, "Medieval Agrarian Society in its Prime: The lands east of the Elbe and German colonisation

The German princes of the east employed (and exploited) the White Monks as their agents in the colonization and cultivation of vast stretches of marsh and wasteland. Throughout the lands which were to become in the thirteenth century the Kingdom of France, disorder, anarchy, and civil wars were endemic during the twelfth century, at least until the reign of Philip Augustus (1180–1223). Unable to extend their royal suzerainty, it was all that the Capetians could do to hold on to what they had, the lands of the Île de France.[88] It was in exactly those parts of the country in which the king's influence was weakest, and the power of the great dukes and counts correspondingly strong — in Burgundy, in Normandy, and in Brittany — that there was the greatest proliferation of Cistercian abbeys.[89]

As I shall demonstrate with respect to England, the probability is strong that the great continental barons who supported the Cistercians did so because Cistercian abbeys required a very small initial outlay of money, because the nobles hoped to learn new agricultural methods from the monks, and in order to exploit the monasteries for financial and feudal reasons. In the German Empire and sometimes in the French territories, the great princes and dukes were able to secure privileges and rights which the English barons would certainly have wanted, but which the strength of the English monarchy prevented them from gaining — the rights of advocacy. Such privileges included political control over monastic dependents, jurisdiction over the tenants of monastic properties, and general governmental authority within the entire monastic territory.[90] It goes without saying that

eastwards," in J. H. Clapham and Eileen Power, eds., *The Cambridge Economic History of Europe*, I (Cambridge, 1941), 361–397.

88 E. Lavisse, *Histoire de France*, tome II, part II (Paris, 1901), 311–329; F. Lot and R. Fawtier, *Histoire des institutions françaises au moyen âge*, tome II: *Institutions royales* (Paris, 1958), pp. 109–110.

89 The feudal lords of Brittany were not at all controlled by the Count of Brittany, and in Burgundy the influence of the duke was checked not only by the lay lords but also by the great clerical and monastic authorities. See Lot and Fawtier, *Histoire*, II, 271, 210–211; Lekai, *White Monks*, pp. 12, 26.

90 Lekai, *White Monks*, p. 278.

such rights, involving such external political pressures on the religious life, were in flagrant violation of the spirit and letter of the Cistercian ideals as expressed in their constitutions. The Order of Cîteaux was established in reaction to the traditional practice of worldly feudal influences on the monastic life. The conditions under which the Cistercian monasteries were founded and endowed on the continent involved them thoroughly in the political and social structure of the territories in which they were established.

It has been shown that the nobles who founded and endowed the first generation of Cistercian houses in England were closely related to one another, either by blood, or by marriage, or by interests; and that they were the very same men who were building up their private power in opposition to the crown. But how does the foundation of a Cistercian monastery serve in any way to enhance the political power or to improve the economic condition of a feudal baron? What was to be the relationship, immediate and long-range, between the monastery and the baronial land-donor? It is to these questions that we must now turn, where we shall be obliged to concur with La Rochefoucauld in finding that generosity was but a cloak for ambition.

chapter two

the cistercians
and their patrons

Let the wilderness and the dry-lands exult,
let the wasteland rejoice and bloom,
let it bring forth flowers like the jonquil,
let it rejoice and sing for joy.

The glory of Lebanon is bestowed on it,
the splendour of Carmel and Sharon;
they shall see the glory of Yahweh,
the splendour of our God.

Isaiah 35:1–2
The Jerusalem Bible

The widespread increase in the houses of the Cistercian Order, an expansion that was evenly distributed throughout the entire island, was truly remarkable in a country where so many great estates were in the hands of the Benedictines. This growth has been considered all the more unusual since it occurred in a period when the Augustinians and the Gilbertines were also multiplying,[1] and in decades marked by bitter civil strife. Yet there was a definite relationship between the disorders of Stephen's reign and the expansion of the White Monks in England; and, when one considers the nature of the early Cistercian endowments,

---

[1] Knowles, *M.O.*, p. 246.

their size, quality, and the general confusion surrounding their beginnings, a less astounding picture of the phenomenon emerges.

The beginnings of a monastic foundation might be haphazard at first or elaborately planned from the start. A house might begin with a lord sending supplies to wandering monks who turned up in his woods or, more probably, with businesslike negotiations between a donor and an established monastery for a nucleus of monks to be sent from the existing house. This last method seems to have been the manner in which most Cistercian houses in England came into being, and preparations were usually made against the arrival of a group of monks. Thus Walter Espec who founded Rievaulx Abbey visited at Clairvaux and made arrangements with St. Bernard before founding that house.[2]

"The basic and indispensable feature of a monastic grant in the twelfth century was the *donatio*, the act of giving. This was a single operation, attested by witnesses, symbolized by some concrete ceremony of law, whether religious or otherwise, perpetuated by a charter, strengthened usually by various other expedients, such as oaths, affidavits and the presence of extra and theoretically impartial witnesses in addition to those of the donor and the monastery."[3] The foundation of a monastery, however, was not a single act. Years might elapse between the first *donatio* of the founder and the actual beginning of conventional life. For the monks, and for the order as a whole, the new house was not considered really founded until the church or part of it was dedicated. At the dedication the intention of the founder was felt to have been realized, and the whole complicated process of foundation would be recorded in writing. Some-

2 Dugdale, *Monasticon*, V, 280. "Anno Domini MCXXII, Gualterus Espec, vir magnus et potens in conspectu regis et totius regni, monachos Cisterciensis observantiae directos a Bernardo abbate Clarevalle recepit, et posuit solutudine Blachomour secus aquam Rie, a qua coenobium eorum Rievallis dicitur, cum quibus missus est Gulielmus primus abbas eorum, vir consummatae virtutis et excellentis memoriae."
3 V. H. Galbraith, "Monastic Foundation Charters of the Eleventh and Twelfth Centuries," *Cambridge Historical Journal*, IV, no. 3 (1934), 214.

times the record of establishment was preserved by a series of individual charters, culminating in a general charter of confirmation when all was finished. But the foundation of the abbey was commonly dated in the monastic chronicles from the moment of the first gift.[4] Whenever a lord founded a monastery on "his" land, both he and the monastery sought a charter of confirmation from the king, since, in theory at least, all the land of England belonged to the king and could only be alienated by him.

What was the legal relationship between the Cistercian abbeys and their patrons? With the older Benedictine houses, patronage often involved custody of the property in vacancies, formal rights in the elections of the abbots, feudal dues and an explicitly stated amount of military service, rights of hospitality, and the usual spiritual services for the donor and his family. These rights of patronage were recognized in common law and in the ecclesiastical courts, with some reservations. The Cistercian houses however, as an exempt order, were theoretically free of these obligations to, and potential interferences from, their benefactors because of their tenure in frankalmoin (see *infra*). The men who established and endowed Cistercian abbeys, although they did not secure the same sort of rights which usually accompanied the patronage of a Benedictine monastery, nevertheless had important feudal and economic interests in their foundations.

There was a considerable difference between the materials necessary for the foundation of a Cistercian monastery and those required for the establishment of a Benedictine house. The ideals of the early Cistercians as set down in the *Exordium Parvum* and the *Carta Caritatis* reflect a deep conviction that life under conditions governed by customs traditional in Benedictine monasteries was a real violation of the Western monastic ideals as defined in the *Rule of St. Benedict*. The Cistercians wanted a life more severe, more retired from the world, and one which practiced absolute poverty. Therefore, they rejected all feudal connections and posses-

4 *Ibid.*, pp. 214–215.

44

sions and sources of wealth, such as manorial mills, bakeries, fairs, courts, and serfs. More strongly, they renounced all income deriving from church possessions. They resolved to choose for their foundations only land far from human habitation,[5] to be tilled and exploited solely for the use of the community, and essentially by the monks' own labors. (Given the social, economic, and political conditions of English life in the twelfth century, the realization of such an ambitious ideal was, as we shall see, virtually impossible.) Because it was impossible for the choir monks, while performing all their liturgical duties, to devote the number of hours necessary each day to the execution of the field and farm work of a great estate, the Cistercians introduced lay-brothers to do the bulk of the manual work. In order to handle the problems involved in the stocking and exploitation of extensive estates without resorting to renting, they introduced a system of isolated granges on those lands at a distance from the abbey, the granges to be staffed by the lay-brothers.[6]

On the other hand, a Benedictine abbey, considered as an economic unit, was for all practical purposes very similar to the barony of any lay or ecclesiastical lord. The lands of a Black Monk house consisted of manors, each with its demesne lands worked by the labor due from the various classes of the rural population, with a small amount held by free tenants; the workers were members of all classes from serf to the totally free.[7]

In contrast to this, the ideal aimed at by the White Monks, an ideal it might be said which was never achieved in England, was to settle on undeveloped land and, instead of holding a number of scattered manors, to be in control of one great bloc of land, in which the center of economic life was the abbey, with the granges as little more than depots.[8]

5 *Consuetudines*, in Guignard, *Monuments*, p. 250. "In civitatibus, castellis, villis, nulla nostra construenda sunt coenobia, sed in locis a conversatione hominum remotis."
6 *Ibid.*, p. 251; Knowles, *M.O.*, p. 211. Here I am dependent on Knowles.
7 Knowles, *M.O.*, pp. 172–190 *et passim*.
8 Guignard, *Consuetudines*, in *Monuments*, p. 251 *et passim*.

From the point of view of the great barons who founded and endowed the Cistercian monasteries, the establishment of a White Monk house was a far less expensive undertaking than the establishment of a Benedictine abbey. In order to begin a Benedictine monastery a large number of buildings furnished with some elaboration were needed, as well as an extensive group of manors already fully exploited and sufficient to bring in produce and revenue for the support of monks, servants, and dependents, and for the upkeep of church, buildings, and libraries. All that the Cistercians needed, however, was a sufficient area of wasteland, capable of being cultivated for the needs of a group of men which did not in the beginning exceed thirty, and was usually only thirteen. It is true that buildings for the community were required, but originally these could be made of wood or mud and twigs, and the monks themselves could build them. The feudal baron made no great sacrifice in founding a Cistercian monastery, because the outlay in costs and in loss of revenue was virtually negligible.[9] And so the Cistercians received just what their constitutions called for, if not what individuals and certain communities would have preferred.

Most, if not all, the land granted to the White Monks in England was called wastelands in the foundation charters. The evidence of the documents on this point is almost unanimous.[10] By wasteland is usually meant soil so rocky or otherwise unsuited to farming that it had never been put to the plow; or forest land; or, as in Cambridgeshire, marshy fenland; or, finally, land agriculturally worn out after centuries of use. Agriculturally exhausted soil seems to have been the type of land the Cistercians usually received, probably because this was the only type of land the barons were willing to part with. But a large part of England was, already in 1135, as the leading authority on medieval English agrarian his-

[9] Knowles, *M.O.*, pp., 246–247.
[10] See for example Dugdale, *Monasticon*, V, 435 (Pipewell), 378 (Ford), 364 (Bittlesden), 512 (Sallay), 388 (Meaux), *et passim*; the early agricultural and economic difficulties of Fountains Abbey are described at length in J. R. Walbran, ed., *Memorials of the Abbey of St. Mary of Fountains*, Surtees Society, XLII (Durham, 1863), I, 48–61.

tory has recently demonstrated for the period 1086–1135, agriculturally "an old country." Anglo-Saxon society had long passed beyond the colonial stage, and although judged by modern standards the population was scanty and the area of woodland large, the farmers of the Anglo-Norman period were not breaking through the edges of an unsubdued wilderness. Villages, hamlets, and farmsteads were to be found throughout the length and breath of the country, and what real waste there was provided supplies of timber, firewood, and a source of food for swine. As regards tillage, "the evidence unmistakably suggests, if it cannot be said to prove beyond all doubt, that the area under the plow in the country as a whole . . . was not much less, and may even have been somewhat greater, than the extent of arable in the early years of the twentieth century." [11]

[11] I am relying strongly here on Reginald Lennard, *Rural England, 1086–1135* (Oxford, 1958), pp. 1–4. Professor Lennard, following the figures of Maitland and Darby, shows that there were 71,785 Domesday plow teams. "At the traditional figure of 120 acres per team, this would mean 8.6 million acres of arable (in 1086), while the official *Agricultural Statistics* give the arable on 4 June 1914 as 7.7 million acres." It can be argued that Lennard has selected the largest possible figure, 120 acres for every plow team, but he demonstrates that if we reckon only 100 acres per plow, we should still be left with 7.2 million acres of arable, which is 93 per cent of the 1914 area. See Lennard's Appendix I, p. 393. Domesday Book also indicates that the old religious orders practiced sheep farming on a large scale, for in 1086 Ely Abbey had 13,400 sheep on its estates in six counties. See Eileen Power, *The Wool Trade in English Medieval History* (Oxford, 1941), p. 33, and Archibald R. Lewis, "The Closing of the Medieval Frontier 1250–1350," *Speculum,* XXXIII (1958), 475–483, which treats general European conditions, but certainly sustains Lennard's conclusions for England. Compare Lennard's thesis with the older, traditional view that there was considerable wasteland as the result of the Conqueror's widespread devastations in the north, and his introduction of the forest laws, in H. C. Darby, ed., "The Economic Geography of England, A.D. 1000–1250," in *An Historical Geography of England Before 1800* (Cambridge, 1936), pp. 166–175. M. W. Barley, "Cistercian Land Clearances in Nottinghamshire: Three Deserted Villages and Their Moated Successor," *Nottingham Medieval Studies,* I (1957), 75–89, using the abbey of Rufford as example, describes how the foundation of a Cistercian monastery often destroyed existing villages and the usual manorial economy in order to achieve the ideal of complete seclusion. This is a most interesting article, which by implication strongly supports Lennard.

47

It was not just with the "old" land that the barons endowed the Cistercians, but with land totally exhausted. Very often the land was so worn out, or so totally unsuited to agriculture when the monks received it, that they were soon obliged to give up their attempts at farming and to seek a new site for their foundations. Thus, the land given to Sawley Abbey in 1147 by William de Percy, the father-in-law of Roger, Earl of Warwick, was so completely irrecoverable for purposes of tillage that the monks "were reduced to extreme want through the ill temperature of the air which permitted nothing to thrive on the ground." The community had decided to give up the foundation when the Countess of Warwick gave the monks a carucate of better lands and rights to certain ecclesiastical income in order, as the chronicler magnanimously puts it, "to prevent her father's charity from being lost." [12]

The abbey of Haverholme was founded in Lincolnshire in 1137, but the land was so wanting in arability that it supported the monks for only two years. Fortunately, Alexander, Bishop of Lincoln (1123–48), came to their rescue and endowed the community with some of his lands at Louth Park, to which the monastery was removed.[13] Further illustration of the nature of the lands given to the first generation of Cistercian houses is provided by the early history of Vaudey Abbey. Vaudey was first founded by William, Earl of York, at Bythan in Lincolnshire, but the monks found their location so inconvenient — perhaps because the land was all swamp and there was no adequate water supply — that they were forced to evacuate. Through the assistance of Geoffrey de Brachecourt or his lord, the Earl of Lincoln, the monks were removed to a more productive spot in the parish of Edenham, called Valle Dei, or Vaudey.[14]

In addition to the fact that the lands which the great

12 J. McNulty, ed., *The Chartulary of the Cistercian Abbey of St. Mary of Sallay in Craven*, Yorkshire Archeological Society, Record Series, LXXXVII (1933), 1.
13 *Victoria County History*: Lincoln, I, 40.
14 Dugdale, *Monasticon*, V, 490; *V.C.H.*: Lincoln, I, 140.

barons gave to the Cistercians during the period of the anarchy were of slight agricultural value, these initial grants were probably quite small in size. It is impossible to prove this beyond all doubt, because the charters of endowment are extremely vague: they usually speak of a baron giving "all his land in," or "a tract of open pasture," or again "a beautiful spot." The amount of these estates in any one part of a county obviously varied greatly, especially during the anarchy of Stephen's reign when the extent of a baron's tenements fluctuated considerably.

The establishment of Kirkstead Abbey provides a typically vague account of the quantity of the land given. The thirteen monks who came from Fountains Abbey in 1139 arrived at "a place of horror like a vast solitude," surrounded by brushwood and marsh. The original site was found to be too small and proved otherwise unsuitable.[15] Or again, the early endowment of Combe Abbey in Warwickshire "consisted essentially of small parcels of land." [16] Those few instances where we do have concrete figures for the amount of land granted to a monastery by its founders confirm the impression that these initial grants were quite small.

The original landed foundation of Thame Abbey in Oxfordshire consisted of only five virgates, about 150 acres.[17] The abbey of Swineshead in Lincoln began her existence in 1135 with 240 acres,[18] and Garendon Abbey, the only Cistercian house in Leicestershire, started with five carucates and three virgates, or about 690 acres.[19] What do these figures mean? The virgate like all medieval measurements varied in size; it might be as small as 15 or as large as 80 acres, but it is now generally understood to have been about 30 acres. A carucate was generally estimated at 120 acres.[20] Thus the

[15] Dugdale, *Monasticon*, V, 418; Walbran, *Memorials of Fountains Abbey*, I, 61–65.
[16] Dugdale, *Monasticon*, V, 582.   [17] *V.C.H.*: Oxfordshire, I, 83.
[18] *Ibid.*: Lincolnshire, I, 146.   [19] Dugdale, *Monasticon*, V, 382.
[20] P. Vinogradoff, *The Growth of the Manor* (London, 1905), pp. 151–162. Vinogradoff stresses the point that hides, carucates, and virgates were not measures in any exact terms. The figures of 120 acres for the carucate and 30 acres for the virgate are only averages.

49

figures given above. The virgate was supposed to be large enough to sustain a peasant; a carucate was considered the amount of land necessary to support one knight and his household.[21] Each Cistercian monastery at the time of its foundation was made up of an abbot and the traditional apostolic figure of twelve monks. A virgate or about 30 acres being necessary to support one peasant, then 390 acres would be necessary to provide sustenance for thirteen. If the thirteen were to be maintained on the meager diet of the peasant, they could not have eked out an existence with the 150 acres with which a monastery like Thame began, nor with the 240 acres which Swineshead had; the 690 acres with which Garendon began should have been sufficient, assuming that the land was arable, which it probably was not. It can be argued that if a peasant could live on a very small holding, a monk should have been been able to do the same. But we know, from one document at least, that the Cistercians, in spite of the austerity of their constitutions, did not and were not expected by contemporary lay society to live on the diet of the peasants. When Geoffrey de Brachecourt, a knight of the Earl of Lincoln, rescued the monastery of Vaudey from collapse due to a small initial endowment and poor soil, he stipulated in his charter of endowment that the monks should supply him and his wife and two servants during their lifetime with all the things necessary for their diet and clothing: he and his wife were to have such food as the monks ate, while his servants were to get such fare as the monks' servants received.[22]

Other difficulties surrounded the foundation of the Cistercian monasteries. Bittlesden Abbey was established in 1147 by Arnold de Bosco, steward of Robert de Beaumont, Earl of Leicester. The account of Bittlesden's beginnings does not reflect much credit on her founder. The lands with which Arnold de Bosco endowed Bittlesden were a gift to him from

[21] P. Vinogradoff, *Villeinage in England* (Oxford, 1892), pp. 148, 238–239.
[22] Dugdale, *Monasticon*, V, 490. "Mihi autem et uxori victum providebunt eodem modo, et mensura quo duobus monachis, et servientibus nostris, sicut duobus ex servientibus suis."

the Earl of Leicester to whom they had escheated during the civil war by the failure of the former tenant, Robert de Meppershall, to do the required homage and service for them. It was said that Arnold determined to found a monastery at Bittlesden in order to avoid the difficulty of a disputed tenure. But when peace was restored, Robert de Meppershall laid claim to the lands and impleaded Arnold. The monks were obliged to buy out Robert's claim and to purchase a charter of confirmation by the payment of the sum of ten marks.[23] This story is a fair illustration of the difficulties of many of the early Cistercian foundations in England. The seemingly generous donations were often, if not always, land which the founder valued least among his possessions, and often, as in this case, land laboring under some kind of legal disability which would severely tax the resources of an obscure and struggling monastery. The simple truth of the matter is that the barons endowed the Cistercians because it cost them virtually nothing to part with the paltry things they gave.

There is a curious and somewhat amusing exception to this generalization in the history of the foundation of Meaux Abbey. William "le Gros," Count of Aumale and Earl of York, sometime in his early manhood had made a vow to go on a pilgrimage to the Holy Land. As the years advanced and he gained in corpulency, William felt indisposed or unable to fulfill his vow. The earl had founded the Cistercian abbey of Vaudey in Lincolnshire, although his original gift to that house was so scanty that it was soon reduced to poverty. In the construction of the conventual buildings at Vaudey, William used the architectural ability of a certain Adam, a monk of Fountains, who had already demonstrated his talents in the development of the cloisters at Kirkstead and Woburn. In several conversations with the earl, Adam detected a certain uneasiness on the subject of the unfulfilled vow, and the shrewd monk so far worked on his patron's disturbed conscience as to advise him to found a monastery as a means of securing papal absolution from his commitment.

[23] *Ibid.*, p. 364; *V.C.H.*: Buckinghamshire, I, 365.

Adam sought out the powerful Abbot of Clairvaux whose good offices naturally succeeded in obtaining the required dispensation from the Cistercian Pope Eugenius III (1145–53). The Earl of York was so relieved that he invited Adam to survey his estates in order to choose a suitable site for the promised foundation. Coming to a place called Melsa or Meaux in Holderness, near Beverley in Yorkshire, Adam found just the situation he desired in an area which the chronicler of Meaux records as "well planted with woods and orchards, surrounded with rivers and waters, and favored with rich soil." In the midst of it was a rising ground, known as the Hill of St. Mary. Going up this hill, Adam struck a staff into the ground, announcing, "Let this place be called a palace of the eternal king, a vineyard of heaven, and a gate of life. Here he established a family of the worshippers of Christ." But the Earl of York became rather alarmed. He had acquired that piece of land only a few days before at very great cost, and he naturally disliked giving it up. He had planned to make it the park of his estate and had already begun to enclose it. He tried hard to bribe Adam with other lands and gave him liberty to select from all of his other properties. But the monk was not to be diverted from his first choice. Eventually the earl, probably realizing that he was cornered, acquiesced and gave the whole property "to God and the Blessed Virgin for the foundation of a monastery of monks." [24]

I have given at some length the history of the foundation of this particular Cistercian abbey, one of the very few specific accounts that we possess, because it illustrates a number of significant points. First of all, Meaux Abbey was not founded in any great gush of religious zeal, but rather because the donor had made a vow which age and health now prevented his keeping, and for which he had to satisfy the Church in some way. Probably the small expense inherent in the foundation of Cistercian monastery was an appealing argument for such "generosity"; the foundation of a house of another

24 E. A. Bond, ed., *Chronica Monasterii de Melsa*, I (Rolls Series, no. 43, London, 1866), 76–82.

order would have cost him far more. The early history of Vaudey Abbey, which Earl William had founded three years before, does not suggest that he was a man of remarkable or genuine charity. He certainly did not want to give the monks his best estates, lands "well planted with woods and orchards, surrounded with rivers and waters, and favored with rich soil." He wanted to keep that for himself. And the history of the start of this house shows that the White Monks themselves were equally anxious to secure the possession of arable lands, fields already under cultivation, and that they did not deliberately seek out poor, rocky soil or wasteland. The truth of the matter is that such was the only type of land they could get, the only kind of land the barons were willing to give them.

All students of the Cistercian movement have considered simple Christian piety to have been the chief, sometimes the only, motive of the great barons who founded and endowed Cistercian monasteries. This has been true of all the research on the subject from the pioneer monograph of Miss Alice Cooke in 1893 [25] down to what is perhaps the definitive general treatment on English monasticism by Dom David Knowles which first appeared in 1940. Miss Cooke praised the barons for their foundations in desert-like "places of horror and dreary isolation." Her explanation for the lords' generosity rested in the nobles' belief that the restless, energetic spirit of the early Cistercians could find expression only in wild and remote valleys.[26] Although the constitutions of the Order had laid it down that Cistercian monasteries should be remote from the habitations of men, as we now know, there was no area so isolated in England in 1135 that half a day's walk would not bring the traveler to some other village, hamlet, or at least homestead. "The unassailable evidence of Domesday Book enables one to assert without hesitation that the great majority of Englishmen lived in villages or hamlets that were associated to form village townships for administrative purposes — and that these were

[25] Cooke, "The Settlement of the Cistercians in England."
[26] *Ibid.*, pp. 647–648.

all within easy reach of other villages." [27] From the evidence cited above relating to the establishment of Meaux Abbey, there is good reason to believe that the monks themselves did not care to begin an already severely ascetic life in barren, desert-like wasteland. Professor Knowles, while he acknowledges the low outlay involved in the foundation of a Cistercian house, suggests that the average feudal magnate "was very willing to atone for his misdeeds by the foundation of a religious house, or by benefactions to an old one." [28] But if their motives were solely penance and piety, who should such a man as William of Ypres, Earl of Kent — who was by no means unique in his behavior — found the Cistercian Abbey of Boxley in 1143, and then, in the same year burn to the ground the nunnery of Wherwell with all the nuns inside; and extort such a high ransom from the abbey of St. Albans that the abbot was forced to convert the sacred vessels of that rich Benedictine house into coin in order to persuade the earl not to burn the town- [29] A recent student of English monasticism states that the moorland settlements of the Cistercians were founded without much thought, and, as it were, "in an enthusiastic fit," [30] implying, perhaps, that the Order of Cîteaux, like the British Empire, grew on a wave of absentmindedness.

Simple, unaffected piety and Christlike generosity perhaps did have their places in the minds and attitudes of the powerful men who supported the Cistercians. But it should always be remembered that the Middle Ages in general, and Stephen's reign in England particularly, was a period of incredible violence and brutality. Fortunately, most churchmen in most ages have sought to temper this disorder, and, given the perverse and corrupt nature of what they have been working with through the centuries, they have had a remarkable degree of success. Piety and penance were not the only motives of the great lords, and even when these virtues

[27] Lennard, *Rural England*, p. 20.   [28] Knowles, *M.O.*, p. 247.
[29] *Ibid.*, pp. 270–271.
[30] Susan Wood, *English Monasteries and Their Patrons in the Thirteenth Century* (Oxford, 1960), p. 4.

appear to be the chief inducements to generosity, they should be understood more as being a possible insurance against future damnation in hell than as a reflection of open simplicity and disinterested love here on earth. The great ideals of the feudal, military nobility of the twelfth century were loyalty and bravery; the Christian virtues of humility and love are almost their direct antithesis. Piety and penance were not the only, or even the main, motives of the great lords. Rich men built monasteries for pride rather devotion, as visible testimony to their power and their position; the monasteries were in many ways the "status symbols" of the twelfth century.

The English barons also built monasteries with a definite desire for, and the sure expectation of, material gain. Wool had been exported from England before the Norman Conquest, and by the beginning of the second quarter of the twelfth century a natural exchange had developed with the manufacturing cities of Flanders, whose climate did not allow the raising of sheep. The evidence of "Little Domesday Book" which covers the counties of East Anglia shows that some of the men who were given English lands by William I turned their minds and estates to sheep-farming. An entry for Forncett in Norfolk states that "then [before the Conquest] there was one sheep, now there are eighty." If the information from East Anglia has any reference to the rest of the country, for which sheep returns do not exist, the Conquest was followed by a general increase in the flocks. There is enormous evidence that the nobility and the upper classes of Henry II's reign were interested in the profits to be made from the sale of the wool from the sheep. If we may argue from the evidence of the early and late twelfth century, it is extremely likely that the great lords of Stephen's reign, who were doing so much to enhance their political power, were also anxious to get what profits they could from the farming of sheep. The barons during the anarchy, sons and heirs of the Anglo-Norman lords who had come to England in 1066, established monasteries in the less settled areas of the west and north where the terrain was especially suited to sheep-farming — temperate, moist, with limestone downs and heather moors ideally suited for grazing. Cistercian monasteries cost the lords virtually nothing in the way of an initial outlay, and the monks themselves provided a most inexpensive labor force. The Cistercians were endowed and supported quite probably because they helped to increase their donors' flocks and the quality of the sheep's wool.

The barons' charters of endowment to the Cistercians, which have not been closely examined before, make it abundantly clear that the patrons of the monks expected definite material gains on their donations.

Throughout the twelfth century, all grants to the Order of Cîteaux were gifts in frankalmoin or free alms tenure. The charters of endowment invariably states that the grant is made to the religious house in free alms (*in elemosinam*) or, more emphatically, "in free, pure and perpetual alms," the purpose or motive of the benefactor being the salvation of his soul and the souls of his relatives and ancestors, or of his lord, or of the king: the land is given *pro anima mea, pro salute animae meae*.[31] According to the customary phraseology of the donor's terms, the gifts are made not to men, but to God. Thus, Thurstan, Archbishop of York (1114–40), made a grant of land "to God and the Church of St. Mary of Fountains and to the abbot and monks there serving God according to the Rule of St. Benedict and the Cistercian constitutions."[32] As the well-known thirteenth-century jurist, William of Bracton, says, such gifts were made *primo et principaliter* to God, and *secundario* to the monks. This form of land tenure, frankalmoin, implied that in the first place, the services required were spiritual, as distinguished from military or some other form of secular services, and in the second place, the prayers of the monastic community were to be continued in time forever. This is the classic

31 For example, see William Farrer, ed., *Early Yorkshire Charters* (Edinburgh, 1914–23), I, 63–64 *et passim*.
32 *Ibid.*

56

definition of Maitland,[33] and here the difficulty begins. The problem of the possession of land in free alms is in many ways as complicated as the very problem of feudalism itself. Certainly, as far as church property is concerned, the holding of land according to frankalmoin tenure is at the heart of the nature of feudalism. As far as there is evidence, it is possible to be specific about the rights, freedoms, liberties — by which is always meant special privileges — and immunities of any particular religious house, but one cannot generalize for the very reason that each charter seems to differ in some way from other written grants. What rights or secular immunities are given by grants in free alms tenure? As F. M. Stenton noticed some time ago, "The precise nature of the immunities enjoyed by a religious house in respect of the lands which it held in alms is an important but also a difficult question. Even if it were true that in the twelfth century land given *in puram et perpetuam elemosinam* should thenceforward be free from all worldly service, the mere statement of this immunity in general terms would tell us little. Charters which promise exemptions from definite burdens are rare." [34]

It is difficult, then, if not impossible, to ascertain in every case which services and the amount of services that went with a grant in free alms. "If the amount of a [lay] tenant's service could be committed to the memory of his peers assembled in a feudal court," [35] very probably the amount of secular service that a monastery owed to a patron for a grant of land was also privately settled between the benefactor and the monastery in a verbal agreement and not recorded in the charter at all. This would account for a large number of gifts which were actually sales or rents in disguise.

If the donor owed no secular service for the land to his

[33] F. Pollock and F. W. Maitland, *The History of English Law Before the Time of Edward I* (2nd ed., Cambridge, 1952), I, 240–247.
[34] F. M. Stenton, ed., *Documents Illustrative of the Social and Economic History of the Danelaw from Various Collections* (London, 1920), pp. cxx–cxxi.
[35] *Ibid.*, p. cxxviii.

lord or to the lord king, then the monastery owed no secular service for it. But the great barons who made benefactions to the White Monks might well have owed some secular service for the land, and the gift of this land to a monastery could not render the land free of the required service. If the land was burdened with knight service, for example, it passed into the hands of the monks burdened with that service.[36] We cannot be definite about the size and the exact location of the estates given to the Cistercians, but it would appear from what evidence does survive that the barons did not owe an appreciable amount of service for the specific lands that they gave to the monks. Nevertheless, in direct contravention of their constitutions, the Cistercians accepted many gifts carrying with them a small or fractional amount of military service. As early as the fifth year of the reign of Henry II (1158–59) Pipewell Abbey paid into the royal exchequer twenty-five shillings in scutage for her holdings of the Earl of Warwick,[37] and Garendon Abbey paid one mark for her military obligations.[38] In 1160–60 Garendon returned the same sum.[39] The monks of Thame in 1161–62 paid five shillings into the exchequer, and in the same years Warden Abbey returned ten shillings for her holdings of the Earl of Bedford.[40]

All studies of Anglo-Norman feudalism, and especially all accounts dealing with specific English fiefs in the first three-quarters of the twelfth century, must to a considerable extent be based on the *Cartae Baronum*, the returns of King Henry II's inquest of 1166 into the military obligations of his vassals. The returns of a number of the barons who had endowed the Cistercians clearly suggest that sometime between the foundation or the endowment of a monastery and

36 Pollock and Maitland, *History of English Law*, I, 241–244. See also for the problem of the alienation of the royal demesne R. S. Hoyt, *The Royal Demesne in English Constitutional History* (Ithaca, 1950), pp. 84–124, esp. 90–92.
37 H. Hall, ed., *The Red Book of the Exchequer* (Rolls Series, no. 99, London, 1896), 18. "Willelmus Giffard reddit compotum de scutagio militum Comitis Warwickae . . . Monachis Pipewelle, XXVs."
38 *Ibid.*, p. 20.   39 *Ibid.*, p. 25.   40 *Ibid.*, pp. 32, 55.

the royal inquest of 1166 some knight service was passed on to the Cistercians. William Ferrers, the grandson of Henry Ferrers who was created earl of Derby by King Stephen in 1138, stated in his return in 1166 that in the time of Henry I the honour of Derby had owed a *servicium debitum* of sixty knights' fees, and that three of those fees were now (in 1166) held by the Cistercian monks of Thame, Combemere, and an unspecified monastery of White Monks.[41] In addition, the abbots of Quarr,[42] Stanley,[43] Kingswood,[44] Woburn,[45] and Revesby[46] were all mentioned in the returns of barons replying to the king's inquest as owing the service of one knight each. In the last forty years of the century, the charters of endowment reveal that many monasteries held land by small or fractional parts of knights' fees. Byland Abbey was given an unspecified amount of land for the service of two knights.[47] Ralph de Adewich gave to Kirkstall one half a carucate which the monks were to hold for eight shillings yearly and by doing the forinsec service where twelve carucates make the fee of one knight.[48] The monastery of Meaux was granted a carucate in 1181 for which the monks were to do the forinsec service for the donor's lord, the Earl of York.[49] Fountains Abbey was given two bovates, with the monks required to do the service for it when ten carucates make a knight's fee.[50] Rievaulx and Kirkstead were also given parcels of land with fractional amounts of military service attached to them.[51]

The method of the multiple division of lands, and of the military services due from them, was a common practice in twelfth-century England, and many feudal barons seem to have combined their pseudo-pious patronage of the Cistercian Order with the attempt to secure assistance for their feudal obligations to the crown by giving the monks land with a small amount of service atached to it. The services owed would be resolved by the monks through the payment

[41] *Ibid.*, pp. 337–338. [42] *Ibid.*, p. 255. [43] *Ibid.*, p. 293.
[44] *Ibid.*, p. 293. [45] *Ibid.*, p. 375. [46] *Ibid.*, p. 378.
[47] Farrer, *E.Y.C.*, III, 410–411. [48] *Ibid.*, II, 165. [49] *Ibid.*, III, 115.
[50] *Ibid.*, II, 148. [51] *Ibid.*, III, 451–452, 419.

of scutage to their patron. Under a weak king or in times of political chaos it was a commonplace for the barons to perform their services when it suited their convenience, or to ignore them altogether. But there was a clear contradiction between the conditions under which their endowments to the monks seem to have been made and the circumstances by which the grants were actually given. Quite probably, there was a deliberate policy on the part of the great lords of Stephen's reign of endowing monasteries with lands and rights to be held, theoretically, in frankalmoin tenure. The barons owed military services to the king for these lands and in order to attempt to escape from their obligations, or to reduce them, the grant was made in free alms tenure. Once they had made such grants, and once the crown had confirmed them to the monasteries, the barons could consider themselves relieved, or at least assisted through subinfeudation, of that percentage of the services with which the land was burdened in the reign of Henry I.

Why did King Stephen acquiesce in the surrender of his lawful rights and confirm baronial charters of endowment which actually weakened his military position? Because the military situation after the first three years of his reign was so weak, and his position vis-à-vis the Church was so strained that he was in no position to antagonize the Church, and especially the Cistercian Order, dominated as both were by the most influential man in Western Europe, Bernard, Abbot of Clairvaux. Those parts of baronial honours which were eternally given to the Church and confirmed in frankalmoin tenure would have been lost to the crown as the genesis of its military strength. The confusion over the amount of service due from his tenants-in-chief was one of the legacies which Henry II inherited from the chaos of Stephen's reign, and the desire to have an exact account of the *servicium debitum* owed to him was one of Henry's reasons for the great inquest of 1166. He was anxious to recover the feudal rights of his grandfather, rights against which the barons had made serious inroads during the twenty years of anarchy. If the great lords had been able to get away with what they undoubtedly tried to do, the military position of the English monarchy would have been much weaker, and the development of strong centralized government much slower in the later years of the twelfth century.

Now, let us look at these endowments from the point of view of the English Cistercians and their constitutions. The question is whether the monks held their estates, or any portion of them, according to frankalmoin tenure or by lay fee. The charters of endowment explicitly state that all lands and rights were given in frankalmoin tenure. The returns of many barons in the royal inquest of 1166, however, state that some monasteries owed them knight service. We know also that these abbeys settled their military obligations by the increasingly customary method of the payment of scutage. Therefore, grants to the Cistercians in free alms tenure were often not what they purported to be, because such gifts frequently carried some stipulation of military service. Some private and apparently lost arrangements must have been made between the patron and the monastery. Perhaps the monks could not acquire the land from the lord on any terms except the military one. Since the barons were responsible to the crown for their quota of knight service, it would seem certain that they would try to gain the service which they admitted was due to them in the returns of 1166 from all possible sources. In a broader context, the evidence of the Cistercian Order unmistakably suggests that the tenure of lands in free alms can be distinguished from tenure by lay fee, not so much by the exemption from military service as by the fact that in addition to military service, religious responsibilities were also required.

From the evidence that has survived, it appears that no one Cistercian monastery owed an appreciable amount of knight service to its patrons, and certainly Cistercian obligations do not begin to compare with the large amounts of service that such older Benedictine houses as Peterborough and Glastonbury owed as tenants-in-chief of the crown.[52] There is

52 See, for the Benedictine obligations, Knowles, *M.O.*, Appendix XV, p. 712.

no evidence of Cistercian monasteries actually summoned to do knight service, but they were obliged, as were the older Black Monk houses, to reckon their service in terms of cash.

The payment of one small cash sum to a feudal lord or to the royal treasury in lieu of knight service would not have been a severe strain on a monastery, provided its firm foundation was assured, and provided it was getting some return on its economic operations. Down to about 1170, however, the primary objective of most Cistercian houses was mere survival. In the aggregate, the small individual amounts paid into the royal treasury as scutage could amount to a sizable sum of money. Even if a religious house held its estates by the obligation of only a tiny amount of scutage, nevertheless, the holding of land by any form of military tenure was a definite contravention of the spirit and the letter of the *Carta Caritatis'* ideal of the complete renunciation of the secular world. An isolated or unique example of such a type of holding among the fifty-odd White Monk houses in England probably would not have had very much effect on the English branch of the Order as a whole. But many Cistercian abbeys, from the famous houses of Fountains and Rievaulx in Yorkshire in the north to the obscure abbey of Quarr on the Isle of Wight in the south, held parts of their estates by feudal tenure; and the practice was apparently widespread throughout England as early as 1166. The result could only be the involvement of the monasteries in the same secular activities and problems which, but a short time before, the very foundation of the institute had represented an attempt to avoid.

II

At the Cistercian General Chapter of 1152 the abbots of the Order decreed that no new foundations were to be made; [1] the death on 8 June 1153 of the Cistercian

1 Canivez, *Statuta*, I, 45. "Anno ab Incarnatione Domini MCLII, statutum est in capitulo generali abbatum, ne ulterius alicubi construatur **nova**

Pope Eugenius III was followed scarcely two months later on 20 August by that of the most powerful religious in Western Europe, St. Bernard of Clairvaux. These events marked the end in England of the period of the rapid growth of the White Monks. In the political sphere, the accession of Henry II (1154–89), marking the resumption of strong monarchy, was a coincidence of no small significance for the Cistercians. Between 1154 and 1200 only six Cistercian abbeys were founded in England.[2] The changing legal position of individual monasteries and of all the houses of the Cistercian Order after 1154 clearly illustrates the shifting balance of power, after the twenty years of feudal anarchy, from local to central authorities or, more precisely, from the local lords to the crown. The further expansion of a powerful religious institute was obviously not to the interests of the crown, basically for three reasons. The Cistercians already held large amounts of property exempt from the obligations of military service. Secondly, the status of Cistercian lands in free alms tenure, fortified as they increasingly were by the protection of papal confirmations, could well deprive the king of valuable revenues. Thirdly, the great influence of the order of White Monks was itself a threat to, or at best an interference with, the prestige of the monarchy at the time when it was anxious to enhance its position through a policy of centralization and consolidation. Nevertheless, as the twelfth century advanced, in the threescore years between the coronation of Henry II and the death of King John, the possessions of the Cistercians continued to increase, and the economic and social importance of their monasteries underwent a marked change. The new benefactors of the monks were from a new class in society; the nature of the landed grants which the monks received was often different, and these new gifts came to be, on the whole, a severe financial burden on the monasteries. The effect of the gifts received in this period on the spiritual climate of the mon-

abbatia nostri ordinis, neque aliquis religionis per subiectionem nostro ordini cosietur."
2 Knowles, *M.O.*, p. 346.

asteries and on the pristine ideals of the Order of Cîteaux as set down in their constitutions was virtually disastrous.

As we have seen, the first patrons of the Cistercians in England, the men who founded and endowed their monasteries in the period 1130–54, were usually barons of the highest rank, tenants-in-chief of the crown. These men made up only a small group in the feudal order, they were closely interrelated, and they often inherited or gained the title and dignity of earl. After 1154, in what might be called the second Cistercian generation, the picture changes considerably. The patrons of the monks came from the class below the barons, from the broad class of knights. As the crown came to rely more on this class for the work of government, and as the prestige of this knightly class increased, so also did its political and social importance. One indication of their "rise" in English society was the knights' patronage of the monasteries.

It is difficult to define with any degree of accuracy the status of the knight in twelfth-century England, and, at any rate, Maitland has said that when compared with tenure, status is unimportant.[3] English society in the twelfth, as in many other centuries, was very fluid, and the increasingly complicated pattern of subinfeudation, in which the knight's fee was by no means a uniform territorial unit, makes generalization dangerous. Late in the reign of Henry II there was a tendency to consider the knight's fee as composed of estates yielding an income of £20 per annum.[4] On the basis of this sum, Round estimated that there were about five thousand knights in England,[5] but Poole considered this almost certainly an underestimate: he would put the figure at between six thousand and seven thousand, which in a population of somewhere under three millions is not a large proportion. Although they formed a relatively small group in the structure of society, nevertheless their position, their prominence, and their power was very great. The knights

[3] Pollock and Maitland, *History of English Law*, I, 407.
[4] Sayles, *Medieval Foundations*, p. 226.
[5] J. H. Round, *Feudal England* (London, 1895), p. 292.

were the principal element in the feudal and the changing legal conception of society.[6]

In the early days of English feudalism, the knight had two military functions; he must fight in the army when summoned to do so, and in peace as well as war he might be called upon to garrison castles. As the twelfth century progressed, however, the exaction of military service was rendered extremely complicated by the splitting-up of fees by subinfeudation. The appearance of small fractional parts of a knight's fee could hardly be explained were it not that the king was taking money in lieu of military service, that is, he was exacting scutage. The knights who compounded for their military obligations found themselves occupied in the administrative work of their counties. The execution of the great judicial reforms of Henry II was largely thrown upon this class. In 1176 the Assize of Northampton established the grand assize, which was increasingly used in the highly litigious decades of thse latter part of the century. This form of inquest was always in the hands of the knights. In addition to serving on juries, the knights were called upon to act as sheriffs, coroners, to perambulate the forests, and to assist in the apprehension and punishment of criminals. Southern has recently studied this class of "new men" who were establishing their family prestige in the shires of England, and he traces the origin of their rise to the patronage they received in the reign of Henry I. Southern compares their social ascent to "the rise of the gentry" in the sixteenth century. The men of this class were willing to shoulder the burdens they did because they wanted to enjoy the prestige and influence which they realized came with their responsibilities.[7] It was this class which in the last four decades of the century endowed and supported the Cistercians.

This new class of donors was made up of poorer men than

[6] A. L. Poole, *Obligations of Society in the Twelfth and Thirteenth Centuries* (Oxford, 1960), p. 36.
[7] R. W. Southern, "The Place of Henry I in English History," *Proceedings of the British Academy*, XLVIII (1963), 127–169; Poole, *Obligations of Society*, pp. 53–56.

the great lords of Stephen's reign, and they apparently could not afford to be very generous. Therefore, they often demanded some financial compensation for their gifts — a practice which, in turn, brought on the White Monks a number of complicated financial, feudal, and spiritual problems.

As in the first half of the century, land — the source and standard of wealth in any aristocratic society — continued to be the most usual type of grant. While we can learn a great deal about the Cistercians and their patrons from the charters of endowment, and while some (few) charters do give the exact amount of the *donatio*, we cannot estimate with any degree of accuracy the total amount of land the monks received because most charters are extremely vague. For example, a gift by a certain Hugh de Bramley to Kirkstead Abbey was composed of "all my land of Bramley except the fields which lie between the top of the hill and the brook of Clementercroft and Sinderhill." [8] The endowment of one Henry, son of Swane, to the monks of Byland consisted of "all his lands in Denby, except for three acres which he gave to the hospital of Jerusalem." [9] This kind of obscurity, which is very common, makes any attempt at the computation of the acreage of any one abbey, and then that of all the English houses of the Order, impossible.

Besides land, and not infrequently together with land, the Cistercians were endowed with a wide variety of gifts and rights. For example, Richard Malebisse gave to the monks of Byland *ca.* 1176 two bovates of land (about 30 acres) [10] on which a church was to be constructed, specifying that the

[8] Farrer, *E.Y.C.*, III, 20–21. "Scientes presentes . . . quod ego Hugo de Brameleia concessi et dedi . . . ecclesie Beate Marie de Kirkstede et monachi ejusdem loci totam terram meam de Brameleia preter illum campum qui jacet in medio a supercilio montis usque ad rivilum de Clementercroft et de Sinderhill. . . ."

[9] *Ibid.*, pp. 420–421.

[10] A bovate was reckoned as an eighth part of a carucate, which was about 120 acres. One bovate, then, would be 15 acres, two bovates 50 acres.

66

revenues of the land were to be applied to the purchase of altar supplies for Mass.[11] William de Stuteville gave to Fountains Abbey a fishery in the waters of the Ure, the services of a fisherman, two boats, and a fishing net.[12] A grant to the monks of Rievaulx included ten acres scattered throughout the donor's holdings, pasture for three hundred sheep, and a small dwelling for the monks on one of his granges.[13] Another grant to Rievaulx was of 15 acres for the construction of iron foundries, all the iron ore discovered on the donor's lands, dead wood for the charcoal to be used in smelting the iron, license to construct a mill, and the right to pasture animals in the donor's common.[14] The financial expenses of Kirkstall Abbey were reduced *ca.* 1159 by the grant of one mark (13s.4d.) for the clothing of the abbot, and one-half mark for the purchase of candles or oil for the sanctuary lamp.[15] A certain Adam de Brus II acquitted the monks of Byland of the toll on all the fish they brought to his markets.[16] Besides the grant of 125 acres to Byland, Roger de Mowbray promised the Cistercians that he and his heirs would exclude from all his territories the men of all other religious orders.[17] There is even an instance in which a human being is found being offered to the White Monks. An interesting charter of endowment to Kirkstall Abbey, dated sometime between 1160 and 1202, grants a man to that house: "Know all both present and future that I, Richard son of Essolfus de Tong, have given by quitclaim to God and St. Mary of Kirkstall and to the monks there serving God, Hugh, son of Daniel de Tong for myself and my heirs. . . ."[18] Such a grant to a monastery in the second half of the twelfth century is indeed unique: in fact it is the only one of its type in the large collection of charters edited by Farrer. It reflects

11 Farrer, *E.Y.C.*, III, 460–461.   12 *Ibid.*, I, 401.   13 *Ibid.*, II, 499–500.
14 *Ibid.*, III, 363–364.   15 *Ibid.*, III, 193.   16 *Ibid.*, II, 7–8.
17 *Ibid.*, III, 439.
18 *Ibid.*, p. 389. "Sciant omnes presentes et futuri quod ego Richardus filius Essolfus de Tong dedi et quietum clamavi Deo et Sanctae Marie de Kirkstall et monachis qui Deo ibidem serviunt Hugonem filium Danielis de Tong de me et heredibus meis abbatie de Kirkstall. . . ."

the great power which a lord had over his villeins and a vestige of the institution of slavery in the high Middle Ages.[19]

Just as they had in the period 1130–54, the charters of endowment show that all grants to the Cistercians in the second half of the twelfth century and down to the accession of Henry III in the thirteenth century were grants in free alms. Such categorical terminology is apt to be very misleading, for very often the donor will add, seemingly as an afterthought, that he expects something in return besides prayer. Not infrequently the patron along with the land gave his body for burial. Thus, Ralph de Adewich gave to the monks of Kirkstall "the land belonging to him within the court of the grange of Bessacar" (a further example of the lack of specifics in the extent of the grant in the language of the charters), and he required that the monks receive his body within the monastery cemetery when he died.[20] Sometimes a patron stipulated that should he ever decide to enter a monastery, he should be accepted as a novice at the monastery which he had endowed. When Robert de Herding gave to Fountains Abbey "land in Great Busby in a corner below the ford between Busby and Dromonby," he stated that when he should take the habit of religion, he wished to be received at Fountains.[21] A gift like this probably would not have an adverse effect on the material condition of the house, although certainly the reception of a man in middle life, when his patterns of thought and behavior had long been set along lines undoubtedly inimical to the desired silent and ascetic atmosphere of the Cistercian abbey, could have a detrimental effect on the spiritual climate of the monastery. Occasionally, the charters imply that in return for his grant a patron shall receive free rights of hospitality at the abbey which he has endowed. When Stephen de Bulmer and Thomas de Muscamp settled their fishery and eight acres of land on the monks of Rievaulx, their charter acknowledged that the monks had received them, their wives,

19 See Vinogradoff, *Villeinage in England*, p. 47.
20 Farrer, *E.Y.C.*, II, 166.
21 *Ibid.*, I, 455.

and their children not only into the full participation of the monks' prayers, but also into the benefits of the house.[22] Likewise, when William de Accum in 1170 notified Roger de Pont de l'Eveque, the Archbishop of York (1154–81), of his grant of nine acres of land, a fishery, and certain pastoral rights for the abbey's sheep, he made the grant in free alms, but observed that the monks had received him, his wife, and his children into the "full fraternity of their house." [23] While the *Rule of St Benedict* specifically states that all guests are to enjoy whatever material benefits the monastery can offer, the founders of the Cistercian Order, in keeping with their ideal of complete seclusion from the world, had emphatically legislated against the presence of powerful benefactors.[24] Violations of this rule came early, and they obviously resulted in a weakening of the ascetic ideal.

A large number of charters show that the knights demanded some material compensation for their gifts, even when the charters of endowment state in the introductory clause that the gift is made in free alms. The patrons sometimes required or expected the monks to make them an offering, usually of cash, sometimes of valuable objects also, in return for the grant itself. A certain Edith Whithaud and William her son gave to Fountains 24 acres of land and dead wood from their forests for building, and charcoal for their smithies. And "in testimony of this our gift the monks of their charity have given to me Edith three marks and four shillings and to me William her son five shillings." [25] When John, a kinsman of a former archdeacon of Cleveland, granted to the abbot and community of Rievaulx lands and houses in an obscure marsh which the dead archdeacon had

22 *Ibid.*, II, 248. "Ipsi monachi receperunt nos et uxores et liberos nostros in participationem orationum, et omnium beneficiorum domus sue."
23 *Ibid.*, II, 50–51. "Monachi receperunt me et sponsam et infantes nostros in plenariam fraternitatem domus sue."
24 Dom Justin McCann, ed. and trans., *The Rule of St. Benedict* (Westminster, Md., 1952), Chapter 53, p. 119; *Consuetudines*, in Guignard, *Monuments*, pp. 256, 265.
25 Farrer, *E.Y.C.*, III, 344–345. "In testimonium hujus nostre donationis monachi dederunt michi Ede tres marcas et quatuor solidos et mihi Guillelmo filio quinque solidos de sua caritate."

bequeathed to him, the monks gave John forty-three marks (approximately £28), and they promised to give annually to the hospital of St. Peter's in the city of York five shillings, and one pound of pepper to the Benedictine abbey of St. Mary's in the same place.[26] Walter Ingram with the consent of his wife gave to Rievaulx five bovates of land, pasture for five hundred sheep, ten cows, and a bull; and although Walter stated in his charter that the grant was in free, pure, and perpetual alms, he required that the monks give him each year 12d. at Pentecost, and for making the grant itself, they paid him fifteen marks, gave his wife a gold ring, and to their sons, two shillings each.[27] An obscure knight called Ralph, son of Swane de Waltershelf, gave to the monastery of Kirkstead all the land which he held of another knight in Pensale on the Lacey fee in Yorkshire. For this grant the monks gave him a gift of eight marks outright, and agreed to produce five shillings annually, 2½ at Pentecost, and 2½ on the Feast of St. Martin's.[28] For another endowment of the same monastery, this time of only one bovate of land, the monks gave their benefactor five marks.[29] Another gift which required an initial payment to the patron was that of a certain Henry, son of Swane of Denby, who granted the monks of Byland all his land in Denby, except for three acres which he gave to the hospital of Jerusalem. The monks were asked to pay him one hundred shillings outright and engaged to give 7s.6d annually.[30]

Throughout the last four decades of the century and in the first two decades of the following one, the stipulation of the payment of an annual sum was attached to a considerable number of grants to the Cistercians. In fact, where information survives beyond the brief notice of a monastery's foundation, its economic wealth in the late thirteenth century, and its value at the time of the dissolution, there is evidence that virtually every English Cistercian house in the later twelfth century accepted grants carrying with them the stipulation of a money payment to their benefactors. Only

[26] *Ibid.*, I, 235.   [27] *Ibid.*, II, 56–57.   [28] *Ibid.*, III, 418–419.
[29] *Ibid.*, II, 18–19.   [30] *Ibid.*, I, 440–442.

a small number of representative grants will be cited, although many examples could be given. Between 1161 and 1171 Bernard de Balliol gave to the monks of Rievaulx pasture land for sixty brood mares in his forest, twelve cows, two bulls, two bovates of arable land, and pasture for sixscore beasts in Westerdale Forest with license to enclose the meadow and to make sheepfolds. All this was given "in pure and perpetual alms, free and open and quit of all services and duties and from all earthly service and secular exaction by rendering to me and my heirs annually two silver marks. . . ."[31] Torphin de Alvestin and Matilda de Fribois his wife, who were very generous patrons of Rievaulx, gave that house one carucate in Allerston, five acres in Gindale, land for a sheepfold, and pasturage for five hundred sheep. This grant in free alms was made on condition that the monks pay the donors twenty shillings each year, ten within the octave of St. Andrew, ten within the octave of Michaelmas.[32] Sampson de Allerton gave to Kirkstall Abbey two carucates, his messuage (a human dwelling with the adjacent buildings for animals and agricultural equipment), and an apple orchard. In return for the gift the monks were to render their benefactor 16s.8d. annually.[33] Another endowment of twelve bovates to Kirkstall by one Geoffrey de St. Patrick, his wife and son, was in free alms except for the yearly payment of eight shillings, to be paid in quarterly installments.[34] When a certain Ralph, son of Nicholas, gave to Fountains scattered estates, dead wood for charcoal for their forges, any iron ore that the monks mined, and pasture land for their swine, oxen, cows, and horses, Ralph asked the monks to return ten shillings annually for his gift.[35] An equally obscure knight, Alan, son of Reinald the archer, presented an estate specified only as land which formerly belonged to Gamel, son of Galle — for which endowment the abbey was to give the donor eight shillings each year.[36] The possessions of Byland were extended by the grant of Geoffrey of Nevill who confirmed a previous gift of land and added

[31] Ibid., I, 440–442.   [32] Ibid., I, 301–303.   [33] Ibid., III, 312–313.
[34] Ibid., II, 158.   [35] Ibid., III, 386–387.   [36] Ibid., I, 389.

to it right of common of pasture for 360 ewes, 20 oxen, 20 cows, and 30 swine within Westceugh, with the stipulation that the monks compensate him with six shillings a year.[37] For the contribution of the town of Murton with all of the donor's rights there, Byland was required to pay the fat sum of 40s. each twelvemonth.[38]

Gifts to Kirkstead Abbey also, in many cases, were not without some financial reservations. When Henry, son of Robert de Lovetot, granted to the monks of Kirkstead the toft (a site, usually on arable land, for a dwelling and outhouse, and used by the Cistercians as a grange and house for the monks living on it), and all the land which he held in Bramley, he asked the monks to give him annually five shillings in silver.[39] The offering of Gerard de Furnival and Matilda his wife of three bovates and certain unspecified amounts of land was contracted for by the abbot and monks of Kirkstall with the annual payment of ten shillings.[40]

It is unnecessary to bore the reader further; many such examples can be given in evidence. For the last half of the twelfth century we have evidence of at least thirty-eight separate grants to the Abbey of Fountains, of which fifteen required some financial recompense. Rievaulx in the same period received fifty-five different landed endowments, of which twenty-two required some cash return; Kirkstall, thirty-one gifts, sixteen at a charge. Of Byland's thirty-six grants, twelve specified a return; thirteen of the eighteen charter-recorded patrons of Kirkstead demanded a money payment; and of the eleven gifts to Meaux, six required some return. An exceptional instance was the monastery of Roche, none of whose six patrons asked any return on their gifts. Roche was always a poor monastery, and the explanation for her small endowment in the period 1155–1215 may lie in the fact that Roche was situated on crown lands, and after her first foundation Henry II was unwilling to alienate any property to her.[41] It appears that only about one-half of the patrons of the Cistercians in the second half of the twelfth

37 *Ibid.*, II, 132. 38 *Ibid.*, III, 447–448. 39 *Ibid.*, p. 21.
40 *Ibid.* 41 *V.C.H.*: Yorkshire, III, 153–154.

century wanted some compensation for their gifts, and the amount of money asked in return for any one grant does not seem to have been extremely large. But again, taken in the aggregate, these single small sums would amount to a great deal of money.

Why then did the White Monks accept this type of grant? Probably because the original endowments which they received from the great barons of Stephen's reign were inadequate for a community of monks to support themselves upon. Secondly, the Cistercians undoubtedly expected to make a financial profit on them. This can be illustrated by one specific type of grant — mills.

In accordance with the ideal that the monks should live on their own labor and produce, mills were permitted by the constitutions only as long as they were used exclusively for *intra*-monastic purposes. The use of mills as a source of income was plainly forbidden. Some of the English houses apparently violated this regulation and acquired mills for purposes of revenue, because in 1157 the General Chapter specifically legislated against any evasion of the rule.[42] But the monasteries continued to acquire mills. Scarcely a year after the Chapter's decree, Woburn secured a mill from the crown.[43] About 1180 Bordesley gained the rights of William de Boker in a mill; and in 1197 Thame acquired two mills, one for grain and one for fulling.[44] Between 1205 and 1210 Warden Abbey was given two mills for a rental fee of three marks per annum.[45]

The question necessarily arises as to whether these grants were made, in the modern understanding, as outright gifts or as rents. On the one hand, all the charters state that the grants are made in frankalmoin tenure, which implies that the legal recipient of the grant, the monastery, owes no

42 Canivez, *Statuta*, I, 1, 65; *Exordium Parvum*, in Guignard, *Monuments*, p. 71.

43 *Pipe Roll* 5 Henry II, 1158–59, p. 18.

44 H. E. Salter, ed., *The Thame Cartulary*, Oxfordshire Record Society, I (1947), 71–72.

45 G. Herbert Fowler, ed., *Cartulary of the Cistercian Abbey of Old Wardon, Bedfordshire* (Manchester, 1931), p. 211.

material to its patron for it, and that the grant is to remain in the donee's possession forever. There are some documents in which a definite distinction seems to be drawn between what we understand as a gift and what is known as rent. When Hugh Chat gave certain lands to Kirkstead Abbey, he stated in his charter of endowment that the monks were to hold one-third of the land in free alms, and the other two-thirds for ten shillings annually.[46] This patron of the Cistercians appears to make an offering which is totally and finally a gift for one part, while for the other part he expects a concrete return.

On the other hand, we understand by the term "rent" the return made by the tenant or occupant of land to the owner for the use thereof, usually a certain sum agreed upon by the tenant and his landlord and paid at fixed intervals. If we substitute the word "holder" for owner in that definition, since according to legal theory the crown was the sole owner of all land in England, we have an interpretation of a frequent type of grant to the English Cistercians. While the monks were technically holding the grant in frankalmoin tenure, in actual practice they were renting it from their "patrons" by a permanent or eternal lease.

Was there a relationship between the amount of property given and the amount of payment expected in return? The amount of the rent seems to have fluctuated widely. Peter, son of Adam de Kirkewaite, gave to Kirkstead Abbey three bovates of land (about 45 acres), for which he asked a return of twenty shillings annually.[47] The gift of 30 acres of arable to Kirkstead from Richard de Acton asked annual rent of only five shillings.[48] The endowment by Peter de Besacle of Kirkstall with two carucates (about 270 acres), pasture for one thousand sheep, and for cows and pigs at will throughout his soc of Brampton required a rent of eight shillings annually.[49] But when Hugh de Doncaster gave to the same

[46] Farrer, *E.Y.C.*, III, 11. "ipsi monachi tenebunt totam tertiam partem predicti terre in puram et perpetuam elemosinam sine omni seculari servitio, et pro reliquis duabus partibus reddent annuatim heredibus Willelmi de Lovetot X solidos."

[47] *Ibid.*, III, 416–417.   [48] *Ibid.*, III, 20.   [49] *Ibid.*, II, 162–163.

house ten bovates (about 150 acres), he asked the monks to produce eleven shillings annually, and for making the grant itself, they gave this patron twenty shillings.[50] A gift of 24 acres of improved land, a tillage, and pasture for two hundred sheep, twenty beasts, and two horses was held by the monks of Byland for three shillings a year,[51] while the grant of one carucate (120 acres) of arable and common pasture for an equal number of animals cost the same monastery only two shillings each year.[52] There does not seem to be any correlation between the size of the estates given and the amount of money due from the monks to their benefactor: the amount of rent seems to have been an arbitrary figure set by the donor. Real charity, the financial security of the donor, or any of a number of other factors could have entered into the motives behind a particular gift. At the same time, as was said above, medieval measurements varied widely, and we have no way of knowing whether in one individual grant the carucate would correspond to 120 acres, which twentieth-century historians take as the average of that measure. Nor can we discover the exact value or the arability of these donations: the gift of a large amount of property at a small annual rental might indicate that the land was of slight agricultural or pastoral value; conversely, the grant of a small parcel of land for a high annual fee could imply that this particular gift was thought by both the donor and the monks to have been very valuable.

In the last four decades of the twelfth century and the first one of the thirteenth, the probability is high that the knights who endowed the Cistercians with pasture land sought to learn from the monks their new methods of sheep-farming. A considerable number of grants included the right of common of pasture. The common pasture lands and meadows of any medieval manor were considered a definite part of the holding, because the means of feeding the cattle and sheep were just as important a part of the landed holding as the arable for the raising of crops.[53] The pasture and meadow

50 *Ibid.*, II, 161–162.   51 *Ibid.*, II, 162–163.   52 *Ibid.*, III, 425–426.
53 Vinogradoff, *Villeinage in England.* The entire essay, "Rights of Com-

lands did not produce a great quantity of hay, and their value was accordingly high. "The right of common of pasture was jealously guarded." [54] Significantly, many grants to the White Monks contained this privilege. The grant to Byland Abbey of Amfrey de Chauncey of lands totalling 74 acres of arable included also pasture for the monks' beasts and for four hundred sheep anywhere on the donor's pastures over his demesnes.[55] William de Stuteville gave to Kirkstall an unspecified amount of arable and common of pasture for 840 sheep with the stipulation that 400 of them should be folded in the donor's sheepfolds.[56] There were two reasons why he required that the monks' sheep be folded with his own. First, crossbreeding would occur, and some of the lambs would accrue to the man in whose fold the ewes gave birth. Secondly, the donor would acquire the sheep dung, an extremely valuable fertilizer. Therefore, by this grant of common pasture, the donor's flock is enlarged, the breed of his sheep is improved, and he gains a valuable fertilizer for his fields. All of these advantages are illustrated in a grant to Rievaulx Abbey. Torphin de Alvestin, Matilda his wife, and Alan their son gave to Rievaulx one carucate of land in Allerston, one acre in Gindale, and other unspecified parcels of land, pasture for five hundred sheep, a sheepfold, and one acre of meadow to supply hay for the fold. And their charter states that "We and our heirs will have for all time a half of the foldage and of the dung of the aforesaid sheep." [57] Students of English agricultural history have pointed out the importance of sheep manure in the later Middle Ages.

mon," pp. 259–277, is valuable, but see especially p. 263. For the Cistercian activities in the exploitation of the land, the standard studies are J. S. Fletcher, *The Cistercians in Yorkshire* (London, 1919); F. A. Mullin, *A History of the Work of the Cistercians in Yorkshire, 1131–1300* (Washington, D.C., 1932); and T. A. M. Bishop, "Monastic Granges in Yorkshire," *E.H.R.*, vol. LI (1936). These studies, although superseded on certain points, are still good general treatments.

[54] Sayles, *Medieval Foundations*, p. 120.

[55] Farrer, *E.Y.C.*, II, 179–180.

[56] *Ibid.*, III, 309.

[57] *Ibid.*, I, 303–304. "Nos autem et heredes nostri habebimus omni tempore medietatem foldicie et fimi berecharie predictarum ovium."

Bennett, in his treatment of conditions in the fourteenth and fifteenth centuries, describes the manorial lord's *jus faldae*.[58] Knowles, in calculating the value of Cistercian wool at the end of the thirteenth century, suggests that the droppings of the animals were worth about one-third of the price of the wool clip itself.[59] But almost all of the standard studies of agrarian conditions before 1250 ignore this subject.[60] Even before the Conquest the place of sheep on the arable had been recognized. Domesday Book contains many references to "fold-soke" — the obligation of the peasants to fold their sheep on the lord's land. By the middle of the twelfth century, the importance of fertilizers and the superiority of sheep manure was common knowledge in England. Sheep manure is richer than the manure of any other farm animal except poultry. It is comparatively dry, and since it is usually allowed to accumulate in the folds where it is trampled hard by the animals, it is less likely to lose the plant food which it contains than any other animal dropping.[61] Certainly the patrons of the Cistercians in asking for a return of the dung as the condition of their grants to the White Monks were fully aware of its importance for farming. This fact illustrates once again that the English barons, who endowed and supported the Cistercians, looked on their grants as investments, and that the lords expected definite material returns on them.

[58] H. S. Bennett, *Life on the English Manor* (rev. ed., Oxford, 1960), p. 77 *et seq.*
[59] Dom M. D. Knowles, *The Religious Orders in England*, I (Cambridge, 1956), 71.
[60] For example, E. A. Kosminsky, *Studies in the Agrarian History of England in the Thirteenth Century* (Oxford, 1956); C. S. Orwin, *The Open Fields* (London, 1931); N. Denholm-Young, *Seignorial Administration in England* (Oxford, 1937); Vinogradoff, *Villeinage in England*; Lennard, *Rural England*. The exception is the invaluable work of Sir John Clapham, *A Concise Economic History of Britain*, I (rev. ed., Cambridge, 1963), 105. For the importance of the Cistercian granges see James S. Donnelly, "Changes in the Grange Economy of English and Welsh Cistercian Abbeys, 1300–1500," *Traditio*, vol. X (1954), which is also concerned with the later period for which records are more abundant.
[61] S. W. Fletcher, *Soils* (New York, 1907), p. 249.

77

The previous reform measures of the monastic order, those of Benedict of Aniane in the ninth century, Dunstan of Glastonbury and Odo of Cluny in the tenth century, and Lanfranc of Canterbury in the eleventh century, contain no conception that the acquisition of properties was in any way a deterrent to the practice of the monastic vocation. But the constitutions of Stephen Harding and the early fathers of Cîteaux strongly insist that any involvement of a monastery in economic activities inevitably threatens the spiritual and liturgical life of the monk, which is his very *raison d'être*. "A monastery, however, could no more isolate all economic interests from its inner life than it could completely avoid political embroilment in its external relations. For the monastery represented its own demand for goods and services in the economy, and the vitality of the monastic life required the adaptation of its resources to this demand." [62]

The relationship between religious houses and their patrons is of great importance as one factor in the relations of Church and State, or of ecclesiastical and lay interests. The Cistercian abbeys in England in the twelfth century were dependent on laymen, first for establishment and survival, and then for economic assistance and growth. The poor quality and small size of the gifts which the White Monks received in the first generation of their existence in England

[62] J. A. Raftis, "Western Monasticism and Economic Organization," *Comparative Studies in Society and History*, III, no. 4 (1961), 458–459. See also Dom Jean Leclercq, "Les Paradoxes de l'économie monastique," *Économie et humanisme*, vol. IV (1945); "La Vie économique des monastères au moyen âge," in *Inspiration religiouse et structures temporelles* (Paris, 1948). C. V. Graves, "The Economic Activities of the Cistercians in Medieval England," *Analecta Sacri Ordinis Cisterciensis*, vol. XIII (Rome, 1957). More recently the economic operations of the White Monks have been analyzed in several very careful studies by R. A. Donkin. See his "The Disposal of Cistercian Wool in England and Wales During the Twelfth and Thirteenth Centuries," *Cîteaux in de Nederlanden*, VIII–IX (1957–58), 109–131, 181–202; and "The Cistercian Settlement and the Royal Forests," *Cîteaux in de Nederlanden*, X–XI (1959–60), 39–55, 117–132. For the unusual but important place of cattle in the Cistercian economy, see Donkin's "Cattle on the Estates of Medieval Cistercian Monasteries in England and Wales," *Economic History Review*, Second Series, XV, no. I (1962), 31–45. All of Donkin's articles concentrate on the middle and late thirteenth century.

virtually obliged them, at first at least, to accept endowments which had feudal and financial strings attached. Although many of them required some financial returns, no single baron or knight who assisted the monks seems to have made a substantial profit from his "gift." From the point of view of the Cistercians, however, when their endowments are studied cumulatively many of them are seen to be economically unsound and destructive of the Order's fundamental ideal of absolute poverty. The continued acquisition of land soon became a drain on their treasuries, because, as we have seen, the charters show that many gifts were sales or rents in disguise. Perhaps the terms at which the land could be had if the lay holder was in some financial distress were too favorable to resist. Perhaps the desire was strong to round out property which the abbey already possessed. The result was that the Cistercians borrowed, and they borrowed heavily, in spite of the prohibition of the General Chapter against it.[63] In the last analysis, whatever the interests of their patrons, it was not to the economic or spiritual advantage of the Cistercians to accept many of the gifts which they did. On the other hand, the ideal of complete poverty and total renunciation of material goods was too unorthodox, too impractical for any institution in the energetic Western civilization of the twelfth century.

The constitutions of the Cistercian Order as they were formulated in the early twelfth century expressed ideals that looked backward to a time in the early Middle Ages when it might have been possible for a monastery to isolate itself entirely from the world around it.[64] The twelfth century, however, was a time of dynamic growth and rapid social change. The political and social forces at work were inherently in conflict with the Cistercian ideals. Professed to ideals of severe asceticism, yet simultaneously pressured by the demands of the world, the White Monks yielded to the world, and in yielding they failed their own profession.

[63] Canivez, *Statuta*, I, 113.
[64] See E. Hoffman, "Die Entwicklung der Wirtschaftsprinzipien im Cisterzensorden während des 12. und 13. Jahrhunderts," *Historisches Jahrbuch*, XXX (1910), 699–727.

chapter three

the congregation
of savigny and
its impact on
the cistercian order

Is not our Mistress faire Religion,
As worthy of all our Soules devotion,
As vertue was to the first blinded age?

John Donne

The Norman Congregation of Savigny had a
markedly significant impact on the Cistercian practice of
the monastic life in England in the twelfth century. The
Congregation of Savigny was united to the Cistercian Order
in 1148, and because the Savignaics had such a pervasive influence on the form and practice of Cistercian monasticism,
it is important to understand the Congregation of Savigny
in order to understand the Cistercians themselves.

The history of the Congregation of Savigny and of its relationship with the Order of Cîteaux has yet to be written.
The lack of interest which students of monasticism both in
England and on the continent have shown in this subject is
indicated by the paucity of contributions to the study of
the Savignaics in comparison to the vast literature on the

Cistercians. Knowles, for example, in his monumental work *The Monastic Order in England* devotes scarcely a page to the Congregation of Savigny, and in the last two centuries only some two or three references have appeared, and these have dealt with peripheral aspects of the Congregation. It is this lacuna in our knowledge of Savigny and the great significance that the Congregation has for an understanding of the Cistercian Order in England in the second half of the twelfth century which justifies this study.[1]

[1] The source materials on this problem are extensive. For the beginnings of Savigny, Etienne de Fougères' *Vie de Saint Vital* is fundamental. Etienne de Fougères was the youngest son of Count Raoul de Fougères who gave to Saint Vital the lands necessary for the foundation of the abbey of Savigny. After serving as a chaplain to King Henry II of England, Etienne was made bishop of Rennes and held this see from 1168 to 1178. He died at the abbey of Savigny to which he had retired. The manuscript life of St. Vital has been lost, but the not inconsiderable fragments which have survived were published by Eugene P. Sauvage in *Analecta Bollandiana*, vol. I (Paris, 1882). This life of St. Vital was translated into French by Hippolyte Sauvage as *Etienne de Fougères, Vie de Saint Vital, premier abbé de Savigny* (Mortain, 1896). Etienne de Fougères had based his account of St. Vital on *Le Rouleau de Saint Vital*, an anonymous account of the saint which circulated in the monasteries of the Congregation of Savigny after his death; the *Rouleau mortuaire du B. Vital, abbe de Savigny* (Paris, 1909) was itself edited by Leopold V. Delisle and is preserved today in the Archives Nationale. Savigny had its own monk-historians, and in *La Chronique de Savigny*, which treats the period 1112 to 1378, we have a narrative description of the fortunes of Savigny which is of great importance. This has been published with all possible guarantees of scholarly exactness by Delisle in *Recueil des historiens des Gaules et de la France*, tome XXIII. The *Gallia Christiana*, ed. D. Sammarthani, tome XI (Paris, 1874), contains many columns on the abbey of Savigny in the diocese of Avranches. There are numerous charters of endowments made to Savigny, as also are there many compilations of the ancient lives of the saints of Savigny. Both of these types of evidence are scattered in the Bibliotheque Nationale, the Archives Nationale, and in several departmental archives.

It was on the basis of the above sources that the seventeenth-century Savignaic monk, Dom Claude Auvry, wrote his *Histoire de la Congregation de Savigny*, collated and edited in three volumes by Auguste Laveille for the Société de l'histoire de Normandie, no. 30 (Rouen and Paris, 1896–99). Little is actually known of Dom Claude Auvry. He was born near Vaux-de-Cernay, probably the scion of an aristocratic family, clothed as a novice at a young age at Savigny, and after serving in a number of administrative positions in several of Savigny's daughter houses, returned to Savigny as claustral prior in 1698. It was during the fourteen years that he held this post, between 1698 and 1712, that he

The origins of the Congregation of Savigny, like those of the Order of Cîteaux, go back to that period at the end of the eleventh century and the beginning of the twelfth so strongly characterized in northwestern Europe by the revival of religious fervor and the renewal of the monastic ideal. Just as the center of Cistercian activity began in northern Burgundy, between Langres and Dijon, so it was on the confines of Maine and Brittany that the Savignaics originated a new approach to the Benedictine life. There, in the woods and heaths which connect Normandy, Maine, and Brittany, lived a large number of hermits who, in order to seek God, had left the world to lead a solitary and heterogeneous life following various inspirations and leaders. Among these men was a certain Vital of Mortain.

He was born *circa* 1050 at Tierceville, a small village in Normandy between Caen and Bayeaux, of pious and humble parents. He was a devout child, probably attracted to the monastic life from an early age, but we must be cautious in crediting the virtues ascribed to young men who grow up to be saints. The late twelfth-century monk who was Vital's

collected the materials and wrote his history of the Congregation. It was, of course, during these same years at the end of the seventeenth and the beginning of the eighteenth centuries that the documentary and critical foundations for the writing of history were being laid — the period which witnessed the publication of those massive and imposing collections of the documents of medieval history that are indispensable to the historian today. With his various means of information, did Dom Claude Auvry produce a history of serious merit? Can you consider his work by itself a sound authority? It may be said at once that this study has a tone of honesty and sincerity which reveals the author as a conscientious analyst. He was not without some critical ability, for he understood and discussed the unequal value of the documents which he possessed, and he evaluated the testimony of his several witnesses. But it is all too easy to agree with M. Laveille that Dom Auvry "was far from possessing all the qualities of the historian." There is very little in these three drawn-out volumes of what we know as "scientific history," and Auvry could not have been familiar with or sympathetic to the critical methods of research which his contemporaries such as Bayle, Dugdale, and Mabillon were establishing. Dom Claude himself acknowledges that "cecy est un livre de bonne foy." The result is an enumeration of pious and edifying tales which go to considerable lengths to enhance the prestige of the monastery and congregation of Savigny. While the *Histoire de la Congregation de Savigny* presents a large com-

biographer undoubtedly projected a later phenomenon backwards when he wrote that St. Vital had, even as a child, a singular devotion to the Virgin.[2] It is true that veneration for the Virgin Mary existed in the Church from early times, but this was largely confined to the Eastern Church, and it was not until the very late eleventh century and early twelfth that Marian piety spread to every part of Western Europe.[3] At a young age Vital left his family and at Paris, Angers, Liege, and perhaps in England also, gained some acquaintance with the humanistic and theological sciences. When, sometime in the last quarter of the eleventh century, Robert, Count of Mortain, discovered the learning of his subject, he drew Vital into his service and made him first his private chaplain, and then, in 1082, one of the canons of the collegiate church which he had just founded at Mortain.[4] At

pendium of information about the foundation, growth, and expansion of Savigny, both as a monastery and as a religious institute, the student must scratch the rocky soil of these didactic recitals very hard to secure a crop of sound information.

There is useful material in J. H. Round, ed., *Calendar of Documents Preserved in France 918–1206*, vol. I (London, 1899), a very rich source for Savigny. There is evidence under the month of October in *Acta Sanctorum Ordinis S. Benedicti*, ed. L. d'Achéry and J. Mabillon, 9 vols. (Paris, 1668–1701). And there is charter information in C. H. Haskins, *Norman Institutions* (Cambridge, Mass., 1918). For the most famous English house of the Congregation of Savigny, Furness, we possess the very revealing, if miscellaneous, collection of notes, charters, calendars, and fragments of chronicles in J. C. Atkinson, ed., *The Coucher Book of Furness Abbey*, 3 vols., Chetham Society, no. IX (Manchester, 1886–1919). This work is a classic example of poor editing. Lacking any logical arrangement of material, possessing few dates, and making no serious attempt to evaluate documents, this collection must be approached with great caution, and the student will find it difficult to use. Finally, for the decades after 1147 when the Congregation was absorbed into the Cistercian Order, there is information on the spiritual state and economic condition of the English Savignaic houses in Canivez, *Statuta*, vol. I. These are the source materials which relate specifically or largely to Savigny. There is also information about Savigny, varying in amount and in significance, in many of the Cistercian sources for the second half of the twelfth century.

[2] Laveille, *Histoire de Savigny*, I, 13–15.

[3] R. W. Southern, *The Making of the Middle Ages* (New Haven, 1953), pp. 246–247.

[4] Eugene P. Sauvage, ed., Vita BB. Vitalis et Gaufridi, primi et secundi abbatum Saviniacensium," *Analecta Bollandiana*, I, 354–355.

the same time Vital began to gain a reputation as a preacher in Normandy, Brittany, and England; but the life of a wandering preacher apparently did not please him, nor did the friendship of the great and the goods they heaped upon him.

Thus, in 1093 Vital left his benefactor and went to live in the woods of Mortain. His retreat soon became known, and gradually a numerous group came to join him from many provinces and apparently from all classes of society. It is significant for later developments in the Congregation of Savigny that the hermits who came to live with Vital did not remain in eremitical isolation, but often went to the neighboring villages to preach to the people. St. Vital himself crossed the channel and preached at the London Council of 1102, and was probably sympathetic to the Gregorian principles which Archbishop Anselm (1095–1109) was trying to enforce in England.[5] Because of the large numbers of men who placed themselves under his protection and sought his guidance in the religious life, Vital decided to unite them and to found a monastery. He went to Raoul I, Lord of Fougères, and asked him to concede to his band of hermits an old castle bordering the forest of Savigny and a small amount of land. Raoul, after what was apparently strong opposition from one of his sons, gave his forest of Savigny to God and Vital and the hermits over which he presided to build a monastery for monks, free and quit of all charges and rents, both lay and ecclesiastical.[6] This grant must have been made by 1112, because in that year it received the confirmation of Turgise, Bishop of Avranches, and Henry I, King of England.[7] But in 1112 the abbey of Savigny had not been founded. Raoul de Fougères gave to Vital, the *hermit*, land where he might establish himself with his companions and found a monastery.[8] In 1115 Guillaume, Count of Mor-

[5] N. F. Cantor, *Church, Kingship and Lay Investiture*, pp. 246–247.

[6] E. P. Sauvage, "Vita B. Vitalis," p. 355.

[7] Sammarthani, *Gallia Christiana*, XI, *Instrumenta*, cols. 110–111.

[8] *Ibid*. The charter of confirmation of Henry I states: "Donationem igitur quam Radulfus Filgeriensis., domno Vitali *Heremitae* in possessionem et coenobiale domicilium monachorum dedit, ego . . . concedo."

tain, gave to Vital, *Abbot* of Savigny, the Neufbourg of Mortain wherein to build an abbey for women. The foundation of Savigny is necessarily placed sometime between these two dates, and the episcopal confirmation granted by Pope Pascal II (1099–1118) in a bull dated at some year between 1113 and 1116 strengthens this hypothesis.[9]

Where was this new abbey situated, and what formal piece of legislation was to direct the lives of its inhabitants? The place where the monastery was to be raised was probably ideally located. It bordered a vast forest where the agricultural energy of the monks could be employed, and was close to three courses of water — the Cambe, the Cambeneste, and l'Eau Noire. Although of probably little importance in themselves, these streams assured the community a steady water supply; and in their inaccessible valley removed the monks from worldly distractions. If Savigny was ideally located for purposes of contemplation, its economic situation was also exceptional. It was at the junction of the three provinces of Normandy, Maine, and Brittany, and this location, combined with the richness of the soil, presented the new monastery of Savigny with commercial as well as agricultural possibilities.[10]

The twelfth century was that period when the Western mind was able and anxious to replace custom and tradition by written law, and to rise from a system of personal dependencies to one of articulated government. This was as true a characteristic of monastic and religious institutions as of political ones. The problem of the constitutional structure of the Congregation of Savigny is a complicated one. St. Vital founded Savigny in reaction to the form of monastic life traditional in the late eleventh century, and Savigny represented, or was intended to represent, one aspect of the new

[9] Laveille, *Histoire de Savigny*, I, 164. Auvry himself gives the date of papal confirmation at 1112, but Laveille shows here that this early date could not have been possible.

[10] *Ex Chronico Savigniacensi*, in M. Bouquet, ed., *Recueil des historiens des Gaules et de la France* (Paris, 1840–1904), XII, 660; Sammarthani, *Gallia Christiana*, XI, *Ecclesia Abrincensis*, col. 542; E. P. Sauvage, "Vita B. Vitalis," p. 350.

religious renaissance. We know that Vital preached a return to the strict observance of the *Rule of St. Benedict*, to the obligation of manual labor, and to poverty and simplicity.[11] All monastic reformers encouraged a return to the strict observance of the *Rule*, but by the early twelfth century this little work, as the sole guide for a religious institute, was no longer adequate. The conditions of life and society in Western Europe had changed considerably since the sixth century. Thus, Lanfranc in his *Constitutions* in the eleventh century, and Stephen Harding in his *Exordium* in the twelfth, had found it necessary to make more elaborate formulations of the monastic ideal; these men in their religious programs reflect the more complex societies in which they lived. This is only as it should have been, because in order for the monastic ideal to survive there had to be reformulations: St. Benedict himself acknowledged that his was just a rule for beginners.[12]

Beyond this, it is impossible to say what customs St. Vital proposed for his monks, for no legislation from the Congregation of Savigny has survived. It is probable that none ever existed.[13] St. Vital had been a hermit for at least ten years, and he is usually referred to as a hermit in the surviving charters and hagiographical accounts.[14] Unlike Robert of Molesme and Stephen Harding, who were first tried in the monasteries of their professions, Vital had no familiarity with the highly structured and routine life of a monastery, and although he was for a time connected with the Collegiate Church of St. Evroul, this foundation was but recently made by the Count of Mortain, and therefore lacked the ordered permanence and tradition of an older house. Moreover, while a canon at St. Evroul, Vital left his monastery frequently to

11 Sammarthani, *Gallia Christiana*, XI, *Abrincensis*, col. 541; E. P. Sauvage, "Vita B. Vitalis," p. 350.
12 McCann, *Rule of St. Benedict*, Chapter 73: "That the full Observance of Justice is Not Established in the Rule."
13 The *Histoire de Savigny*, p. 173, maintains that Savigny never (before the union with Cîteaux) had any rule besides the *Rule of St. Benedict*.
14 *Ex Chronico Savigniacensi*, in Bouquet, *H.F.*, XII, 781; H. Sauvage, *Etienne de Fougères, Vie de Saint Vital*, pp. 29–30, 58–59, for example.

go on preaching expeditions, exhibiting, perhaps, the unstable qualities of those monks whom St. Benedict called gyrovagues. The *Rule of St. Benedict* was probably the sole guide to the early monks of Savigny.

Some writers have said that from its origin Savigny was in its customs very close to the Cistercians,[15] but this could not have been possible. Savigny was founded sometime between 1112 and 1115, and she could not originally have followed the Cistercian practices because Cîteaux itself, although established in 1098, did not formulate and promulgate its principles in the *Carta Caritatis* until 1120.[16] Mlle. Buhot accepted this theory that from the start the abbey which St. Vital founded leaned strongly in its practices, habit, and rule to those of the Cistercians, but she has perhaps overlooked the fact that the early lives of St. Vital, even that of his earliest biographer, Etienne de Fougères, were written by Cistercians in the late twelfth century, long after the Congregation of Savigny had been united with Cîteaux. It is likely that these hagiographers read the Cistercian customs and practices by which they themselves lived into the early history of Savigny.

It is very difficult to agree with Mlle. Buhot that Vital was in complete accord with the reforming founders of Cîteaux and that he preached a return to the strict observance of the *Rule of St. Benedict*, to manual labor, and to absolute poverty.[17] Aside from the fact that Vital was continually absent from his monastery (which is always a dangerous sign — even in the case of St. Bernard because, as many commentators on the *Rule* have remarked, "a monk out of his monastery is as

---

15 *Ex Chronico Savigniacensi*, in Bouquet, *H.F.*, XII, 781. "His beatus vir modernas institutiones in aliquibus Cisterciensibus similes monachos suis imposuit, virtutibus et miraculis claruit."

Ordericus Vitalis criticized Savigny for using the new observances: "Ritus Cluniacensium vel aliarum imitatus non est sed modernas institutiones neophytorum prout sibi placuit amplexus est." *Historia Ecclesiastica*, pars. III, liv. VIII, in Migne, *P.L.*, CLXXXVIII, col. 643–644.

16 Canivez, *Statuta*, I, 2.

17 Jacquelin Buhot, "L'Abbaye normande de Savigny, chef d'Ordre et fille de Cîteaux," *Le Moyen Age*, XLV–XLVI (1935–36), 8.

a fish out of water"), as early as 1118 Vital was involved in a complicated quarrel over property with the Benedictine Abbot of Saint Etienne of Caen. The matter went all the way to the royal court where the king, Henry I, himself settled it.[18] This does not reflect a tremendous devotion to absolute poverty, and this particular incident seems to have started a dangerous precedent, for the history of the congregation which Vital founded is full of acrimonious disputes over property.

Perhaps Vital did found Savigny in reaction to the less stringent monastic observance of the Cluniacs, whom he may have known well from his many travels, and perhaps in the hope of being one of the champions of the religious renaissance. But we have no definite way of knowing. The fact that the early monks of Savigny wore white habits has been taken as a characteristic symbol of this relationship with the Cistercians and of their return to the strict observance of the Benedictine *Rule*.[19] Against the evidence that the early Savignaics wore gray habits,[20] and in spite of the fact that it is not known what the color of the clothes of the monks of St. Benedict's monastery was, the color of the habits of the monks of Savigny was probably dictated more by relative expense than by anything else. Unbleached material is cheaper than dyed cloth. And if St. Vital was as steeped in the *Rule* as his biographers suggest, then he was certainly familiar with St. Benedict's admonition that monks should not be concerned about the color or coarseness of their clothes, but should be content with what was to be found in their district and could be purchased cheaply.[21]

Vital governed the abbey of Savigny from its foundation to 1122. We know little about his life during these years, except that he continued his preachings, travelling across Normandy, France, and England. He was sufficiently in-

18 The notification settling the matter is printed in Haskins, *Norman Institutions*, Appendix F, p. 294.
19 Buhot, "L'Abbaye normande," p. 8.
20 Laveille, *Histoire de Savigny*, I, 173.
21 McCann, *Rule of St. Benedict*, Chapter 55: "The Clothes of the Brethren," p. 125.

fluenced by the new Marian piety and obedient to ecclesiastical discipline that he carried out at Savigny Pope Urban II's injunction that the Office of the Virgin be added to the liturgy.[22] But the part played by Vital in the creation of the monastic institute is minimal. He founded an abbey for women at Neubourg through the generosity of the Count of Mortain, and he established a priory at Dompierre in the diocese of Mans at a place for which he had a special predilection, since he had passed much time there as a hermit. This priory owes its origin to a grant of King Henry I, who endowed it with land, established a prior and monks there, and visited the house frequently.[23] St. Vital had originated the idea of a new religious institute, and he founded the monastery of Savigny, but he brought neither to any real fruition, because he was never basically or temperamentally a monk to begin with, and, spending so much time away from the monastery, he could not have given it the organization and direction which any new foundation requires. When Vital died in 1122, significantly at Dompierre, his former hermitage, he was succeeded by Geoffrey, the Prior of Savigny and the man who much more than Vital was the monastic saint and reformer.[24]

Geoffrey was first clothed in the religious habit at the Cluniac monastery of Cerisy-la-Forêt where he had tested his vocation in a monastery and had gained a knowledge of the regular life. At the time when Vital's reputation was spreading, Geoffrey apparently thought he could better achieve his salvation if he followed the more severe rule of Savigny, and so he requested and obtained permission to leave Cerisy-la-Forêt for the new foundation. Perhaps Savigny was not quite what he anticipated, certainly not what one would expect of a new monastery in the first flush of religious fervor. The author of Geoffrey's life tells us as much about the spiritual atmosphere of Savigny as he does about Geoffrey's virtues: "For in his monastic development he had

22 Laveille, *Histoire de Savigny*, I, 251 *et seq.*
23 Buhot, "L'Abbaye normande," p. 8.
24 Laveille, *Histoire de Savigny*, I, 379–81.

such humility that he confounded the pride of all who saw him; he extinguished their irascibility with his gentleness; he aroused their lukewarm fervor with his spirit of obedience; and he subdued their troubled dispositions with example of an encouraging and constructive attitude."[25] This may be part of the typical formula of a saint's life, but this passage also suggests a spirit of discord, disagreement, and disorder within the monastery which came to characterize the Congregation of Savigny throughout the later twelfth century.

The government of Abbot Geoffrey (1122–39) was perhaps the most constructive period in the early history of Savigny; certainly the rule of a man who had had experience as a monk was valuable for the new institute. What Vital had founded, Abbot Geoffrey developed and organized. He began by rendering more severe the rules laid down by his predecessor. He made definitive the establishment of his monastery at Savigny, enlarged the little church begun by Vital, and constructed the permanent conventual buildings to replace those that the first abbot had built in a temporary and haphazard fashion.[26] At the same time, because of his growing reputation for holiness and his able leadership, Geoffrey attracted to Savigny many recruits. It was Geoffrey then who was the real creator of the Congregation of Savigny.

When the number of monks became too great for the house to provide for their material sustenance, the practical solution was to send some monks to begin new foundations. And it was at this logical moment that the Congregation of Savigny was forced for the first time to formulate principles of government, both internal and external. The problem necessarily arose as to which of the contemporary formulas should be used, the Cluniac or the Cistercian.

Students of the Congregation of Savigny, both medieval

25 E. P. Sauvage, "Vita B. Vitalis," p. 401. "Nam in sua conversatione tantum habuit humilitatem, quod omnium ipsum intuentium confundebat superbiam; ejus patientia aliorum extinguebat iracundiam; ejus obedientia tepiditatem excitabat aliorum; ejus mansuetude turbatos aliorum animos gratia consolationis atque aedificationis mitigabat."
26 Sammarthani, *Gallia Christiana*, XI, *Abrincensis*, col. 544.

and modern, have maintained that the customs of this institute were predominantly Cistercian in orientation. Perhaps this is because both orders were established at about the same time and were parts of the religious revival of the early twelfth century. Thus, Dom Claude Auvry wrote that "the type of life of the first religious of Savigny and the statutes and rules that St. Vital gave for their conduct had a great deal in common with the usages and practices of the Cistercian Order."[27] More recently, Mlle. Buhot held that "one should not wonder that the first two abbots of Savigny showed a certain hesitation between the Cluniac customs and the Cistercian observances before definitely adopting the latter."[28] There were indeed similarities between the Savignaic constitutions and those of the Cistercians, but these are insignificant: the Cistercian influence was *not* very great. It was, in fact, the Cluniac approach to the monastic life which most determined the constitutional structure of the Congregation of Savigny. First of all, it must be repeated that our sources are, or are based on, the writings of Cistercian monks who would be inclined to see a link between the two institutes as early as possible, to read Cistercian practices into Savigny since she was soon absorbed into Cîteaux. Secondly, the monastic character of Abbot Geoffrey, under whom legislation was drawn up, was formed in a Cluniac monastery, and as far as we know he was, with one exception, the only monk at Savigny who had previously led a monastic life. He would very probably rely on his knowledge of the regular life at Cerisy-la-Forêt in his preparation of rules for Savigny.[29] Of course, the same observations could be made about the early Cistercians, but they did produce concrete and new legislation which made stringent changes in the nature of the monastic life. Most damning of all to the theory that the monks of Savigny were from the start very close to the principles of the White Monks is the fact that on every fundamental point,

27 Laveille, *Histoire de Savigny*, II, 200.
28 Buhot, "L'Abbaye normande," pp. 12–13.
29 Laveille, *Histoire de Savigny*, I, 240–243. The third abbot of Savigny, Ewan (1139–40), was a monk with Geoffrey at Cerisy-la-Forêt.

Savigny adopted the observances and practices of Cluny, not of Cîteaux. The very title *Congregation* of Savigny is suggestive of Cluny because Cluny founded this form of ecclesiastical organization.[30]

It is true enough that both the Savignaics and the Cistercians constructed their monasteries in isolated areas, far from towns and villages. Both professed to maintain a strict observance of the *Rule of St. Benedict* (although in fact the Cluniacs made the same claim),[31] and both Cistercians and Savignaics adopted the liturgical office of the Virgin.[32] Abbot Geoffrey attempted to establish the Cistercian practices of the abbatial visitation and the General Chapter, but he did not do this until 1132,[33] *after* many houses had already been founded. It is probable that the Savignaic chapters, like the Cluniac, were very irregular.[34]

The differences between Savigny and Cîteaux are very striking. The abbot of Savigny, like the all-powerful abbot of Cluny, governed absolutely all the houses of his Congregation in matters both spiritual and temporal; there were no constitutional checks whatsoever on him.[35] The abbot of Cîteaux, on the other hand, was held responsible for his government of the order to the abbots of his four eldest daughter houses.[36] Secondly, the monasteries of the Congregation of Savigny were, from the very beginning, exempt from the jurisdiction of bishops and, like the Cluniac houses, subject directly to the pope at Rome.[37] The White Monks

30 L. M. Smith, *Cluny in the Eleventh and Twelfth Centuries* (Oxford, 1930), p. 148; Kassius Hallinger, *Gorze-Kluny*, Studia Anselmiana, XXII–XXIII (Rome, 1950), I, 53.
31 This is perhaps more of a tribute to the flexibility and modality of the *Rule* than it is to the "one sure road" of any of the three institutes. The best comparative treatment of the Cluniac position is that of Knowles, *Cistercians and Cluniacs*.
32 Laveille, *Histoire de Savigny*, I, 251.
33 Sammarthani, *Gallia Christiana*, XI, *Abrincensis*, col. 544. "Visitationes et capitulum generale totius generationis apud Savigneium per tridium quotannis in fest sanctissimae Trinitatis instruit an 1132. . . ."
34 Buhot, "L'Abbaye normande," p. 13.
35 Laveille, *Histoire de Savigny*, I, 205.
36 *Carta Caritatis*, in Guignard, *Monuments*, p. 81.
37 Laveille, *Histoire de Savigny*, I, p. 204.

in the first half-century of their history were not exempt from the authority of the diocesans. While the period of Cistercian expansion occurred before the bishops actually pressed their claims of disciplinary control over religious houses, the first Cistercians and then the entire Order as represented in the person of St. Bernard of Clairvaux, high Gregorian that he was, protested vehemently their submission to the bishop and their opposition to exemption.[38] It was only in the last third of the twelfth century when the White Monks had gained considerable possessions in land, tithes, and advowsons that they secured almost total exemption from episcopal authority; and in the protection of the papacy they gained support against attacks on their property and liberty.[39] Thirdly, from her very foundation Savigny had accepted the patronage of churches; she took tithes, and she received gifts from the faithful who accordingly associated themselves with the monastery.[40] These forms of endowment St. Stephen Harding had most violently rejected for the Cistercians as dangerous to the peace and solitude of the monastery and as destructive of its desired economic austerity. Needless to say, such gifts were the means by which Cluny had attained her great wealth in the late years of the eleventh century. Finally, the monks of Savigny, imitating St. Vital, went out of their monastery to preach, to care for the sick, and even to perform pastoral functions, from the beginning of their establishment.[41] If these merciful works were good in themselves, they were foreign to the spirit and general practice of the early Cistercians. Indeed, in all of these practices and characteristics the Congregation of Savigny had little in common with "the new model of Cîteaux," and in-

[38] Knowles, *M.O.*, pp. 633–634; Watkin Williams, *St. Bernard of Clairvaux* (rev. ed., Manchester, 1953), pp. 159–189. Although St. Bernard was involved in the appointment of many bishops and energetic in condemning the laxity of others, he was respected by them because of his vast prestige, and his relations with them were at least externally cordial.
[39] See the important chapter "L'Exemption et le gouvernement de l'ordre cistercienne" in Mahn, *L'Ordre cistercien*, pp. 119–155.
[40] Laveille, *Histoire de Savigny*, I, 207.
[41] *Ibid.*, 208.

stead Savigny bore a marked similarity to the Congregation of Cluny.

In one respect the Savignaics differed considerably from both the Black Monks and the White. Through the influence of their hermit founder they apparently retained a definite eremitical quality so that Ordericus Vitalis could refer to them as both "monks and hermits." Since St. Vital had never led any type of stable communal life for any length of time, the eremitical character of his own monastic experience would certainly leave an imprint on his congregation.

One of the thorniest problems in the constitutional structure of Savigny is that of filiation — the nature of her relationship with her daughter houses: was it comparable to that of Cluny,[42] or to that of Cîteaux? The question is made all the more complex by the fact that Cluny at the beginning of the twelfth century had no logical constitution like that of the Cistercians but the Congregation was a hierarchical system of relationships culminating in a personal dependence upon the abbot of Cluny. When Cluny intended to make a foundation, she sent some monks under a superior to form a priory, and when once the new monastery was founded, all aspects of its conventual life were modelled on those of its parent. The priory thus formed, even if it increased in num-

[42] The only work which makes a serious attempt to study this problem is Hallinger, *Gorze-Kluny*. The extensive diagrams showing the complicated filiation of Cluny's subject houses are very useful, but this is not an adequate history of Cluny because social and economic problems and the impact of Cluny on the life of the Church in the period between 1050 and 1150 are subordinated to the monk-author's liturgical and theological interests. E. Sackur, *Die Cluniacenser* (Halle, 1892–94), closes with the death of the Abbot Odilo in 1049 and does not give a thorough account of the tendencies then developing. The scope of Joan Evans' *Monastic Life at Cluny* (London, 1931) is indicated by its title; so far as it goes it is a useful book. Smith, *Cluny in the Eleventh and Twelfth Centuries*, belabors the point that Cluny had very little to do with the Investiture Conflict. The chapter entitled "Cluny and Its Subject Houses," pp. 114–164, describes the gifts which gradually came to make up the large congregation, but it contains little information on the constitutional relationship between Cluny and her daughters. Rose Graham's "Life at Cluny in the Eleventh and Twelfth Centuries," in *English Ecclesiastical Studies* (London, 1929), is interesting, but, like Miss Evans' work, limited in scope.

bers and in wealth and was eventually elevated to the status of an abbey, remained under the direction, if not the domination, of the abbot of Cluny. A Cluniac abbey could attain great wealth, and it could make new foundations, but these dependent priories could not attain the same importance. The monks of all houses of the Congregation of Cluny ranked as monks of Cluny and when at Cluny were considered children of the house. Over all houses the abbot of Cluny exercised, in theory at least, supreme and immediate power, and was therefore constantly occupied in journeys and visits, but no kind of legislation fixed the frequency and procedure of these visits, nor was there any machinery by which these responsibilities of the abbot could be reduced by a delegation of powers.[43] One final point deserves mention. The custom developed of exacting from the houses founded or adopted by Cluny an annual tribute, varying in amount and in itself of no great significance, but which in the aggregate brought in what must have been an enormous sum.[44] This must have been one of the reasons why Cluny held such a tight control on her "vassal" abbeys and was reluctant to grant them independence. This was very comparable to the census paid to the Holy See by the churches which were under its special protection. In a very real sense this entire Cluniac organization was typical of the feudal system of personal dependencies which characterized all government in Western Europe in the eleventh and early twelfth centuries.

The Cistercian method of filiation was otherwise. When a White Monk abbey numbered sixty solemnly professed monks, the abbot could, with the approval of the General Chapter, send twelve monks under the leadership of a thirteenth who was designated the superior — the significance of the figure is apparent — to found a new establishment. A suitable place for the building of the new monastery had usually been chosen or given to the monastery from which

[43] The entire section entitled "Entwicklungsgeschichte des Gedankens der zentralen Zusammenfassung der monastichen Einzelgemeinschaften" in Hallinger, *Gorze-Kluny*, II, 746–764, is very useful.
[44] *Ibid.*; Knowles, *M.O.*, p. 148.

the thirteen came. The monks themselves built the conventual buildings — church, dormitory, refectory, guest house. When this new foundation contained more than sixty professed, it in turn would establish a new house. And each new house, once established, was independent of its parent house and of the abbot of Cîteaux. Thus the filiation of Cîteaux.[45] This procedure was established by the *Carta Caritatis*, whose important contributions to Cistercian government were the provisions for a yearly visitation of each abbey by the abbot of the founding house, and for a yearly assembly of all heads of houses for General Chapter at Cîteaux.[46] The maintenance of a uniform discipline was thus secured by means of a single code enforced by visitation, examination, and additional legislation.

The system of filiation which Savigny adopted at first — that is, until the death of Abbot Geoffrey in 1139 — seems to have had strong elements of both systems. The parent houses were responsible for the material maintenance and religious direction of any foundation, and thus each daughter house was dependent on the parent. Because abbeys founded by Savigny had at their beginning neither funds nor rents, they were dependent on the charity of the abbots of Savigny.[47] The offspring, therefore, were not autonomous houses, and the position of the abbots of Savigny must have resembled the monarchic position of the abbot of Cluny. Savigny, like Cluny, did not develop concrete legal and administrative machinery to implement her rule. Experience had shown not only that the efficient exercise of such wide powers was beyond the capacity of one man, but also that the very existence of such a central authority paralyzed the healthy action of those dependent upon it. Yet, the structure of the Congregation of Savigny had some Cistercian elements. After 1132, Abbot Geoffrey did begin visitations of the houses dependent on Savigny, but there is no indication that these were made annually, or that they were a definite part of the constitu-

45 *Carta Caritatis*, in Canivez, *Statuta*, I, xxvii.
46 *Ibid.*
47 Laveille, *Histoire de Savigny*, I, 210.

tional structure of the Congregation. He also began the General Chapter to be held each year at Savigny on the feast of the Holy Trinity for the correction of abuses that might arise, and to be attended by all the abbots of the institute, but there are indications that attendance, particularly of the English superiors, was very casual.[48] According to one source the English abbots maintained that if they wished to attend these assemblies, they would have to be away from their monasteries for as long as six months of the year.[49] There may be some truth to this explanation, but it is curious that we do not initially hear it from the Cistercian abbots, even those located on the barbarous fringes of Wales and Scotland. The entire program of the Cistercians as formulated by St. Stephen Harding had been a reaction to the feudalization, if not the secularization, of the monastic ideal by Cluny and her daughters; the early fathers of Cîteaux had attempted to put into distinctive form a new approach to monasticism which cut away all the "feudal" accretions of the Cluniac system. Unfortunately, the first two abbots of Savigny failed to take a definite stand on this matter. In fact, it was their refusal or inability to make a decisive choice between the Cluniac and the Cistercian methods of filiation which was to be the source of tremendous contention and disorder before, during, and after the union with Cîteaux.

Under Abbot Geoffrey the size of the community and the possessions of Savigny increased to such a degree that he was forced to make new foundations. In 1123 he sent under a certain Ewan d'Avranches a group of monks who settled first at Fulket in Lancashire in England. The credit for supporting the first permanent English foundation goes to Stephen, Count of Mortain and later King of England, who in 1127 gave the monks his vast forest of Furness in Lancashire together with various privileges and appurtenances.[50] It was J. H. Round who first observed how the possession by Ste-

48 Sammarthani, *Gallia Christiana*, XI, *Abrincensis*, col. 544.
49 d'Achéry and Mabillon, *Acta Sanctorum*, October, VIII, 1011.
50 Round, *Calendar of Documents*, I, no. 804, p. 291; Dugdale, *Monasticon*, V, 247.

phen of lands on both sides of the channel led to the introduction of the Congregation of Savigny into England.[51] Other members of the Anglo-Norman baronage soon followed Stephen's example, and by the death of Henry I in 1135 there were six more English houses founded directly from Savigny: Neath (1130), Basingwerk (1131), Quarr (1132), Combemere (1133), Stratford Langthorne (1135), and Buildwas (1135); and in 1135 Furness herself sent out three foundations: Calder, Rushen, and Swineshead. King Stephen and Queen Matilda supported the foundation of Coggeshall, which was colonized from Savigny in 1140. Calder sent a group of monks to Byland in 1138. Finally, the abbey of Quarr on the Isle of Wight sent a community to Stanley in 1151, and Combemere established the monastery of Dieulacres in the last year of Stephen's reign.[52] Thus, between 1124 and 1153 thirteen houses of the Congregation of Savigny were founded in England.

The history of the foundation of Byland Abbey is an example of that spirit of acrimonious contention and querulous litigation with which the history of the Congregation of Savigny abounds, and which is testimony to the fact that the Congregation of Savigny never had an adequate constitutional foundation, especially in regard to the problem of filiation. Calder Abbey was the third house which the great Norman family of Ranulf de Gernons, Earl of Chester, founded in Cumberland. Calder was founded from Furness in 1135, and the lands and privileges with which the Earl of Chester endowed Calder — pasture land, fishing rights, burgage rights — were extensive, if of uncertain value. The political troubles which followed the death of Henry I in 1135 were disastrous to the monastic seclusion and the economic security of the new community at Calder. King David of Scotland (1134–53) sent his grandnephew, William, south

[51] J. H. Round, *Studies in Peerage and Family History* (London, 1910), p. 168, n. 2.
[52] See the table of filiation in d'Achéry and Mabillon, *Acta Sanctorum*, October, VIII, 1007; Dom L. Guilloreau, "Les Fondations anglaises de l'abbaye de Savigny," *Revue Mabillon*, V (1909), 298–301; J. H. Round, "The Abbeys of Coggeshall and Stratford Langthorne," pp. 139–140.

with the Picts of the Scottish army. They came unexpectedly and with great fury on the new house of Calder, devastated it, and took away all they could carry. The monks, under Abbot Gerald, sought refuge at the gate of Furness, but this unnatural mother refused to admit them. The unfortunate monks wandered about until finally they were taken under the protection of Thurstan, Archbishop of York, who recommended them to Roger de Mowbray. Roger de Mowbray, son of Nigel d'Albini and nephew of the powerful Earl of Arundel, established them first at Thirsk Castle, then at a hermitage at Hood, and then in 1142 at Old Byland, close to Rievaulx. But the proximity of Old Byland and Rievaulx was so great that the monks of both houses were confused by the ringing of each other's bells, and a removal was again necessary. This time Roger de Mowbray's foundation near the town of Byland proved suitable, and Byland Abbey rapidly grew in members and estates. This was not without distress for Abbot Gerald who, fearing that the Abbot of Furness would now attempt to exercise a paternal jurisdiction, crossed to Normandy and laid the matter before Serlo, Abbot of Savigny (1140–48). A General Chapter of the Congregation on 24 June 1142 released Byland from the jurisdiction of Furness and declared her directly subordinate to Savigny. Gerald died soon after his return to Byland.

Now, Furness who had refused to attend this General Chapter felt that she had been unjustly deprived of a daughter house. Accordingly, Furness sent the monk Hardred at the head of another community in 1143 to occupy the deserted house at Calder; in this way the original succession resumed. Once in possession of Calder Abbot Hardred set up a claim to jurisdiction over Byland and argued that Savigny had unjustly obtained her (Byland's) subordination. Roger, Abbot of Byland, replied by reminding Hardred of Furness' behavior at the time of the Scottish invasion. Ultimately, an amicable agreement was reached between Byland and Calder, and Calder abandoned her claim.[53]

The squabble was by no means settled here. Several years

53 *V.C.H.*: Cumberland, II, 174–75.

later Furness challenged Savigny for possessing unlawful jurisdiction over Byland. This affair, which must have been the monastic *cause célèbre* of the mid-century, dragged on for years. Finally, in 1154 after the absorption of Savigny into the Cistercian Order, Lambert, Abbot of Cîteaux, appointed a commission of thirteen English Cistercian abbots to be presided over by Ailred of Rievaulx and Godfrey of Garendon[54] to settle the matter. Ailred summoned witnesses, investigated the difficulties, and heard the arguments on both sides. The representatives of Savigny for their part asserted that Byland was a *gift* which Roger de Mowbray had made to Savigny; that Gerald, first abbot of Byland, although a monk of Furness, had been appointed to rule by the abbot and chapter of Savigny; and that Gerald had undertaken the charge of Byland as a special subject of the Abbot of Savigny and had remained in obedience to him until his death. The present abbot of Byland, Savigny maintained, had only followed in his predecessor's footsteps. To all these allegations Furness could make no reply. Nor could she produce any suitable witnesses. After the judges had heard the evidence of Savigny's witnesses who supported their remarks with definite proofs, the judges awarded the subjection of Byland to the Abbot of Savigny, and Furness accepted the decree with apparent humility.[55]

This sorry account of the establishment of Byland Abbey, which is not without parallel in the early history of the Congregation of Savigny in England,[56] is a commentary on this religious institute and especially on its lack of real constitutional structure. It suggests, first of all, the type of dissension and confusion which arose over the problem of filiation. It shows that the abbots of the Congregation of Savigny, like the abbots of Cluny, regarded their daughter foundations as gifts, as property, over which they held a sort of imperialistic power for purposes of exploitation. Finally, this affair

54 Powicke, *The Life of Ailred of Rievaulx*, pp. lxiii-lxiv.
55 Round, *Calendar of Documents*, I, no. 819, p. 297. The entire case is set forth in a letter of Ailred's to the Abbot of Cîteaux.
56 See Laveille, *Histoire de Savigny*, I, 287–295.

reflects the fact that Savigny had no effective control over the houses of the Congregation whose obedience was sporadic, and that the General Chapter was not an effective instrument of control over the Congregation. The first fifty years of the Cistercian Order contained none of this type of internal disorder, and it could have been the mission of the White Monks to give a stronger code of observances to this lesser institute without the law.

At the death of Abbot Geoffrey in 1139 the Congregation of Savigny numbered twenty-seven houses, of which ten were English.[57] Geoffrey was succeeded by the Englishman Ewan, who had founded Furness Abbey, but his reign was very brief, lasting only from 1139 to 1140.[58] The fourth abbot of Savigny was Serlo, under whose rule there occurred the great event in the early history of the Congregation — the union with Cîteaux. One of the reasons for this union was the great influence St. Bernard exerted on Abbot Serlo. Serlo imitated the Abbot of Clairvaux not only in the conduct of his life and in the direction of his monastery, but even in the style of his writing.[59] This literary imitation is, according to one student, so servile in the number of writings which Serlo has left that they make ridiculous some of the best sermons and letters of St. Bernard.[60] Serlo's greatest desire, apparently, was to live under Bernard, and he believed that he could do so if he surrendered to Cîteaux the houses over which he presided. There was also a material reason for union which seems much more decisive. The wealth and expansion of Savigny was also the cause of its growing decadence, and reform was necessary; the growth of the Congregation had been too rapid, and there is no question but that material success had spoiled it.[61] In order for such a widespread organization to have retained some integrity, it would have been essential to have at its head a powerful abbot: peace and order in this monastic institute depended, as in the feudal world in which it existed, on a strong leader, and

[57] Buhot, "L'Abbaye normande," p. 17.
[58] Laveille, *Histoire de Savigny*, II, 304–312.   [59] *Ibid.*, p. 313.
[60] Buhot, "L'Abbaye normande," p. 179.   [61] *Ibid.*, p. 180.

while the first four abbots of Savigny were holy men, they were not men of great executive and administrative ability. The number of monasteries established in the space of twenty years was indeed large, but the abbot of Savigny, theoretically responsible for their moral and material welfare, was unable to exercise effective control over them. The Cluniac custom, which Savigny adopted, of an annual visitation by the *abbé père* of all the houses descended from him — monasteries scattered across England, France, and Normandy — was naturally an impossible ideal for any one man to carry out in practice. The journey to England was certainly long and dangerous, coupled with the fact that both Normandy and England were wracked with the disorders that accompanied the anarchy of Stephen's reign. To a considerable extent, however, these are but rationalizations for the Savignaic failure to adopt sound constitutional safeguards. The Cistercians, who had grown much more rapidly and were extended far more widely across Europe, had solved these problems by making the abbot of each monastery responsible for the moral and material welfare of all its daughter houses; and these in turn responsible to the abbot of Cîteaux for them. It is true that the political conditions of the times were very chaotic and the routes of travel, both land and sea, were fraught with danger, but one finds it hard to believe that these weak and mundane matters could have daunted such a man as the Abbot of Clairvaux.

Moreover, the English houses of the Congregation of Savigny had the support of what political protection the crown could provide. King Stephen had established the abbey of Furness, he confirmed the foundation of Buckfast, and he placed the entire Congregation under his protection.[62] His fond generosity for Savigny undoubtedly goes back to the fact that he had been lord of the area in which Savigny was founded, Mortain. However awkward Stephen's position had been, there can be little doubt that Savigny stood high in his favor.

[62] Round, *Calendar of Documents*, I, no. 800, pp. 290–291; Dugdale, *Monasticon*, V, 244 *et seq.*

The internal difficulties created by these constitutional shortcomings were not long in rising to the surface. The abbey of Furness, established by Stephen in the deep and hidden valley of Bekanesgill and endowed by him with the entire forest of Furness, Wolney Island, and several manors, was from its early beginnings a bulwark of the honour of Lancaster. The isolation of this monastery increased a power possessed by few religious houses in the north of England; the abbots ruled vast territories with almost total feudal independence. "The historical importance of Furness springs from its feudal ascendancy and . . . its independent lordship over a large self-contained tract gave political importance to the abbey for more than two centuries. So far as England was concerned, Furness was like an island. . . ."[63] In spite of the anarchy — or perhaps because of it — and because of the special protection of the king, Furness had been able to acquire a certain hegemony over the other English houses of the Congregation of Savigny. We have seen that Furness sought to keep control over Calder and Byland, that she refused to attend the General Chapters, and that she denied the Chapter's jurisdiction. In short, she found the surveillance of Savigny burdensome and sought to renounce it. Abbot Serlo at Savigny obviously found this a greater problem than he alone could contend with, and brought it to the attention of Rome. In 1144 Pope Lucius II (1144–45) wrote to Savigny:

"If indeed any of the abbots, or monks or conversi of your congregation shall depart from your command and order, and if having been warned a second and a third time he shall remain incorrigible, if an abbot let him relinquish his office without obstruction, and be at the disposal of him who is abbot of Savigny at the time and let another, more suitable be substituted in his place; if a monk should be so contumacious, let him undergo correction according to the Rule." In this way the pope sought to prevent any abbot from daring to cause schism in the order or from removing himself or his monastery from the jurisdiction of the higher authority of the abbot of Savigny.[64]

[63] F. M. Powicke, "The Abbey of Furness," in *V.C.H.*: Lancaster, II, 114.
[64] Sammarthani, *Gallia Christiana*, XI, *Abrincensis*, col. 544. "si quis vero ex abbatis, monachis quoque vel conversi vestris, inquit, congre-

As time went on Serlo had increased difficulty with some of the abbots who refused to carry out his orders and became more slow and more intermittent in attendance at the General Chapter. The movement for independence which had so strongly manifested itself in the case of Furness was spreading to the other English homes, and then to Norman and French monasteries. There was a crisis in the order, and Serlo, realizing that he could not handle it alone, and desiring the union of Savigny with Cîteaux, sought the aid of Bernard of Clairvaux.

The reaction of the Abbot of Clairvaux must have been favorable, and Serlo may have secured Bernard's promise of support. Next, Serlo submitted the question at the General Chapter at Savigny, and the Norman and French abbots present voted on Trinity Sunday, 1147, for union with Cîteaux.[65] The General Chapter of the Cistercian Order which met on 14 September 1147 was apparently no ordinary session; none of the sources fail to mention the fact that the Cistercian Pope Eugenius III (1145-53) was present.[66] Abbot Serlo requested that his institute be absorbed into the Cistercian Order, and the General Chapter, pressured by Bernard and with the approval of the pope, accepted the union. Serlo surrendered all the houses of the Congregation of Savigny to the Abbot of Clairvaux.[67] Five days later, on

gationis a proposito et ordine exorbitavarit, et secunde tertiave commonitus incorribibilis remanserit, abbate absque ulla contradictione retanto, juxta providentiam Savigneiensie abbatis qui protempore fuerit, loco ipsius alius idoneus substituatur, monachus vero, si contumax fuerit regulariter corrigatur. Ad haec vetat pontifex, ne ullus abbas schisma in isto ordine facere ausit, aut commisum sibi monasterium absque assensu communi alterius subjicere."

65 Laveille, *Histoire de Savigny*, II, 370-371.
66 Bernard Pignatelli of Pisa had entered Clairvaux in 1135, and, having received all of his monastic training under St. Bernard, was made abbot of the Cistercian abbey of St. Anastasius in Rome. He was in France in 1147 to commission the preaching of the Second Crusade, to hold synods at Paris, Trier, and Rhiems, and to secure support against the Roman Senate. See A. Fliche and V. Martin, *Histoire de l'Église*, IX, part 1 (Paris, 1944), 87-89.
67 Canivez, *Statuta*, I, 114. "Instabat tempus capituli generalis, nec quidquam aliud Eugenius praestolabatur. Igitur eodem anno apud Cistercium iuxta morem, abbatibus congregatis praedictus papa venera-

19 September, Pope Eugenius officially confirmed the union at the abbey of Saint-Seine to which he had removed on leaving Cîteaux.[68]

This is not the place to go into the very interesting but complicated legal ramifications of this union, both for the Cistercians and the Savignaic houses in England. But certain issues must be raised here. Did union promote reform among the English houses of the Congregation of Savigny? What effect did union have on the spirit and the letter of the observances of the abbeys of the English Cistercians?

Unfortunately, the union of Savigny and the Cistercian Order did not result in that feast of reason and flow of soul that was hopefully anticipated. As soon as the news of the union had crossed the channel, the English houses of the Congregation of Savigny created great difficulties; they re-refused to accept the union of Savigny with Cîteaux. Led by Furness Abbey, finding the yoke of Savigny not at all to their taste and the burden of her observances too heavy, they renounced obedience to the Congregation of Savigny. It is not surprising that a man of such power and possessions as the Abbot of Furness should resist the union with Cîteaux, whose customs if observed would certainly have reduced the vast suzerainty to which he was accustomed. The annual General Chapter and the visitations from Savigny would have placed checks and responsibilities on the Abbot of Furness, checks which he preferred to avoid. The matter was promptly referred to Pope Eugenius who expedited a special

bilis adfuit, non tam auctoritato apostolica praesidens, quam fraterna charitate residens inter eos, quasi unus ex eis. Caeterum illud adhuc singularius in hac capitulo cui non simile invenias, ex vix speres; integram, numerosamque congregationem (ordinem potius dixeris) monasteriis constantem supra triginta, per Galliam, Angliam, Normaniamque sparsam; illustrem viris, nec obscuram ecclesiis et possessionibus, relictu habitu relictis institutis, quae per plures iam annos observarent, in iura, et leges Cistercii transisse, sub clarevallis visitatione."

Sammarthani, *Gallia Christiana*, XI, *Abrincensis*, col. 545; it was undoubtedly the enormous prestige of St. Bernard which facilitated this merger. Yet it is interesting to note that the submission of the Congregation of Savigny to the Abbot of Clairvaux rather than to the Abbot of Cîteaux was certainly a transgression of the Cistercian rules.

68 Buhot, "L'Abbaye normande," p. 184.

bull at Reims on 10 April 1148, a letter in which he called on each abbey by name to submit.[69] But the English houses again refused, and the pope promptly excommunicated them. Thereupon, the English Savignaic abbeys sent a delegation, headed by the strongest secessionist, Peter, the fourth abbot of Furness, to lay their position before Pope Eugenius. The pope placed the matter in the hands of Hugh, Archbishop of Rouen, and Arnulf, Bishop of Lisieux, directing them to hear and settle the matter at Michaelmas (29 September) 1148; but Eugenius first stipulated that Abbot Peter must swear to abide by the decision of the two Norman bishops before the sentence of excommunication could be raised. This apparently Peter did. On the way back from his conference with the pope, Peter stopped in Scotland and at York, seeking the support of the King of Scotland and the Archbishop of York. As a result of this procrastination, when Peter failed to appear at the court of Michaelmas, the bishops postponed its meeting until Martinmas (11 November). Again, the Abbot of Furness reneged. This time (Martinmas, 1148) Archbishop Hugh and Bishop Arnulf held their court, heard the testimony of the Abbot of Savigny, accepted the sworn evidence of "many religious persons" that Furness should be subordinate to Savigny, and in a letter to Peter, Abbot of Furness, ordered him "wholly to desist, at the sight of this letter, from his presumptuous rebellion, and to allow the abbot of Savigny free power to dispose of the property and possessions of Furness according to his will and choice."[70] Under threat of total excommunication, Furness and the other abbeys were given fifteen days to submit. At the renewal of this dire threat, Peter yielded and submitted to Savigny.

This was not to end the division between Savigny and her English daughters. The proof of the great disorder at Fur-

[69] Sammarthani, *Gallia Christiana*, XI, *Abrincensis*, col. 545. "Anno sequenti in concilio Remensi idem pontifex bulla solemni data IX idus Aprilis 1148, valuit observantia Cisterciensis ordinis in Savigneiensi monasterio, et ab eo dependentibus teneretur. Sola quidem recenset monasteria Anglicana, quia soli unioni refragabantur Angli."
[70] Round, *Calendar of Documents*, I, no. 813, p. 294.

ness is that as soon as Abbot Peter submitted, the monks of his monastery rebelled. In a letter addressed to the monks and lay-brothers of Furness, Archbishop Hugh of Rouen warned them that "Obedience and humility are the duties of religion and right behavior; arrogance and disobedience are to be avoided." The archbishop commanded them, under penalty of anathema, to submit to higher authority.[71] At the same time, he sent off a letter to his colleague at York, reviewing for Archbishop Thurstan the entire case and warning him not to be deceived by the lies and guiles of the rebellious monks of Furness.[72] Ultimately, sometime in 1149, the monks submitted. Peter was removed from the office of abbot, and a monk of Savigny was sent to restore Furness to discipline and to teach her rebellious monks the observances of the Cistercian Order.[73]

The Holy See was not unaware of the fact that, in other respects, monasteries of the former Congregation of Savigny were not living up to their obligations as members of the Cistercian Order. In a letter which is not dated but which Holtzmann believes may have been written as early as 1166 and certainly no later than 1179, Alexander III wrote to the abbots of Swineshead and Furness:

It is know to us that you have reverently entered the Order of the Cistercian Brethern, but you have by no means observed the laws which they themselves require as proper. Accordingly, we have heard that you possess manors and serfs, that you take those things into possession for illegal gain, and that according to the custom of lay lords you sell the use of patronage rights which is church property. Hence, wishing to protect the aforesaid Order

71 *Ibid.*, no. 814, p. 294.
72 *Ibid.*, p. 295.
73 Atkinson, *The Coucher Book of Furness Abbey*, part I, p. 9. The Furness chronicler relates that Abbot Peter on his return from Rome was captured by the monks of Savigny and incarcerated at Savigny. He was then deprived of his office, and the Cistercian Richard of Bayeux was installed in his place. This is a fabrication. First of all, Pope Eugenius was not in Italy in 1148 and was not able to return to Rome until the following year. If Peter was taken to Savigny he certainly escaped, because we know that he visited Archbishop Thurstan of York before returning to Furness. Finally, if he were at Savigny, why would the Norman bishops address him at Furness?

from such abuses, since it appears to us to be threatened by all kinds of other difficulties, relying on your good judgment and by apostolic writ, we counsel and warn you, accordingly, because so we have heard that although you have undertaken to observe the laws of the same Order in every respect, you have surrendered nothing in the way of ecclesiastical properties, retaining both manors and serfs and even the churches of prelates . . . as you acquire more, the next thing [will be that] you will scandalize the brothers in whose Order you have entered. Because if you do not wish to correct the aforesaid situation according to our admonition, you should know that we have placed it in the hands of our venerable brother, the archbishop of York so that he can bring it to the attention of the Cistercian General Chapter and, if that [assembly] will not improve these conditions, he (the archbishop) should hasten quickly to inform us.[74]

This letter clearly reveals that the papacy knew that the economic practices of some English Savignaic abbeys were in blatant violation of canon law and church practices. Moreover, these abuses were a serious transgression of the spirit of poverty and the law of reform in the Cistercian constitutions, which, as the pope interpreted the union, the Congregation of Savigny in merging with the Cistercian Order had *ipso facto* pledged to observe. If Alexander III knew of the special conditions under which the Congregation of Savigny

[74] W. Holtzmann, ed., *Papsturkunden in England*, in Abhandler Akademie der Wissenschaften in Göttingen, Philologisch-Historische Klasse, II (1935), 366, n. 174. "Alexander episcopus seruus seruorum Dei. Dilectis filiis de Swynesheued(e) et de Forneys abbatibus salutem et apostolicam benedictionem. Relatum est nobis, quod uos religionis intuitu Cistercensium fratrum ordinem suscepistis, set ipsum sicut decuit et eius exigunt instituta nullatenus obseruatis. Audiuimus siquidem, quod uillas et rusticos habeatis et eos in causum ducentes notis pecuniariis condempnatis et more secularium dominorum ius patronatus in dandis ecclesiis uendicatis. Unde iamdictum ordinem in parte seruare uolentes, quem in detrimentum aliorum infringere nobis omnino periculosum existit, discretioni uestre per apostolica scripta consulimus et monemus, quatenus, quia eundem ordinem, sicut audiuimus, suscepistis, instituta illius per omnis conseruetis et uillas et rusticos quietantes in dandis ecclesiis uobis nichil uendicetis, ne forte prelatorum ecclesias . . . exinde acquiratis aut fratres, quorum ordines suscepistis, in aliquo scandalizetis. Quod si predicta secundum commonitionem nostram nolueritis emendare, noueritis nos uenerabili fratri nostro Eboracensi archiepiscopo in mandatis dedisse, ut hoc capitulo Cisterciensi significet et, si id per eum emendatum non fuerit, nobis studeat celerius intimare. Dat. Lat. XI kal. febr."

108

had been united with the Cistercian Order, he did not approve of them, and this letter would seem to imply that he was rescinding them. At the same time, Alexander III's fears that the Cistercians would be scandalized implied not only that they would be morally disedified, but that the White Monks might adopt the same acquisitive spirit and moneymaking practices. He therefore called on the Cistercian General Chapter to correct these abuses, threatening to rectify summarily the situation if the Cistercians did not put their own houses in order.

As the second half of the twelfth century went its course in the five decades between 1150 and 1200, it became increasingly apparent that the union of the Congregation of Savigny with the Cistercian Order not only failed to achieve reform among the Savignaics in England but, on the contrary, promoted disorder, dissension, and decline among the Cistercians themselves. Obviously, it is impossible for the modern student to make a direct correlation between what the English Savignaics did and their impact on the Cistercians. It is significant, however, that there is no evidence, certainly no repeated evidence, for the disorder among the English Cistercians before the union of the White Monks with the Gray. Again, this is not to say that the union of the two institutes was alone responsible for the corruption of the Cistercians, because other factors were involved. The probable truth is that the union did the Cistercians absolutely no good and was a prominent cause of their corruption.

This theory may be demonstrated with respect to two problems: the issue of tithes and property disputes in general; and the subjects of the General Chapter and the Cistercian annual visitations.

"The tithe was a tax of a variable amount, but generally of a tenth, levied first on the fruits of the earth and later on all licit gains, intended to assist the exercise of worship and, in consequence, the support of its ministers, as also the care of the poor. . . . Paid first only to parish priests, it was as early as the ninth century levied by monasteries and even by the lay proprietors of churches and chapels." [75] In the eleventh and twelfth centuries the number and variety of tithes possessed by monks increased enormously, and for many religious houses tithes were the chief source of wealth.[76] "As property rights all over Europe became more clearly defined and laid down in writing, usurpation and tithes . . . became relatively less important to monasteries than gifts and sales of tithes and fractions of tithes belonging to established churches or from lands and revenues." [77] Within the Cistercian Order in England the acceptance of tithes soon became the source of difficult dissension and lengthy litigation.

The early Cistercian constitutions and legislation had shown uncompromising opposition to the acceptance of tithes. The *Exordium Parvum*, expressing the attitude of the Fathers of the Order, states that because the first Cistercians

read neither in the Rule nor in the life of St. Benedict that the same learned man possessed churches, elaborate altars, oblations, burial rights, tithes from other men, or ovens, mills, manors or serfs, or that women had entered his monastery, or that he had buried the dead there with the exception of his sister, therefore they renounced all these things, saying: When the blessed Father Benedict teaches that a monk should separate himself from all worldly matters, he clearly bears witness there, for these affairs ought not disturb the activities or the hearts of monks, who by their very name ought to leave behind what they have fled. And the Holy Fathers, who were the agents of the Holy Spirit, had distributed tithes (which the law considered a sacrilege to keep) into four portions, one for the bishop, another for the priest, the third portion for guests and those coming to churches, for widows or the poor having nowhere else to eat, and the fourth part for the fabric of the church. And because under these circumstances they found no reference to the monk who possessed his own lands,

[75] R. Naz, "Dime," in Bernard Loth and Albert Michel, eds., *Dictionnaire de théologie catholique, Tables générales*, IV (Paris, 1955), 995.
[76] Giles Constable, *Monastic Tithes from Their Origins to the Twelfth Century* (Cambridge, 1964), p. 107. The entire section "Monastic Possession of Tithes," pp. 99–136, is extremely valuable. Constable's achievement will long remain the definitive treatment of the subject.
[77] *Ibid.*, p. 99.

from which he supported himself by his own labor and that of his animals, they therefore refused to usurp illegally for themselves those things which rightly belonged to others.[78]

The rejection of the property and the property rights which monastic tithes represented as a source of revenue was an important part of the monastic reform program of the eleventh and twelfth centuries. As Constable put it, "it fitted the desire of the reformers to be poor both communally and individually and to support themselves by the labours of their own hands and animals. Secondly, it was in accord with their frequently expressed ideal of returning to the primitive, pure church of the apostles. . . . Lastly, and in practice perhaps most important, the rejection of other men's tithes kept the reformers from involvement in secular affairs and particularly from litigation, the avoidance of which was an important part of their program." [79] The Cistercian constitutions specifically forbade the acceptance of this form of property, but one of the stipulations which the Congregation of Savigny made as condition to the union with the Cistercians was the confirmation of all the privileges which she had previously enjoyed.[80] Savigny not only continued to collect her tenths after the union with Cîteaux,

[78] P. Canisius, ed., "Exordium Parvum," *Analecta Sacri Ordinis Cisterciensis*, VI (Rome, 1950), 14. Et quia nec in regula, nec in uita sancti benedicti eundem doctorem legebant possedisse ecclesias uel altaria, seu oblationes aut sepulturas uel decimas aliorum hominum, seu furnos uel molendina, aut uillas uel rusticos, nec etiam feminas monasterium eius intrasse, nec mortuos ibidem excepta sorore sua sepelisse, ideo hec omnida abdicauerunt, dicentes: Vbi beatus pater benedictus docet ut monachus a secularibus actibus se faciat alienum, ibi liquido testatur, hec non debere uersari in actibus uel cordibus monachorum, qui nominis sui ethimoloyam hec fugiendo sectari debent. Decimas quoque aiebant a sanctis patribus, qui organa erant spiritus sancti, quorumque statuta transgredi sacrilegium est committere, in IIII portiones distribuas, unam scilicet episcopo, alteram presbitero, terciam hospitibus ad illam ecclesiam uenientibus, seu viduis siue pauperibus aliunde uictum non habentibus, quartam restaurationi ecclesie. Et quia in hoc computo personaum monachi, qui terras suas possidet, unde per se et per pecora sua laborando uiuat, non reperiebant, idcirco hec ueluti aliorum ius iniuste sibi usurpare detrectabant."

[79] Constable, *Monastic Tithes*, p. 142.

[80] Buhot, "L'Abbaye normande," p. 250.

but she accepted new ones.[81] Disputes were not long in aris-
ing. In a letter dated between 1152 and 1160 Archbishop
Theobald of Canterbury (1139–61) was writing to Rome:

We have, after frequent and lengthy pleadings, been entirely
unable to settle the dispute between the abbot of Coggeshall
(Savignac house in Kent) and the prior of Rumilly (a Cluniac
priory in the diocese of Therouanne), since after many citations
and delays they at last appeared before us, and each party cited the
other to your Apostolic presence. The prior of Rumilly appealed
the abbot on the ground that he was depriving him of the Church
and tithes of those parishoners, whom the monks of Coggeshall
have driven from their lands and homes. . . . The monks of
Coggeshall pleaded their poverty and declared that they had
appealed to your court in the presence of the bishop of Therouanne, and had appointed the Feast of St. Luke as term for
their appeal, and they renewed the appeal in our presence.[82]

How this case was eventually resolved we have no way of
knowing, but certainly the acceptance of the patronage of
churches and the accompanying revenues soon became a
practice among the Cistercians, bringing a great amount of
litigation. About 1158 Archbishop Theobald was forced to
reprimand and threaten Boxley, a Cistercian house in his
metropolitan area, for what was their unlawful possession
of tithes:

It is the virtue of obedience which links mortal things to things
divine . . . and those who scorn obedience . . . rend asunder
the unity of the Church . . . Nothing can cause greater wonder
than the fact that you have thus far despised the command of
the lord pope and of ourselves. For whereas we with fatherly care
and in accordance with the mandate of the Apostolic See had
warned you often, as was right, that you should restore the tithes
of the church of Rochester to Paris the archdeacon as justice demands, we not only failed to secure the performance of our repeated commands, but could not discern even a trace of humility
or obedience among you . . . we therefore instruct and command
that you should without gainsaying or delay restore the aforesaid
tithes to the archdeacon in accordance with the mandate of the
See Apostolic . . let none of you presume to enter a church so

81 See for example Round, *Calendar of Documents*, I, no. 853, p. 307.
82 W. J. Millor and H. E. Butler, eds., *The Letters of John of Salisbury,
1153–1161*, I (London, 1955), 6.

long as by your criminal disobedience you continue the sin of witchcraft and idolatry.[83]

Sometime before 1170 Pope Alexander III (1159–81) wrote to the archdeacon and dean of Lincoln ordering them to admonish those parishioners who had unjustly deprived the Cistercian monks of the diocese of their reasonable tithes, and to protect the monks from violent attacks.[84] Again, in 1179 the monks of Rufford Abbey appealed to Pope Alexander for his assistance in the recovery of the tithes of which they felt they had unfairly been deprived.[85] The practice of accepting tithes or ecclesiastical tenths began among the Savignaics and rapidly spread to the Cistercians, but it was the cause of only one type of acrimonious dispute which led to litigation over property. In 1188 the Cistercian abbey of Merevale and the Savignaic abbey of Bordesley in Warwickshire entered a fierce struggle over a piece of pasture land. Four abbots, two Savignaic and two Cistercians, were assigned to settle the quarrel.[86] When the two litigants refused to accept the decision of the arbiters and the case had dragged on for some years, the Cistercian General Chapter finally resolved the matter by dividing the land equally between them.[87] Between 1157 and 1160 the monks of Meaux Abbey came into bitter conflict with the Austin canons of nearby Merton Priory over some adjoining lands. Both sides appealed to Rome, which returned the case to the jurisdiction of Archbishop Theobald. Theobald decided for the Austin canons and hit the White Monks with a heavy fine for illegal acquisition of property.[88] Now it is commonplace to students of medieval history that the great revival in the study of the law in the twelfth century resulted not only in a more peaceable means of settling quarrels but in the obvi-

[83] *Ibid.*, pp. 218–219.
[84] W. Holtzmann and E. Kemp, eds., *Papal Decretals Relating to the Diocese of Lincoln in the Twelfth Century*, Lincoln Record Society, XLVII (1954), 5.
[85] *Ibid.*, pp. 24–27.
[86] Canivez, *Statuta*, I, 137.
[87] *Ibid.*, p. 153.
[88] Millor and Butler, *Letters of John of Salisbury*, I, 164–165.

ous corollary of a great increase in litigation. What is significant to the student of monastic history in this case of the Cistercians and the Savignaics is the fact that the absorption of Savigny into Cîteaux, permitting Savigny to maintain all her particularistic rights and privileges, creating in effect an *imperium in imperio*, almost inevitably involved the Cistercians in the type of feudal possessions — and litigation over these possessions — which she had originally sought to avoid. And just as a separatist spirit had early appeared among the English houses of the Congregation of Savigny, this too very rapidly spread among the abbeys of the White Monks.

One of the two chief means for maintaining discipline and uniformity in the Cistercian abbeys was the institution of the annual General Chapter. Here the problems of individual monasteries could be settled and the affairs of the entire order discussed. In the last quarter of the twelfth century it became increasingly apparent that this organization was weakened by the failure of the English abbots to attend. The Savignaic abbots were consistently the greatest offenders.

For example, in 1190 the abbots of the Savignaic houses of Quarr and Stanley did not come to the General Chapter and were to undergo punishment for three days, one of them on bread and water.[89] In 1194 the General Chapter of the Order decreed: "Abbots who ought to have come to the chapter this year and have not come, and not for reasons of illness, are not to celebrate mass, are not to occupy the stall (in the choir) of abbot, and in all six ferial seasons in the year are to receive only bread and water until they are reprieved by Cîteaux." The Abbot of Savigny denounced this or said it ought to be reduced for the abbots in England, Scotland, Ireland, and Wales.[90] But this statute went without obedience, for in 1195 the Savignaic Abbot of Combemere, though specifically ordered by Savigny to appear, failed to do so. In the same year the Cistercian Abbot of Rievaulx put himself at the mercy of the Chapter for having

[89] Canivez, *Statuta*, I, 126.　　[90] *Ibid.*, p. 179.

secured a royal excuse for his failure to come in the previous year. He was to undergo punishment for six days, one of them on bread and water.[91] The same punishment was meted out to the abbots of Ford and Furness in 1198 for their failure to attend the General Chapter.[92] Many examples can be given. This failure to appear at the annual meetings on the whole shows the increasing growth of disorder and the decline of discipline.

The same type of disorder is reflected in the visitation made to the English Cistercian and Savigniac houses. In 1187 the visitors removed the Abbot of Waverley and, perhaps not trusting the ability of any monk of the same house, replaced him with a monk of Bruern.[93] In 1188 the visitors sent by the General Chapter dismissed the abbots of Tintern, Bordesley, and Dore.[94] In 1195 the Abbot of Garendon was removed, and in 1199 the Abbot of Bordesley was dismissed.[95] And so it goes. In any individual case we have no way of knowing whether a specific deposition was for financial maladministration, for departing from the observances of the Order, or for moral difficulty. But it is certain that there was considerable disorder in the English houses of the Cistercian Order.

One of the chief causes for the spiritual decline of the White Monks in the second half of the twelfth century was their union with the Congregation of Savigny. Union in itself could have been valuable for both institutes, but the acceptance of Savigny on her own terms with the preservation of all her particularistic rights and observances not only failed to reform Savigny but introduced and encouraged the same problems in the Order of Cîteaux.

91 *Ibid.*, p. 191.
92 *Ibid.*, p. 230.
93 H. R. Luard, ed., *Annales Monastici*, II (Rolls Series, no. 36, London, 1866), 244.
94 *Ibid.*, p. 245. "Hoc anno descenderunt in Angliam visitatores, missi a capitulo Cisterciensi, in quorum visitatione dimiserunt abbatias suas Willelmus de Tinterna, (et successit Vido abbas de Kingeswoda, eique successit in Kingeswoda Willelmus, prior ejusdem loci), et Willelmus abbas de Bordesleia dimisit abbatiam suam. . . ."
95 *Ibid.*, pp. 250, 252.

chapter four

the english cistercians and the gregorian reform

| 1st Gent. | Our deeds are fetters that we forge ourselves. |
| 2nd Gent. | Ay, truly: but I think it is the world That brings the iron. |

George Eliot

The connection between the Cistercian Order and the Gregorian Reform movement has long been assumed by students of the medieval Church. Within the monastic order it was under Pope Gregory VII himself (1073–85) that the various movements of reform, including the departure of the Abbot Robert and Stephen Harding from the monastery of Molesmes and the foundation of Cîteaux, gained the support of the papacy. The study of the active involvement of the Cistercians in the practical work of reform, however, has usually been associated entirely with St. Bernard and thus thought to have ended with the death of the Mellifluous Doctor in 1153. The zealous participation of the White Monks in the reforming program strengthened the authority and extended the influence of the papacy; it involved the Cistercians in the study of canon law and in the application of that law. The sad result was that these activities took them out of their monasteries and away from their original ideals and constitutional principles.

It is now well known to medievalists that the Gregorian Reform was a movement beginning within the Church in the late eleventh century which had as its object not only the centralization of the Church under the sovereign authority of the papacy and the moral regeneration of the clergy; but also the freedom of the Church, by which was meant the freedom to obey the newly codified canon law of the Church, freedom from royal control and interference from laymen. This last objective, in which the entire problem of lay investiture played the most important part, has given its name to the entire movement.[1] From one point of view the papal reformers of the eleventh and twelfth centuries revealed a very strong faith in the divine origin of their mission. They intended to destroy two ancient and powerful elements of clerical society: first, they desired to abolish simony and with it theocratic kingship and lay control of ecclesiastical patronage; second, they tried to destroy the family life of the clergy. This platform has been considered by one medievalist, who knows it well, as nothing less than

[1] G. Tellenbach, *Church, State and Christian Society at the Time of the Investiture Controversy*, trans. R. F. Bennett (Oxford, 1959), p. 162 *et passim*. See also the fundamental A. Fliche, *La Réforme grégorienne*, which remains the starting point for all serious study of the subject. W. Ullmann, *The Growth of Papal Government in the Middle Ages* (London, 1953), develops in a highly technical study Fliche's idea that the writings of popes Gelasius I (492–496) and Gregory I (590–604) were the sources of the Gregorian view of church-state relations. Cantor, *Church, Kingship and Lay Investiture*, develops some of Tellenbach's ideas and stresses the revolutionary aspects of the Gregorian Reform program. The best study for English conditions is Z. N. Brooke, *The English Church and the Papacy from the Conquest to the Death of John* (Cambridge, 1952). The most recent discussion of some aspects of the movement in England is in Southern, *Saint Anselm and His Biographer*, which seems to return to the older view of Fliche. Southern's book is, however, essentially a study of monastic life and thought. These titles do not constitute even the beginnings of a bibliography of the subject, because such a list would differ little from one of late eleventh- and twelfth-century European history in general.

a world revolution similar in many ways to the revolutions of modern Western history — the Protestant revolution of the sixteenth century, the liberal revolution of the eighteenth century, and the Communist revolution of the twentieth century.[2] From another point of view, the Gregorian reformers were only doing what every policeman does: they were trying to maintain and enforce the long-stated but largely ignored law of the Christian Church. In England, the ideals and principles of the Gregorian Reform movement were spread to no small degree by the Cistercians, whose order was originally one expression of the whole movement.

The Cistercians in England, as the White Monks all over Europe, were strongly influenced in their thinking by St. Bernard of Clairvaux. Thirty years ago the French historian Augustin Fliche pointed out that St. Bernard's course of action was based on a very categorical and well-defined set of principles, and that these were none other than those which in the eleventh century had led to the elaboration of the ideals of the Gregorian Reform — the moral regeneration of the clergy and the establishment of the pervasive influence of the pope throughout the Church.[3] St. Bernard inter-

[2] Cantor, *Church, Kingship and Lay Investiture*, pp. 6–7.
[3] A. Fliche, "L'Influence de Gregoire VII et des idées grégoriennes sur la pensée de St. Bernard," in *St. Bernard et son temps*, I (Dijon, 1928), 138; see also *Commission d'histoire de l'Ordre de Cîteaux* (Paris, 1953), Chapter IX: "St. Bernard: The Principles of His Activity." A recent interpretation suggests that the period in which St. Bernard dominated papal policy — from the Concordat of Worms in 1122 to the election of Pope Hadrian IV in 1154 — constituted a deviation from the line of development inaugurated by the Gregorian reformers and the era of papal monarchialism which followed it. St. Bernard believed that the highest authority in the Church should be placed not in the canonists, nor even in the sacerdotal hierarchy where it would legally rest according to the implementation of the Gregorian principles of papal rule, but in the monks, those who stood at the top of the spiritual hierarchy. See Hayden V. White, "The Gregorian Ideal and St. Bernard of Clairvaux," *Journal of the History of Ideas*, XXI, no. 3 (1960), 321–348, esp. 339–346. While it is true that St. Bernard in setting forth his views on the basis of papal power attacked the institutions which almost inevitably developed from the Gregorian reforms — bureaucratic administrative techniques, curialism, and abstract legalism — and emphasized the

vened in English ecclesiastical difficulties at least twenty-five times between 1120 and 1150 concerning matters directly related to the issues of the program of reform.[4] That his ideals and those of the monasteries which he pressured into support of the program were Gregorian is nowhere better illustrated than in the election to the northern primatial see of York in 1141.

It is not necessary to relate in detail here the long and complicated story of the York election and the subsequent controversies because they have been more than adequately dealt with elsewhere.[5] The death of Archbishop Thurstan in 1130 began a struggle for the control of the north which had political as well as religious overtones. After prolonged negotiations and the involvement of many candidates, William Fitzherbert, the treasurer of York, was elected under circumstances which gave strong grounds for the charge of simony. In addition, the elect had a reputation for unchaste living. Opposition to William soon came from a group of church reformers in the south directed by the growing influence of Archbishop Theobald.[6] But swamping all other influence was the zeal of the newly founded Cistercian houses of Yorkshire, whipped into action by William, Abbot of Rievaulx, and Henry Murdac, Abbot of Fountains, both of them urged on by the impatient reform-

monastic virtues of humility and holiness of life; yet, in the correction of existing evils within the church, St. Bernard's aim was identical with those of the Gregorians — moral reform. Bernard's views from the point of view of professional administrative leadership did encourage the intrusion of influences which are essentially irrational, unpredictable, and thus destructive of orderly development. White's excellent monograph points up the need for a complete reevaluation of St. Bernard and his influence on papal government in the twelfth century.

4 Knowles, *M.O.*, Appendix IX, pp. 705–706.

5 Dom M. D. Knowles, "The Case of St. William of York," *Cambridge Historical Journal*, II (1936), 162–164. This article contains a detailed narrative and references to all previous literature on the subject. C. H. Talbot, "New Documents in the Case of St. William of York," *Cambridge Historical Journal*, X (1950), 1–15, presents new sources which serve to confirm Knowles's position. See also G. V. Scammell, *Hugh du Puisset, Bishop of Durham* (Cambridge, 1956), pp. 8–21.

6 Avrom Saltman, *Theobald, Archbishop of Canterbury* (London, 1956), pp. 90–91, 100.

ing fervor of Bernard of Clairvaux. Unfortunately, all but two of the letters which Bernard apparently wrote about the election have been lost. In 1145 he wrote to Pope Innocent II: "The archbishop of York [William Fitzherbert] is coming to see you, the same man about whom I have repeatedly written to Your Holiness. He is a man who puts not his trust in God his helper, but in the abundance of riches. His case is a feeble one, and I have it on the authority of trustful men that he is rotten from the soles of his feet to the crown of his head. . . ."[7] Between 1145 and 1147, and probably because of the continual attacks of Bernard and his fellow Cistercian abbots in Yorkshire, and their influence at the Curia, William Fitzherbert was first suspended and then disposed by the Cistercian Pope Eugenius III,[8] a disciple of St. Bernard's who had made his novitiate with Henry Murdac of Fountains. Not long after the final disposition had been pronounced on William Fitzherbert, another election was held in which Henry Murdac himself was chosen. Under the confused circumstances, with the deposed archbishop still alive and spending his retirement with his uncle Henry, Bishop of Winchester; with the refusal of the cathedral chapter at York and of King Stephen to receive Murdac, it was not to be expected that the Cistercian archbishop was to have a quiet pontificate. Such a combination of opposition compelled the archbishop to spend five of the six years of his episcopate in retirement.[9]

It may well have been in the bitter winter of his discontent that Gerald of Wales quoted Pope Alexander III (1159–81) as saying that "when God deprived bishops of sons, the devil gave them nephews."[10] This sardonic comment was

[7] Bruno Scott James, trans., *The Letters of St. Bernard of Clairvaux* (Chicago, 1953), no. 187, pp. 261–263.

[8] Walbran, *Memorials of Fountains Abbey*, I, 101.

[9] This treatment of the York election is based on Knowles, *M.O.*, pp. 255–256.

[10] J. S. Brewer, ed., *Giraldi Cambrensis Opera*, II (Rolls Series, no. 21, London, 1862), 304. "Unde papa Alexander III, facetum hoc, ut fertur, verbum emisit: 'Filios episcopis Dominus abstulit, nepotes autem diabolus dedit.' "

not without justification because, in spite of the repeated publication of the canons against nepotism, in the second and third quarters of the twelfth century ecclesiastical dynasties still progressed as do knights on a chessboard. The office of archdeacon was usually the recognized step towards episcopal rank, and it was very common for bishops to appoint their nearest kinsmen to this important office. So many examples can be given that it is difficult to discover any bishop who was influential in the life of the English church or state in the middle and later twelfth century who had not first held the office of archdeacon. Archbishop Theobald gave the archdeaconry of Canterbury to his brother Walter; Bishop Nigel of Ely made his son Richard his archdeacon; at Hereford, Gilbert Foliot secured the appointment of his kinsman Ralph; Alexander, Archdeacon of Salisbury, was the nephew of Bishop Roger; and at York, Geoffrey, the archdeacon, was the nephew of Archbishop Roger Pont de l'Éveque. In 1173 when King Henry II allowed the large number of vacant sees to be filled through free elections, almost all of the bishops elected were at the time archdeacons. Richard, Archdeacon of Poitiers, became bishop of Winchester; Geoffrey, Archdeacon of Canterbury, was elected to the see of Ely; Geoffrey, Archdeacon of Lincoln, succeeded to the throne of Lincoln; Reginald, Archdeacon of Salisbury, became bishop of Bath; and Robert, Archdeacon of Oxford, was elevated to the bishopric of Hereford. The general prevalence of this practice suggests that it was in the twelfth century that archdeacons acquired what was almost a right to succession to an episcopal throne; [11]

[11] An archdeacon had administrative authority delegated to him by the bishop for all or part of the diocese. The duties of archdeacons varied widely but they usually included the responsibility for the administration of ecclesiastical property of the archdeaconry and a general disciplinary supervision of the clergy. Cross, *The Oxford Dictionary of the Christian Church*, p. 79. For the office of archdeacon as the recognized step to episcopal rank, see Wm. Stubbs, ed., *Radulfi De Diceto Opera Historica* I, (Rolls Series, no. 68, London, 1876), xxvi–xxvii, 367–368: "Ad instantiam cardinalium Alberti et Theodini, Henricus rex pater regis in Anglicana ecclesia fieri liberas electiones et permisit et scripsit. Proinde vacantium ecclesiarum conveniente clero, sub paucorum inter-

and the system seems to have met little opposition except when the moral character or the administrative ability of the candidate was called into question.

Thus it was that the death of William of St. Barbara, Bishop of the palatine see of Durham, on 13 November 1152 was followed by the election of the king's nominee, Hugh du Puisset. Hugh du Puisset held several archdeaconries in plurality, his character seems to have been formed by the violence of feudal faction and molded by the luxurious extravagance of his patron William Fitzherbert, archbishop of York (1143–53), and, given this background, his promotion by his uncle Henry of Winchester could only raise up charges of corrupt nepotism.[12] Hugh du Puisset's character and career combined all those evils which the reformers were trying to eradicate from the Church: lay interference, clerical immorality, nepotism and simony. The Cistercian Henry Murdac spent the last six years of his life unsuccessfully fighting this election. He died on 14 October 1153, a matter of weeks after the demises of St. Bernard and Pope Eugenius. Both of these episodes are significant because they show the Cistercians in the vanguard of the papal reform in the north of England on the issues of clerical morality and the honest election of bishops. While Henry's death was a factor in the decline of the relationship of the northern Cistercians with the reforming program of the papacy, it by no means ended the identification of the English White Monks with the ideals of the Roman Curia.

One concrete and obvious indication of the progress of the reform in England with which the Cistercians were connected is in the decline of a married clergy. In the twelfth century, the numbers of the regular clergy increased considerably. Knowles and Hadcock have estimated that there were scarcely one thousand monks in England in 1066; by

stitio dierum, Ricardus Pictavensis archidaconus ad Wintoniensem, Gaufridus Cantuariensis archidiaconus ad Helysensem, Gaufridus Lincolnsiensis archidiaconus ad Lincolniensis, Reginaldus Saresbiriensis archidiaconus ad Batoniensem, Robertus Oxenefordensis archidiaconus ad Herefordensem. . . ."

12 Scammell, *Hugh du Puisset*, p. 15.

1200 the number of regular clergy had increased to more than ten thousand.[13] This is probably the most concrete indication of the success of the campaign for celibacy.[14] The English population itself may have increased, but not on this scale. And, the greatest cause of the growth of the numbers of the regular clergy was due to the Cistercians: more than half of the English regulars in the last quarter of the twelfth century were Cistercians. In 1200 there were over six thousand choir-monks, which does not account for their lay-brothers.[15] This increase was not made entirely at the expense of the secular clergy, because we know that as the century advanced large numbers of secular were involved in the work of the royal government. Undoubtedly, the appeal of the monastic profession increased in a century under the spell of Peter Damian and Bernard. In the second half of the century, the married bishop was very rare, and by the first quarter of the thirteenth century, married clergy at any level seem to be the exceptional problem.[16] The ideals of the Gregorian Reform had had over a century and a half considerable effect. And, significantly, the English Cistercians, by the sheer force of their numbers, made a great contribution to the success of this reform.

A recent interpretation of the Cistercian influence on the Gregorian Reform movement maintains that the movement was a failure, and that the association had a catastrophic effect on the entire future of Western monasticism. The Cistercian ideals of ascetic piety and total withdrawal from the world, Cantor suggests, influenced all subsequent religious orders of Western Europe with the result that monasticism no longer provided the educational leadership, the bishops who were also royal administrators and professional bureaucrats; in fact, Western monasticism lost all its political influence and social utility about the year 1130. Finally, this

13 Dom M. D. Knowles and R. N. Hadcock, *Medieval Religious Houses: England and Wales* (London, 1953), pp. 359–365.
14 C. N. L. Brooke, "Gregorian Reform in Action: Clerical Marriage in England, 1050–1200," *Cambridge Historical Journal*, XII (1956), 7–8.
15 Knowles and Hadcock, *Medieval Religious Houses*, p. 360.
16 C. N. L. Brooke, "Gregorian Reform in Action," pp. 7–8.

student maintains that St. Bernard became restless, torn and ill-tempered because of the psychological tension produced by the ideals of his high-Gregorian position and the realization that Cistercian renunciation from society and the feudal world would inevitably lead to the decline of monasticism and the collapse of the Gregorian Reform program for the Church.[17]

Cantor has exhibited important insights into the relationship between the Cistercian standards and the ideals of the Gregorian movement. The Cistercian ideals of total withdrawal from the world, apostolic poverty, and severe asceticism — ideals adopted by most subsequent orders — damaged their public prestige because they implied the rejection of traditional monastic responsibilities. The absolute withdrawal into the cloister of some of the best minds in Europe contributed to the monks' loss of education leadership. Although the tempo of that decline was much more gradual and the factors involved were much more complicated than Dr. Cantor suggests, the decline in the close relationship between the kings and monastic houses did result in the weakening of the power of, and the belief in, sacramental kingship, and thus aid the development of the bureaucratic secular state. On the other hand, the evidence is overwhelming that the Cistercians, by the spiritual example of their lives and by their active participation in the work of reform, contributed to the achievement of the practical, the moral objectives of the reform program. The monk-historian is apt to judge the Cistercians entirely by the inner spiritual achievement of their lives, thus making a sublime judgment on the basis of data which are hardly calculable, a judgment that is perhaps best left to the Almighty. The wholly secular or secular-minded student is likely to render his judgment solely on the practical standard of social utility, forgetting that the fundamental objects of the monk's life are always otherworldly. If the historian may judge the ideals and achievements of the Cistercian Order by the political

17 N. F. Cantor, "The Crisis of Western Monasticism," *A.H.R.*, **XLVI** (1960), 65–67.

needs and educational achievements of twelfth-century Europe, he must conclude that the new order was a failure. Judged by the improved climate of moral life and by the development of inner piety at the end of the century, both lay and clerical, the Cistercians made valuable contributions to the success of the Gregorian Reform program.

Most of Cantor's material is based on the example of England. His argument that the number of monks holding bishoprics declines after 1130 is open to question because it rests on the hypothesis that there were many monastic prelates in the period between 1066 and 1130. This impression may perhaps be given by the great significance in English and Norman church history of Lanfranc, Anselm, and a few other monastic prelates, but in fact the proportion of bishops of monastic background was never so great under the Conqueror as it had been in the last years of the Confessor. Only five of William's seventeen appointments went to the monks, and two of these were to the relatively unimportant see of Rochester. Moreover, in the entire period between the Norman Conquest and the death of King John there was no decline in the number of monks holding bishoprics; the figure remained constant. From three in 1070 it rose to five for a few months in 1090–91, from which it fell to zero in 1124–26; another maximum of six Benedictines and the Cistercian Henry Murdac was reached in 1147–53, from which the figure declined to zero again at the death of the Carthusian Hugh of Lincoln in 1200. Thereafter until the death of King John there was no monk in the episcopate.[18] The point to notice here is that there never had been a great number.

In the later years of the century monks continued to be assigned active parts in crown councils and in the work of royal government. Samson, the aggressive but attractive Abbot of Bury St. Edmund's who is most familiar to us from the romantic but historically inaccurate picture of Carlyle, may not have been typical, but he was hardly unique. Samson was one of the most important tenants-in-chief, an officer

18 See the statistics in Knowles, *M.O.*, p. 710.

who held the power of royal sheriff in the vast liberty of St. Edmund's.[19] It should be remembered that the strongest and most consistent supporter of the king in the great politico-ecclesiastical struggle of the century, the conflict between King Henry II and Archbishop Thomas Becket (1162–70) was Gilbert Foliot, monk of Cluny and Abbot of Gloucester, before he was promoted to the episcopate. A letter to Bishop Gilbert in 1163 refers to him as, first and foremost, a monk: "Fortunate, indeed is the Church of Cluny who has deserved to have such a son, who is the flower of the learned, the mirror of religion and an ornament of the present world."[20] In 1193 the justiciars, Walter of Coutances, Archbishop of Rouen, and William Longchamp, singled out two Cistercian abbots, those of Boxley and Robertsbridge, to go to Germany to search for King Richard whom they found on Palm Sunday at the town of Oxefer in Bavaria.[21] Why this mission should have been assigned to these particular monks is difficult to say. An

[19] H. E. Butler, ed., *Chronicle of Jocelin of Brakelond* (London, 1951), pp. xxxiv-xxxvi. See also R. H. C. Davis, ed., *The Kalendar of Abbot Samson of Bury St. Edmund's*, Camden Society, Third Series, LXXXIV (1954), xv–lvii.

[20] J. C. Robertson and J. B. Sheppard, eds., *Materials for the History of Archbishop Thomas Becket*, V (Rolls Series, no. 67, London, 1881), 30. "Felix, inquam Cluniacensis ecclesia, quae meruit talem habere filium, qui esset flos doctorum, religionis speculum, et praesentis saeculi decus."

This is probably the kindest characterization, contemporary or subsequent, of Gilbert Foliot. See the recent work by Dom Adrian Morey and C. N. L. Brooke, *Gilbert Foliot and His Letters* (Cambridge, 1965), which is probably as judicious a study of this "complex" and "enigmatic" figure as we are likely to get. Although Gilbert Foliot was highly respected by Archbishop Theobald and Henry II (pp. 96–98), and for a time even by Thomas Becket (p. 248), he was an accomplice to forgery (pp. 124–246, which contain an excellent treatment of the entire subject of forgery in the twelfth century) and a blind and bitter opponent of Becket (pp. 149–187).

[21] Wm. Stubbs, ed., *Memoriale Fratris Walteri De Coventria*, II (Rolls *Series* no. 58, London, 1873), 25. "Audita itaque regis captione, Waltherus Rotomagensis archiepiscopus, et caeteri domini regis justiarii, miserunt abbatem de Boxelya, et abbatem de Ponte Roberti, in Alemanniam, ad quaerendum regem Angliae. Qui cum totam Alemanniam peragrassent, et regem non invenissent, Baveriam ingressi sunt, et obviaerunt regi in villa quae dicitur Oxefer, ubi ducebatur ad imperatorem, habiturus cum eo colloquium in die Palmarum."

explanation may rest in the fact that the two monasteries were in Kent, not far from the eastern coast. The Abbot of Boxley was present at a church council held in London in 1175, presided over by King Henry, at which the Archbishop of Canterbury, Richard (1174–84), promulgated canons against clerical fornication and marriage;[22] and the Abbot of Boxley, because of the proximity of his monastery to London and Canterbury, may have played a larger role in royal councils than the surviving evidence would indicate. At the turn of the century the Cistercian Abbot John of Ford in Devon became confessor to King John and thus gained a position in which he may have been able to exercise some influence on the king. John of Ford resigned his duties (which to King John were probably rare) and nominated as his successor the abbot of a daughter house, Henry of Bindon.[23] After 1204, then, two Cistercian abbots were associated with the royal court, perhaps involved in some way in the work of government, and perhaps as able as anyone to exercise some weight on that paranoiac head of state, King John. Finally, as late as 1221 we know that at least two of the six judges who heard the pleas of the crown for the County of Gloucester on the General Eyre of that year were monks.[24] These are but a few examples of the participation of monks in the royal government. The decline in the number of monks in the royal administration was a slow one stretching over the last half of the twelfth century and the first half of the thirteenth.

Essentially, Cantor's thesis is based on the unique example of Lanfranc and the Anglo-Norman state; but even the instance of Lanfranc is not a strong one. Lanfranc seems to have followed what we would call a middle-of-the-road policy. He came to Normandy before the reformed papacy had begun to take a strong stand on the reform of the

[22] *Ibid.*, I (1872), 239.
[23] Dom Maurice Bell, ed., *The Life of Wulfric of Haselbury*, Somerset Record Society, LXVII (1933), xx–xxxix.
[24] F. W. Maitland, ed., *Pleas of the Crown for the County of Gloucester*, (London, 1884), pp. xi–xiii.

Church, before the full force of the Gregorian program of centralized and direct church government from Rome was pushed; and in Normandy, the ideal state of affairs appeared to be a strong hierarchy under a strong king. For these reasons, Lanfranc seems to have had little sympathy with the *political* implications of Gregory VII's program. But it is a great exaggeration to state that Lanfranc of Canterbury was "forced to conclude that Gregory was a dangerous man and his policy mistaken." The policy of *moral* reform that Lanfranc laid down in England was the very same as that of Pope Gregory. Given a free hand in England, Lanfranc left a deeper mark upon the Church in England than did any archbishop between the learned Theodore and the toady Thomas Cranmer. Part of his objectives were undoubtedly aimed at the type of moral and spiritual revival that any conscientious bishop of the time would have desired, but the long-range achievements of his ministry were something quite different. The impetus for these innovations probably stemmed from his legal training in Italy and his administrative experience at Bec. The lasting results of Lanfranc's rule of the English Church: his series of "national" councils,[25] the introduction of cathedral chapters, his increase in the number of territorial archdeaconries[26] — all of these tied the Church into an organic

[25] The first council for which we have a definite record was the Council of Winchester of 1072 where the issue of the supremacy of Canterbury over York was settled. See Giles, *William of Malmesbury.* By 1075 the conciliar revival was well established. At the great London Council of that year, the proceedings of which were set down by Archbishop Lanfranc, all but two of the bishops of England were present. See J. D. Mansi, ed., *Sacrorum Conciliorum Nova et Amplissima Collectio,* XX (Paris, 1778), col. 450; J. Earle and C. Plummer, *Two of the Saxon Chronicles Parallel,* I (Oxford, 1892), 287. This admirable edition containing "The Acts of Lanfranc" shows that the primate held church councils in 1076, 1077, 1078, and 1080, in addition to the great councils of 1072 and 1075. See also Heinrich Boehmer, *Kirche und Staat in England und in der Normandie im XI und XII Jahrhundert* (Leipzig, 1899), pp. 62–64.

[26] When Lanfranc became archbishop there were few archdeaconries in existence, but by the beginning of the twelfth century five archdeacons had been appointed in the York diocese, seven in Lincoln, four in Salisbury, one in Wells, and an unknown number in the dioceses of Chi-

whole. "Above all, Lanfranc was responsible for the institution which was to have the most far reaching consequences: ecclesiastical courts.[27] Church courts applied canon law, and canon law thus gained an entrance into England at the moment when it was to develop from being a general directory of church discipline into a potent instrument of high policy and papal propaganda."[28]

As for the Abbot of Clairvaux, the probability is strong that St. Bernard did, like the warring class of feudal nobility from which he sprang, enjoy the pomp and circumstance of glorious war. It is also unquestionable that his letters reveal long periods of serious pessimism and profound depression, perhaps brought on by physical illness.[29] Thoreau

chester, London and Canterbury. See Boehmer, *Kirche und Staat*, pp. 44, 91; and A. J. MacDonald, *Lanfranc* (2nd ed., London, 1931), p. 122. The use of this very carelessly executed study is a constant reminder of the need for a scholarly treatment of this most important churchman.
[27] Sometime between 1070 and 1076 Lanfranc secured from the Conqueror the now well-known law that any matter involving clerics or ecclesiastical property must be tried before the bishop at such a place as he shall arrange, and according to canon and episcopal law. See Wm. Stubbs, *Select Charters* (rev. ed., Oxford, 1913), pp. 99–100. Lanfranc's letters, with their many references to canon law, illustrate the way in which he encouraged churchmen, especially bishops, to study the decrees of the Roman pontiffs and the sacred canons. For example, he wrote to Bishop Herfast of Thetford (an episcopal see removed in 1091 to the cathedral of Norwich): "Postpositis alies, ut majora taceam ludisque saecularibus, quibus per totam diem vacare diceris, divinas litteras lege, decretisque Romanorum pontificum, sacrisque canonibus praecipue studium impende: ibi quippe invenies quod nescis, perlectis illis frivolum duces, unde ecclesiasticam disciplinam effugere te confidis." This letter is printed in J. A. Giles, ed., *Lanfranci Opera*, I (Oxford, 1844), 47. See also Z. N. Brooke, *The English Church and the Papacy*, pp. 57–83.
[28] Dom M. D. Knowles, ed., "The Twelfth and Thirteenth Centuries," in *The English Church and the Continent* (London, 1959), pp. 32–34.
[29] See for example James, *The Letters of St. Bernard*, no. 469, p. 521, to the Abbot of Bonneval. "What room can there be in me for pleasure when suffering claims me completely for her own? The only sort I have is in eating nothing. So that the suffering may never be absent from me, even sleep has left me. I take a little liquid food frequently during the day and night, so as to keep up my strength, but I cannot take anything solid. The little that I do take causes me great suffering, but I fear that it might be worse if I took nothing at all. . . ." Williams, *St. Bernard of Clairvaux*, p. 9 *et passim*, discusses the problems raised by this gastric condition. His sympathetic study is still the best treatment of St. Bernard.

is probably right: most men (in monasteries or out) live lives of quiet desperation. Yet, even if psychology is our next assignment, there is something misplaced about the application of psychological terminology to a man seven hundred years dead — without extensive study of his background and theological vocabulary.

In the second half of the twelfth century the entire legal machinery of the Gregorian papacy was operative in England. It is now an established fact that the English Church in the later twelfth century was well abreast of the developments which everywhere resulted in the growing uniformity and centralization of ecclesiastical procedure, from the work of Gratian and his school, and from the ever increasing number of authoritative responses and appellate decisions rendered by the popes in their decretal letters.[30] More than sixty years ago Maitland observed that "in no age since the classical days of Roman law has so large a part of the sum total of intellectual endeavour been devoted to jurisprudence."[31] And the significance of the great increase in canonical processes and the study of canon law rests in the fact that the law of the English Church as elsewhere emphasized the primacy of the Church of Rome, the sovereign authority of the pope over all Christian courts and over all ecclesiastical things and persons.

It was again the Cambridge professor of law who first pointed out the importance of the system of delegate jurisdiction whereby cases were referred back by Rome to the country of their origin.[32] Now in the traditional process of ecclesiastical jurisdiction, suits began in the court of the bishop of the diocese, the bishop being the ordinary for his diocesans alone. From here appeal might be made to the court of the metropolitan. From the archbishop's court, a further and final appeal could be made to Rome. The canonists had developed the theory that the papal court was an

30 Z. N. Brooke, *The English Church and the Papacy*, pp. 94–105, esp. 105; S. Kuttner and E. Rathbone, "Anglo-Norman Canonists of the Twelfth Century," *Traditio*, VII (1949–51), 279.
31 Pollock and Maitland, *History of English Law*, I, 111.
32 *Ibid.*, p. 114.

omnipotent court of first instance for all of Christendom, the pope thereby becoming judge-ordinary of all men. Were it not for the papal practice of delegating jurisdiction, the diocesan courts would have remained immune from constant competition with the Roman court. Papal authority was assigned most often by delegating jurisdiction to one, two, and sometimes three individuals for the purpose of judging a particular case. The direct and personal appeal from one of the interested parties to Rome is generally thought to be the way in which suits began, whereupon the pope would issue an order appointing judges-delegate to try the case in the appellant's native country.[33] The judges acted with full papal authority, for as Alexander III instructed the Bishop of Chartres, "a judge so delegated acts in the pope's stead and therefore obtains a plenary jurisdiction over all things and persons who affect the case."[34] Moreover, the jurisdiction of judges-delegate would overcome the problems of geographical and diocesan boundaries which would hinder the bishop. From the point of view of the Roman Curia, the return of litigation to the countries of their origin had the strong merit of reducing the amount of work which increasingly clogged the machinery of the Curia.[35]

There were two fundamental reasons why occasions for the English to have recourse to the Roman Curia multiplied. First, innumerable rights — in lands, in tithes, and in the patronage of churches — were becoming the endowments of religious houses. Each grant was a potential cause of dispute, particularly since grants were not usually recorded at once or ran counter to the customary rights of feudal inheritance. In the course of the twelfth century the number of religious

[33] Dom Adrian Morey, *Bartholomew of Exeter, Bishop and Canonist: A Study in the Twelfth Century* (Cambridge, 1937), pp. 46–47. See also Z. N. Brooke, "The Effect of Becket's Murder on Papal Authority in England," *Cambridge Historical Journal*, II, no. 3 (1928), 213–228, which describes how the number of appeals to Rome from England was increased and the system of commissions of judges-delegate was expanded after 1172.

[34] Cited in Morey, *Bartholomew of Exeter*, p. 50.

[35] C. R. Cheney, *From Becket to Langton: Studies in English Church Government* (Manchester, 1956), p. 69 *et seq.*

houses doubled, as Knowles has described, and this greatly increased the chances of litigation. Moreover, old, established monasteries sought new privileges or falsified old ones.[36] The Cistercians, of course, obtained episcopal exemptions for their houses,[37] and this meant that disputes with the bishops, who were anxious to prevent any infringement on their diocesan jurisdictions, were virtually unavoidable. Conflicts between the exempt houses and the jealous bishops would go to the Roman tribunal in the first instance. Secondly, in the middle of the twelfth century the Church was attempting to gain for her courts an exclusive right to pronounce on the validity of marriage. But with only a few brief Biblical texts, a few passages in the writings of the Fathers, and a few canons and decretals, which were often contradictory, the Curia was not then equipped with any doctrine of wedlock sufficiently definite to serve as a legal theory. Gratian writing *ca.* 1139–42 evolved a theory which held that the *sponsalia*, the agreement to marry, constituted an "initiate marriage" which only became a "consummate marriage" at the moment of physical intercourse. At about the same time Peter Lombard was working out a definition. Espousals by words of present time, which are contracted if man and woman express the agreement to be from henceforth husband and wife, constitute a perfect marriage, though the *copula carnalis* is necessary to introduce into the union the sacrament of Christ and His Church. The definition which eventually evolved, if definition it can be called, seems to have been a combination of the two. Gratian's view that by consummation a marriage gained an additional quality of indissolubility and perhaps sacramentality was grafted onto Peter Lombard's doctrine that consent *per verba de praesenti* constitutes a marriage.[38] This is generally

---

36 *Ibid.*, pp. 49–51.

37 Mahn, *L'Ordre cistercien*, pp. 81–101.

38 F. W. Maitland, "Magistri Vacarii Summa de Matrimonio," *Law Quarterly Review*, vol. XIII (1897). There is no more difficult or complex problem in canon law, medieval or modern, than the problem of what constitutes under all circumstances and in all places a valid marriage. What Maitland has said about medieval England — "Suppose that

taken to be the present law of the Church. Because of the variety of disputes over religious endowments and because of the complex and large number of marriage cases, the system of delegate jurisdiction both from the point of view of the popes in Rome and the litigants in England was very important. The involvement of the Cistercians in the work of this system has previously gone unobserved.

Between 1160 and 1200 a considerable number of Cistercian abbots served as papal judges-delegate in England. It is Baldwin, Abbot of Ford (1174–80) and afterwards Bishop of Worcester (1180–85) and Archbishop of Canterbury (1185–90), who appears after 1175 with the greatest frequency in the addresses of decretals produced by English cases.[39] Baldwin first appears in English history in 1160 when he was clerk to the Bishop of Exeter. Yet, he must have had some reputation for his learning ten years earlier because when he was presented to Pope Eugenius III in 1150 at Ferentino, the pope appointed him tutor to Gratian, a nephew of Innocent II.[40] In 1160 the new bishop of Exeter, Bartholomew, made Baldwin archdeacon of Totnes, a division of the diocese of Exeter, and in this capacity he was a close friend not only of the bishop but also of John of Salisbury. Bishop Bartholomew, it might be noted, was an expert canonist and theologian, and he participated in the London Synod of 1159 which was convoked to decide the claims of the papal rivals Victor IV and Alexander III.[41] As a bishop he maintained contact with the great minds of his age, and through the school which he supported at Exeter he encouraged a tradition which had made that cathedral city a

we want to find the English marriage law. We shall certainly not find it . . . there is no English law of marriage" — can be applied, with rare qualification, to any time or place in the history of the Roman Catholic Church. See F. W. Maitland, *Roman Canon Law in the Church of England* (London, 1898), pp. 38–39.

[39] See Appendix herein.

[40] R. L. Poole, "The Early Lives of Robert Pullen and Nicholas Breakspear," in *Essays in Medieval History Presented to Thomas Frederick Tout* (Manchester, 1925), p. 69.

[41] Knowles, *Episcopal Colleagues of Archbishop Thomas Becket*, p. 28.

133

center of learning.[42] Gerald of Wales states that Pope Alexander III called Bartholomew of Exeter and Roger of Worcester the two great luminaries of the English Church, and that Alexander had such a high opinion of their goodness and learning that he entrusted to them almost all the causes in England which required the appointment of judges-delegate.[43] While it is an exaggeration to say that Bartholomew heard almost all the judicial causes in England, it is nevertheless true that he was employed more than any other English bishop before 1175 as a judge-delegate; on many occasions Archdeacon Baldwin acted with the bishop as judge-delegate, probably at the bishop's own desire.[44] Certainly, Baldwin gained considerable legal knowledge and judicial experience while he was archdeacon. And the best example of the intimate connection between Bartholomew and Baldwin during the period of Baldwin's archdeaconry can be seen in the dedicatory letter which Baldwin prefixed to his treatise *De Sacramento Altáris*, which he wrote while abbot of Ford. Baldwin recalls his debt to the bishop at whose wish the treatise had been composed and says "Under God, all that I am or can be, I owe to you."[45]

In 1169 or 1170 Baldwin resigned the prospects of a very promising career and entered the Cistercian abbey of Ford in Devonshire. This move may be explained, in part at least, in that the years 1169–70 witnessed the height of the Becket controversy, and the probability is that Baldwin shared the strong sympathies of his preceptor, Bartholomew of Exeter, a friend, if one of equivocal conduct, of the Archbishop of Canterbury.[46] By 1175 Baldwin was abbot of Ford, and again it was very probably at the instigation of his patron and friend, the Bishop of Exeter, that Alexander III

42 Morey, *Bartholomew of Exeter*, pp. 101–126.
43 J. F. Dimock, ed., *Giraldi Cambrensis Opera*, VII (Rolls Series, no. 21, London, 1891), 57.
44 Morey, *Bartholomew of Exeter*, p. 120.
45 Migne, *P.L.*, CCIV, col. 641.
46 Knowles, *Episcopal Colleagues of Archbishop Thomas Becket*, p. 104. In the great crisis between the king and the southern primate, Bartholomew first hesitated, probably because of Becket's own indecision, and then firmly supported him.

commissioned him as judge-delegate [47] during his years as abbot. It was probably not because of the sermons and treatises which he produced as monk and abbot that Baldwin's reputation grew — as Knowles has stated.[48] Rather, it was Baldwin's earlier experience as judge-delegate (coupled no doubt with the support of Bartholomew) which prompted Alexander III, a lawyer himself, to promote Baldwin to the see of Worcester in 1180.

Now it is a generally accepted fact among canonists that from the time of the Conquest all the collections of ecclesiastical law, complete or abridged, in England included or made prominent the extreme claims of papal authority being put forth at Rome.[49] One of the three main groups of decretal collections into which all primitive collections composed in England are classified, is the Worcester Family. It has recently been shown in a very learned study that of all the primitive collections of canon law, the Worcester Family is the most advanced in technical construction.[50] This collection may well have been begun at Ford during the years that Baldwin was abbot and serving as a judge-delegate. It was definitely completed by him at Worcester before his elevation to the primacy of Canterbury in 1185.[51] Baldwin, therefore, was familiar with and shared responsibility for the spread of canon law and the principles of the Gregorian Reform in England.

In addition to the Abbot of Ford, at least eleven other Cistercian abbots held commissions as papal judges-delegate.

[47] Holtzmann, *P.V.*, III (1952), 341–342.
[48] Knowles, *M.O.*, p. 317.
[49] Z. N. Brooke, *The English Church and the Papacy*, p. 166; Kuttner and Rathbone, "Anglo-Norman Canonists," p. 279.
[50] Charles Duggan, "The Trinity Collection of Decretals and the Early Worcester Family" *Traditio*, XVII (1961), 515. I am much indebted to Professor Duggan of King's College, London, for his kindness and the generous amount of time he spent introducing me to some of the complications of twelfth-century canon law. Compare his article with F. M. Stenton, "Acta Episcoporum," *Cambridge Historical Journal*, III (1929), 3.
[51] Hans Eberhard Lohmann, "Die Collectio Wigorniensis, ein Beitrag zur Quellengeschichte des Kanonischen Rechts im 12 Jahrhundert," *Zeitschrift der Savigny-Stiftung für Rechtsgeschichte*, LIII (Weimar, 1933), 53.

On the one hand, the popes in the later twelfth century probably chose these abbots for the same reasons they selected
other high ecclesiastics: all the popes of the second half of
the century were themselves canonists and chose their dele-
gates for their legal experience.[52] But why were Cistercian
abbots chosen? The English Cistercians in the later decades
of the twelfth century, although they often possessed considerable wealth and lived in easier circumstances than their
founders, were still influenced by the high Gregorian principles of St. Bernard. They still enjoyed some reputation for
sanctity, and their lives differed from those of the members
of the old and most of the new religious institutes. For this
reason, they may well have been nominated by one of the
litigants. The frequent use of Cistercian abbots is, then,
partially explained by their prestige in the public community. Moreover, the ambition of great Cistercian abbeys to
be exempt from episcopal control made them the natural
supporters of papal authority,[53] and they were anxious to
secure papal protection and confirmation of their possessions.[54] Finally, it was very probably through the influence,
both at Rome and in England, of Baldwin of Ford that
Cistercians were given commissions. There is no record
of a Cistercian abbot serving as a papal judge before Baldwin
entered the monastery of Ford in 1169.

As was said above, the abbots of at least twelve Cistercian
monasteries served as judges-delegate. They were the abbots
of Ford, Fountains, Rievaulx, Boxley, Bruern, Thames,
Buckfast, Wardon, Kirkstall, Combe, Stanley, and Vaudey.

52 Morey, *Bartholomew of Exeter*, pp. 48–49; see also C. R. Cheney,
From Becket to Langton, pp. 68–69. Cheney is closely following Maitland, *Roman Canon Law*, p. 122.
53 Mahn, *L'Ordre cistercien*, pp. 81–101, esp. 96–99.
54 The papal registers contain frequent references to confirmation of
properties of the English White Monks. See Ph. Jaffe, ed., *Regesta
Pontificum Romanorum*, vol. II (2nd ed., Lipsiae, 1888). 20 November
1160: "Alexander III Monasterium S. Mariae Rievallense tuendum suscipit et eius bona ac iura confirmat," p. 151; 25 December 1162: "Monasterii
S. Mariae de Fontibus tutelam suscipit bonaque et iura confirmat, petente
Ricardo abbate," p. 164; 2 February 1165: "Monasterii Cisterciensis
protectionem suscipit possessionesque confirmat, petente Gilliberto
abbate," p. 189 *et passim*.

On the basis of the materials hitherto published by that very careful student of the papal relations with England, Holtzmann, we may calculate that the abbots of Rievaulx were called upon five times, the abbots of Vaudey three times, the abbots of Fountains, Bruern, and Thames twice each, and each of the other abbots once.[55] It is likely, however, that the abbots of these monasteries, and perhaps those of other houses, served much more frequently. For example, as far as the surviving documents will prove concretely, the Abbot of Fountains was the recipient of only two papal commissions between 1170 and 1185. There is very good indication, however, that he was repeatedly delegated jurisdiction.[56] It is probable that a considerable number of commissions have been lost and that the Cistercians played a larger part in the process of delegate jurisdiction than the surviving records suggest.

It is possible to speculate as to the reason that the abbots of these particular monasteries were selected to be judges delegate. Baldwin of Ford was obviously selected because of his own legal knowledge and practical experience. Ford was a daughter house of Waverley Abbey, as were also the monasteries of Bruern, Thame, and Combe. Although fourteen Cistercian foundations were made from Waverley, she was never well known in the Middle Ages, and, as Knowles observed, "there is a certain irony in the posthumous celebrity which her name has received as the result of its adoption by Sir Walter Scott."[57] The observance of the Cistercian constitutions would bring the abbots of these houses together at least once a year; the annual visitation of the abbot of Waverley to his daughter houses and the journey of all those abbots together annually to the General Chapter at Cîteaux would imply a close relationship between Bruern, Thame, Combe, and Ford; and the abbots of these monasteries would certainly have come in contact with Baldwin.

55 See Appendix herein.
56 See below, pp. 144–45.
57 Dom M. D. Knowles and J. K. S. St. Joseph, *Monastic Sites from the Air* (Cambridge, 1952), p. 62.

The abbey of Rievaulx in the North Riding of Yorkshire was not the first Cistercian foundation in England; but it was founded from Clairvaux by St. Bernard's own monks, it quickly became in the general public opinion of the times the most famous monastery of the Order in England, and its reputation was further enhanced by the prestige of its third abbot, Ailred (1147–66), called "the Bernard of the North." Ailred had gained widespread recognition for his leadership and sound judgment after 1154 when he was chosen as arbitrator in the most difficult monastic dispute of his time, the rival claims of Savigny and Furness for the obedience of Byland.[58] It was during the later years of Ailred's abbacy that the great Italian lawyer and canonist Vacarius was living in York, and Ailred must have known him because together they witnessed an agreement between the churches of Durham and York in 1159.[59] Vacarius had been brought to England to help Archbishop Theobald in his struggle to wrest the papal legateship from Bishop Henry of Winchester. From the end of Stephen's reign, Vacarius devoted his long life to the work of an ecclesiastical lawyer in the northern province, especially in the service of Archbishop Roger of York.[60] Vacarius' presence in the north of England, where he came in contact with other Cistercians besides Ailred and the monks of Rievaulx, undoubtedly stimulated the study of the developing canon law among the White Monks there. Sometime between 1171 and 1181 Silvanus, the fourth abbot of Rievaulx, served as a judge-delegate with Bishop Bartholomew of Exeter,[61] and this association must have brought to Rievaulx further knowledge and practical experience. A combination of all these factors, then, prompted the Roman Curia to assign judicial commissions to the later abbots of Rievaulx.

The close constitutional relationship between Rievaulx

58 See previous chapter.
59 Farrer, *E.Y.C.*, II, 276; Powicke, *The Life of Ailred of Rievaulx*, p. xcii.
60 Joseph de Ghellinck, S.J., "Magister Vacarius," *Revue d'histoire ecclésiastique*, XLIV (1949), 173–178; *D.N.B.*, XX, 80–81.
61 Holtzmann, *P.U.*, III, 445.

and her earliest foundation, Wardon, and the fact that they were founded by the same man, Walter Espec, help to explain why the abbot of obscure Wardon would be summoned to assist the papacy. Boxley Abbey in Kent was founded directly from Clairvaux in 1145. When, the day after his murder, the rumor circulated that the corpse of Thomas Becket would be thrown outside the walls of the city for the birds and dogs to feed upon, it was the Abbot of Boxley with the prior and community of Canterbury who in 1171 hastily buried the archbishop.[62] This particular incident might well suggest several things: that the Abbot of Boxley was associated with Becket and sympathetic to his position; and that Boxley Abbey, founded directly from Clairvaux, had over the years retained a connection with and an affinity for high-Gregorian principles — principles for which Thomas Becket was martyred; and it offers one reason why an abbot of Boxley would be called upon to help reduce the law's delay.

Since the abbey of St. Mary's of Fountains competed with Rievaulx for prestige and fame among the English Cistercian houses, it would seem only to be expected that the papacy would call upon abbots of Fountains to serve as judges-delegate. There is evidence to indicate that the abbots of Fountains served as papal judges far more frequently than the actual surviving number of papal commissions would indicate. The development of an extensive collection of decretals at Fountains, as has recently become apparent, would indicate a much greater participation by the abbots of Fountains. One of the seven twelfth-century collections of decretals which compose what Professor Duggan calls the "English" family of decretals is the Fountains Collection.

[62] Frederic Madden, ed., *Matthaei Parisiensis Historia Anglorum*, I (Rolls Series, no. 44, London, 1866), 365. "Sequenti vero die, videlicet Mercurii, summo diluculo rumor increbuit, quod nefandi carnifices corpus archiepiscopi abstrahere ab ecclesia condixerant, et extra muros civitatis illud projicere avibus et canibus discerpendum; sed abbas de Boxsleia, cum priore et conventu ecclesiae Canturariensis, illud marturiori tradentes sepulturae, nec abluendum illud fore judicabant, quod sanguis notabilia concurrebant."

This was transcribed at Fountains sometime after 1181 and shows considerable familiarity with the Worcester and Exeter collections, to both of which it was certainly indebted.[63] The survival of a learned collection of decretals at Fountains, which was fully acquainted with the most advanced decretal collection (the Worcester) in England, obviously presupposes that the monks of the house had or gained a sophisticated knowledge of the latest developments in the canon law of their time. Moreover, the Abbot of Fountains in 1177 must have known Master Vacarius because in June of that year he was assigned by Alexander III to serve with Vacarius on a judicial commission to settle a complicated marriage problem. A combination of these factors, therefore — the presence of Master Vacarius in York for several decades, the participation of the abbots of Fountains and Rievaulx in the process of delegate jurisdiction, and the preservation of a collection of canons and decretals at Fountains Abbey — would suggest that there was considerable study and activity in the development of a universal ecclesiastical law among the Cistercians of northern England.

Again, so fundamental in the structure of the Order was the principle of kinship that it is not surprising that the abbots of two Fountains' daughter houses, Vaudey and Kirkstall, should each receive several commissions as judges-delegate.

The case of Stoneleigh Abbey is similar. In January, 1195, Pope Celestine III (1187-91) requested the abbots of Stoneleigh and Combe to settle a dispute between two religious houses over the tithes of a parish church.[64] Both Stoneleigh and Combe were descended from Waverley — Combe, a daughter of Waverley; Stoneleigh, a daughter in the second generation — and both monasteries were situated in Warwickshire.

Finally, the abbey of Buckfast in Devonshire was the only

[63] Charles Duggan, *Twelfth Century Decretal Collections and Their Importance in English History* (London, 1963).
[64] Holtzmann, *P.U.*, I (1930-31), 619.

member house of the Congregation of Savigny to participate among the Cistercians in the papal system of delegate jurisdiction. The popes may well have hesitated to call upon abbots of the Congregation of Savigny because of the conflicts and disorders within and among the houses of the Congregation, and because of the notorious disregard for the law which the English abbots of the Congregations of Savigny had displayed. One can find no familial or legal reason why the Roman Curia would select the Abbot of Buckfast. Of course, as was stated above, the abbot might have been selected by one of the suitors in a particular case. Buckfast lies, however, in the county of Devon geographically very close to the episcopal seat of the diocese, Exeter, and only a short distance from the abbey of Ford. It is likely, then, that the Abbot of Buckfast knew either Bartholomew of Exeter or Baldwin of Ford, or both of them, and on their recommendation was assigned to serve on a papal commission.

Almost all of the cases which these Cistercian abbots decided concerned, as far as we know, property disputes. A few examples will illustrate this. Sometime between 1170 and 1181, Pope Alexander III assigned the Abbot of Rievaulx and the Dean of Lincoln to settle the complaint of one P., a clerk, who had protested to Rome that he had been violently dispossessed of the church of Sprotborough in the diocese of Lincoln.[65] In 1192, Pope Celestine III requested the abbot of Wardon, the Prior of Chicksands, and Archdeacon Robert of Huntington to investigate the dispute between the nuns of Harrold in Bedfordshire and the clerk Baldwin over the church of Stevington.[66] Again in 1195, Celestine III called on the abbots of Kirkstall and Swainby and the Prior of Malton to decide the struggle between the prior and canons of Guisborough and two clerks of the diocese of York over the tithes of Wivelsich and certain lands which these two clerks had seized.[67] The only recorded dele-

[65] Holtzmann and Kemp, *Papal Decretals*, pp. 40–41.
[66] Holtzmann, *P.U.*, III, 587–588.
[67] Ibid., I, 625.

gation of jurisdiction which did not involve property was related to that other type of subject which has always filled the ecclesiastical courts, marriage. On 30 June 1177, Alexander III ordered the Abbot of Fountains and Master Vacarius to settle a complicated problem. It appeared that William de Roumare, first earl of Lincoln, captured a man, put him in chains, and compelled him to marry a certain woman. The prisoner, after his escape, married another woman and by this second wife had sons. The judges were to determine (1) whether the man had been compelled to marry the first woman and (2) if, when he was married to the first wife, he had carnal knowledge of her. If he had been forced to marry the first wife, so Pope Alexander ordered, but did not sleep with her, then he could return to his second (and lawful) wife. But if the reverse was true, he must put aside the second wife.[68] The Abbot of Fountains was important in the evolution of what was to be one fundamental legal theory of the Western Church: marriage is established only by a promise to marry, followed by consummation.

What effect did these judicial activities have on the Cistercian Order? First of all, the entire involvement of Cistercian abbots in the program of delegate jurisdiction can be traced to Baldwin of Ford. The judicial duties of Ailred of Rievaulx ten years earlier concerned matters intimately related to difficulties within the Cistercian Order, and it was only after Baldwin entered the abbey of Ford that White Monk abbots are found serving as papal judges all over England. Baldwin may have been a profound thinker, because he wrote the treatise *De Sacramento Altáris*, which a recent student has called a great and remarkable work.[69] Moreover, he was a man of considerable practical experience in the application of law; and the production of theological treatises represents a real achievement for one so busy

[68] Holtzmann and Kemp, *Papal Decretals*, pp. 20–21. The classic account of the expansion of canon law in England after the death of Becket is Mary Cheney, "Compromise of Avranches and the Spread of Canon Law in England," *E.H.R.*, LVI (1941), 177–197.
[69] C. J. Holdsworth, "John of Ford and Early Cistercian Writing, 1167–1214," *T.R.H.S.*, 5th Series, II (1961), 125.

in the ecclesiastical courts and in making a collection of canon law. But Baldwin became a Cistercian late in life; he certainly spent no more than ten years at Ford, during which time he was frequently occupied with judicial responsibilities; and he could have been only partially formed by Cistercian ideals. Baldwin was a monk, nevertheless, and that is how his contemporaries looked upon him. Gerald of Wales lists Baldwin among the six most praiseworthy bishops of his age: Thomas of Canterbury and Henry of Winchester, Bartholomew of Exeter and Roger of Worcester, and Baldwin of Canterbury and Hugh of Lincoln. The Cistercian Baldwin then was linked with the Carthusian Hugh, because both of them were monks.[70] In an age when the Cistercians held a position of no small reputation in the English Church, it is significant that it was Baldwin, the canon lawyer, who rose to be archbishop of Canterbury.

Baldwin's learning brought him a considerable reputation within the Cistercian Order, and it was undoubtedly because of his example and influence that Ford became almost a literary center, in direct opposition, it should be noted, to Cistercian tradition. In 1178 Cardinal Peter, the papal legate, wrote from France to Alexander III recommending Baldwin for the cardinalate: "There is however Master Baldwin, Abbot of Ford, and although we have not seen him, he is distinguished throughout the entire Cistercian Order for his great learning, his character and his religion."[71] His impact on the Cistercian Order in England in the last three decades of the twelfth century was profound. A number of abbots, serving, as papal judges, gained considerable knowledge and experience in canon law. Contact with men of

[70] Dimock, *Giraldi Cambrensis Opera*, IV (1877), 67–68. "Fuerunt autem in Anglia, non longe post horum tempora, duo de ordine monastico, alter Cisterciensis, alter vero Cartusiensis, in episcopos, rege procurante, Wigorniensem qui et post Cantuariensis, et Lincolniensem assumpti. . . . Fuerat autem his duobus, ut videbatur, bonitas propemodum et religio par, sed via virtutum valde dispar."

[71] Bouquet, *H.F.*, XV, 962. "Magister autem Balduinus abbas Fordenus, quamvis eum non viderimus, a toto ordine Cisterciensi de multimoda literatura, honestate et religione potissimum commendatur."

such learning and reputation as Master Vacarius and arch-deacons, whose legal experience prepared them for positions in the hierarchy, undoubtedly widened their horizons and deepened their learning in the law. A collection of canons and decretals was transcribed at Fountains Abbey perhaps to serve as a text for future students, probably to serve as a reference work for the abbots of the monastery who might be called upon to act as papal judges. But these activities imposed grave burdens on the judges involved, taking them outside of their monasteries for lengthy periods of time in contradiction to the spirit of the *Rule of St. Benedict* and the letter of the Cistercian statutes. Thus, Abbot John who succeeded Baldwin at Ford lamented the extent to which administrative duties took abbots away from their monasteries on matters of litigation, exhausted their energies, and left them little time for pastoral direction.[72] At the same time, it does not appear that papal judges-delegate had any recognized means of recovering the expenses in which their commissions involved them. Presumably, the abbots had to regard this as a charge on their ecclesiastical revenues. The complaints of the brethren of Fountains about the difficulties that resulted from the responsibilities laid on their abbot were acknowledged in a letter that Pope Lucius III (1181–85) wrote that abbot in 1185:

From some of the monks of your community it has been brought to our attention that as a result of our commissions, their house is burdened with expenses and they themselves together with you for the most part have gained the anger and hatred of great men; therefore for you and for themselves they have humbly asked that the Apostolic See mercifully make some provision for this situation. Thus, by witness of this document, we announce that we shall take care, with the help of God, that responsibilities are not assigned to you by us, so that other graver problems do not develop, unless by chance some other greater problem should arise which we do not think can be settled suitably without you. If indeed it should happen that at some time, through forgetfulness, we should delegate a case to you alone, or with another, or with others, you would not need to accept the mandate unwillingly, but the

72 Holdsworth, "John of Ford," p. 132.

others who by chance have been assigned with you, let them (alone) resolve what we have assigned you and them.[73]

How this promise was kept we have no way of knowing, but it is clear that the system of delegate jurisdiction was detrimental to monastic observance, peace, and financial good order. We do not know when the study of canon law began in the English Cistercian monasteries. From the end of the eleventh century and throughout the twelfth and thirteenth centuries there were repeated papal decrees prohibiting juridical studies in all the houses of the regular clergy. The popes felt that the study of law would introduce a profane spirit into the cloister, encourage an immoderate love of money, and result in frequent and prolonged absences from the monastery. On the other hand, theology, the popes believed, was the science especially important for the education of monks, canons, and all the regular clergy. The result was that throughout the Cistercian Order, obedient to Roman discipline, the study of Holy Scripture and the writings of the Church Fathers constituted the preponderant and almost the only part of the monks' intellectual development in the early years.[74]

In 1188, almost forty years after the publication of Gratian's *Decretum*, the Cistercian General Chapter made its first restrictive pronouncement concerning the study of

73 Holtzmann, *P.U.*, III, no. 368, p. 470. "Lucius episcopus etc. Dilecto filio abbati de Fontibus salutem et apostolicam benedictionem. Ex parte fratrum tuorum relatum est nobis, quod occasione commissionum nostrarum domus eorum grauatur sumptibus et ipsi plerumque tecum indignationem et odium magnarum personarum incurrunt ideoque tibi et eis super hoc de apostolice sedis clementia prouidere humiliter postularunt. Quocira significatione presentium intimamus, quod auctore Deo prouidere curabimus, ne tibi a nobis negotia delegentur, nisi forte aliqua maiora emerserint, que non putemus sine te congrue terminari. Si uero per obliuionem quandoque contigerit, ut causam tibi soli uel cum alio aut aliis delegemus, non suscipias mandatum inuitus, sed alii, qui tecum forte fuerint delegati, quod tibi et eis scripsimus, exequantur. Dat. Veron. kal. aprilis."

74 P. Colomban Bock, "Les Cisterciens et l'étude du droit," *Analecta Sacri Ordinis Cisterciensis*, VII (Rome, 1951), 7–10, esp. 10.

law.[75] The Chapter advised against placing Gratian's work indiscriminately at the disposal of all.[76] The implication of this *statuta* is that persons serving as judges-delegate or involved in some way with the juridical work of the papacy might study Gratian's fundamental text. At Ford Abbey in England the study of canon law was undoubtedly connected with the presence of Baldwin, and at the other English monasteries it was probably connected with those abbots who held commissions as papal judges. By the end of the century, Dom J. M. Canivez has written, "It is incontestable that our abbots and our monks enjoyed at the Roman court a very good reputation for their juridical knowledge."[77]

As papal judges-delegate the Cistercians in England played an active and important role in the application of the program of the Gregorian Reform. They tried to enforce the principles of canon law, and this required them to promote the study of canon law. In so doing they undoubtedly strengthened the authority of the Roman papacy in England. On the other hand, and in the last analysis, these activities had what can only be called a damaging effect on the ideals and the practices of the English Cistercians.

[75] Canivez, *Statuta*, I, 108. Liber qui dicitur Corpus canonum et Decreta Gratiani apud eos qui habuerint secretius custodiantur, ut cum opus fuerit proferantur; in communi armario non resideant, propter varios qui inde possunt provenire errores."
[76] I have followed the interpretation of this statute given by Block, "Les Cisterciens," pp. 14–15, in his very learned study, which is concerned, however, with the theories of juridical studies among the medieval Cistercians, rather than the actual judicial activities of the monks.
[77] Dom J. M. Canivez, "Cîteaux," in R. Naz. ed., *Dictionnaire de droit canon* (Paris, 1935–), III, col. 777.

chapter five

conclusion

And right action is freedom
From past and future also.
For most of us, this is the aim
Never here to be realised;
Who are only undefeated
Because we have gone on trying;
We, content at the last
If our temporal reversion nourish
(Not too far from the yew-tree)
The life of significant soil.

T. S. Eliot

In religion, nothing fails like worldly success, and the development of the English Cistercians in the twelfth century illustrates this rather cynical maxim. The history of the White Monks differs hardly at all from that of most male religious orders in Western civilization. A small group of reformers, dissatisfied with existing conditions because they believe the current expression of the monastic life to be too broad, attempts to establish a new religious organization which is to be governed by what the reformers consider a strict interpretation of the *Rule of St. Benedict*. From poor and difficult beginnings, the new order grows and expands. As it does, it accumulates property and great wealth. The result is the rapid departure from the original ideals of

147

the founders until the "new" institute appears in its way of life no different from any other contemporary religious order.

The first Cistercians who came from Clairvaux in Burgundy to Waverley in England had nothing to recommend them but their reputation for severe asceticism. In the long run, even in the short run, this reputation was to be the cause of their undoing. Their penitential piety brought them respectful prestige among the general public, aspirants from the very devout, and large donations of property from the wealthy. Ardent young men entered the Order, for one reason — because they believed that monasticism, especially Cistercian monasticism, was the surest road to salvation. The rich and propertied, who had chosen the middle way of tepid souls, supported the monks out of a desire to make reparation for sins committed in the past, or as an insurance for salvation in the future. Even more, their motives were inspired by the fact that since the Order of Cîteaux enjoyed the greatest popular reputation in Christian Europe, it was socially and materially advantageous to be associated with that reputation. At the same time, concrete financial and material returns were often expected on this investment. The patron of one or several monasteries enjoyed a fame among his contemporaries because of his association with the Order of Cîteaux, and the monks in turn promised him that his generosity insured the prayers of "his monks," which, accordingly, promised his eternal salvation.

While most houses of the Congregation of Savigny in England were founded in the last years of Henry I, the monasteries of the Cistercian order were established against the background of the anarchy and civil wars of Stephen's reign. The men who endowed the Cistercian and Savignaic abbeys down to the accession of Henry II in 1154 were almost all barons of the highest rank, tenants-in-chief of the crown, or persons closely connected with the great barons. Of the fourteen foundations made by members of the royal family, seven were houses of the Congregation of Savigny. The feudal barons who founded Cistercian monasteries were frequently related to each other, either by blood, or marriage, or interests. These men made up only a small group in the feudal order, and they all bore or gained the title and dignity of earl. The fact of their close familial relationship helps to explain the establishment of *Cistercian* monasteries. The Cistercians were usually given small parcels of land which the barons valued least among their possessions. Yet, sometime between the foundation of the monasteries and about 1166, many barons required the White Monks to compound for their gifts by small amounts of rent and/or the payment of scutage.

After 1154, in what may be called the second Cistercian generation, the pattern of endowment changed considerably. The patrons of the monks came from the class below the great barons, the broad class of knights. The knights were poorer men than the great lords of Stephen's reign, and they could not afford to be very generous. Very frequently, therefore, they demanded some compensation for the estates with which they endowed the monks — money or a fractional part of knight service. Although the obligation for any one gift was never very great, in the aggregate they brought on the Cistercians a great number of problems: the feudal obligation of scutage, the financial debt of rents, and the spiritual difficulties resulting from these political and economic responsibilities. The capacity of custom in the Middle Ages to transform precedents into permanent rights tended to perpetuate the seignorial demands and the monastic obligations. The Cistercians, therefore, became inextricably involved in the economic and social structure of the land. The acceptance by the White Monks of many gifts carrying with them financial obligations was as economically unsound as it was destructive to the Cistercian ideal of total separation from the lay world.

In a broader perspective, the issues raised by this situation are part of the inherent conflict between ecclesiastical and lay interests. When we understand the conditions surrounding the foundation of the monasteries, when we realize the material needs of the monks and the spiritual aspirations of their benefactors, it rapidly becomes impossible to specify with any degree of reality what are in practice the things of Caesar and what are those of God.

The absorption of the Congregation of Savigny into the Cistercian Order in 1148 was most unfortunate, and a major cause of the loss, by the greater monastic institute, of her prestine fervor and ideals. The Congregation of Savigny never had a written constitution, and even from what we know of her early history, the Savignaic expression of the monastic life never approached the high ideal of the *Carta Caritatis* nor in practice the ascetic life led by the first White Monks at Cîteaux. Within ten years of her foundation, the monks of the Congregation of Savigny were involved in the wholesale acquisition of churches, tithes, and secular rights; the quest of property for its own sake; and above (or worst of) all in ambitious schemes for which money was raised by lending at interest, that is, by usury.[1] The most unfortunate aspect of the union of Savigny and Cîteaux, a union of which St. Bernard was the chief architect,[2] was the

[1] R. Genestal, *Rôle des monastères normands comme établissements de crédit* (Paris, 1901), pp. 64–150. The business dealings of many abbeys of the Congregation of Savigny appear to be as corrupt as they were complicated; certainly, these houses flaunted the Church's prohibition against usury as egregiously as any contemporary "capitalistic" layman.

[2] St. Bernard was probably one of the greatest mystics that the Church has produced, but here, as in several other instances, his interference was destructive of sound constitutional development and good order.

St. Bernard also had a strong hand in the foundation of the Order of Knights Templars, for his *Liber de Laude Novae Militae* was written at the request of Hugh de Payens, the first master of that order. This book demonstrated the possibility of reconciling the monastic profession with the military life in the Holy War against the Muslims. Bernard further manifested his interest in the Templars by attending the Council of Troyes in 1128 where he took a large part in the framing of the Rule of the Knights Templars. The text of the *Liber de Laude Novae Militae ad Milites Templi* is printed in Migne, *P.L.*, CLXXXII, cols. 921–940. See also Williams, *St. Bernard of Clairvaux*, pp. 234–240. The influence of St. Bernard on the Templars and the absorption of the Congregation of Savigny into the Cistercian Order probably served as precedents for the union of the Spanish military Order of Calatrava with the Order of Cîteaux in 1158. This order, whose members were required to produce patents of nobility for entrance, went through a rapid decline, and by the beginning of the fourteenth century was notorious for its sexual immorality and for the number of bastards its monk-knights left behind.

fact that the Savignaic monasteries were allowed to retain all their special practices and privileges, as full members of the Cistercian Order, although the Cistercian constitutions specifically forbade such practices in theory, and in practice condemned them with bell, book, and candle. The results were virtually inevitable. Very soon after the union of the two monastic bodies, the Cistercians were involved in the same difficulties that had plagued the Savignaics. The 1150's and 1160's were filled with Cistercian disputes over property, tithes, and jurisdictions, to say nothing of a spirit of acrimonious contention. These were all very serious departures from the monastic ideal as set forth in early Cistercian legislation. The union of the two institutes presented an exceptional opportunity to the Cistercians with their great influence and St. Bernard with his great prestige. By insisting that the members of the Congregation of Savigny give up their old practices and accept entirely the Cistercian regulations, St. Bernard could have promoted reform in the lesser order and raised its standards. But the acceptance of Savigny on her own terms resulted in the creation of a dual standard, and the lower standard spread through and corrupted the Cistercian Order.

The rapid growth and increase of prosperity of the Cistercian Order in England, and on the continent as well, had what can only be called a damaging effect on the original spirit and ideals of the Order as a monastic institute. When one reflects on Lord Acton's famous dictum on the corrupting effect of power, and wealth is power in any age, the effect of the Cistercian prosperity is all too apparent. The chief institution for the maintenance of the Cistercian ideals was the annual General Chapter because of its power to discipline. The *instituta* of many chapters in the last quarter of the twelfth century reflect the decline in the spirit and observances of the English Cistercian monasteries. The *insti-*

See J. F. O'Callaghan, "The Affiliation of the Order of Calatrava with the Order of Cîteaux," *Analecta Sacri Ordinis Cisterciensis*, vol. XV (Rome, 1959–60). The impact of this order on the Cistercians in Spain could not be called edifying.

tuta promulgated by the General Chapter at some time between 1173 and 1191 cover most aspects of the Cistercian life, but they lay emphasis on one particular matter. The work of the monks — whether it be manual labor, the sale of the monastery's produce, or trading at fairs — is to be limited to the needs of the community: Cistercian monks, this ordinance stresses, are not to work and trade for the purpose of making a profit. The frequent repetition of this statute would indicate that the law was not being observed and that the Order was having difficulty enforcing it.[3] The statutes of 1173 do not refer specifically to English houses of the Order, but other evidence shows that the English houses were guilty of the same abuses.

The enormous increase in the numbers of the monks themselves could only increase the possibility of internal disorder. Knowles had indicated that there may have been as many as five thousand Cistercian monks in England at about 1160, counting both choir monks and lay-brothers.[4] The hundreds of novices who entered Fountains and Rievaulx and a few other houses in the middle decades of the century could not all have had genuine vocations, and the toleration of so many of the lukewarm could only have had a detrimental effect on the spiritual climate of the house. The one monastic order which has never been reformed, the Carthusian, has always guarded carefully the numbers of those who sought to enter. When the Cistercians allowed so many to remain, they lost as much in zeal as they gained in members.

During the last two decades of the twelfth century, and possibly before, the English Cistercian abbots seriously

3 Migne, *P.L.*, CLXXXI, cols. 1725–40; Watkin Williams, "The First Cistercian Era," in *Monastic Studies* (Manchester, 1938). This issue is mentioned only three times in the "Instituta" of the General Chapter as printed by Migne, but Williams cites the subject eight times in the Dijon manuscript from which he worked.
4 Knowles and Hadcock, *Medieval Religious Houses*, p. 360. I think this figure is a modest estimate from the tables deductible in Knowles and Hadcock. See also J. C. Russell, "The Clerical Population of Medieval England," *Traditio*, II–III (1944–45), 177–212, esp. 194–196, which is an older but still valuable study.

weakened the power of the entire order by failing to attend the annual General Chapter at Cîteaux. The abbots of the former Congregation of Savigny were the earliest and most flagrant offenders, but the White Monks' abbots soon followed suit. The result was that the ability of the General Chapter to punish offenders, to correct abuses, and generally to maintain discipline was gravely impaired.

The impact of the Cistercian development on the English nation was indeed very great. Many students have stressed the importance of the White Monks as builders of the vital wool trade and as reclaimers of the soil. Here, as tillers of the land, the Cistercians were not as important in England as they were on the continent, in eastern Germany for example, because when they came to England the island was far more advanced agriculturally than most parts of continental Europe. In the realm of Church-State relations, a number of Cistercian abbots served the papacy as judges-delegate and thereby participated in the development of canon law and church discipline which characterized the century. As servants of the pope, they strengthened the power of church courts and the authority of the Roman pontiff in England, at the very moment, it might be said, when King Henry II was trying to reduce the papal authority and the jurisdiction of its courts in the land. But the Cistercians as twelfth-century papal "shock troops" quickly discovered that their judicial responsibilities entailed a considerable financial burden, and these duties took them away from their monasteries for lengthy periods of time, to the destruction of good discipline and ancient ideals.

It is a commonplace to medievalists that medieval society was an organic, united civilization, in which all institutions were connected with and dependent on all others. In the sphere of her constitutional life the essential difference between the *original* Cistercian ideal and that of all other monastic and lay institutions is to be found in the desired detachment of the Cistercian monasteries from the social life of the country. The Cistercian abbey was to be an entirely self-contained unit, separated from all outside influences whether ecclesiastical, politico-feudal, or social, in which the monks and officials were to exist solely for the life of their community. Here lies an essential reason for the rapid decline of the Cistercian ideal. While the monks were regarded by their lay contemporaries as intercessors for the rest of society, separated from those who gave it livelihood by toil and those who defended it by arms, and while prayer was regarded as an indispensable social service, in so organic a society it was virtually impossible for one institution to remain completely apart from any active social service. St. Bernard himself, for all that he seems to have personified the Cistercian ideals, was continually involved in ecclesiastical and political peregrinations. The papacy itself summoned Cistercian abbots into its service to the detriment of the very ideal for which the White Monks stood. Stephen Harding and the early fathers of Cîteaux achieved in the *Carta Caritatis* a constitution which influenced all later religious institutes in the Western Church, but it attempted to create what can only be called an impossible ideal for operation within the feudal world for which it was written. The machinery of the *Carta Caritatis* continued in operation but of itself was powerless to prevent a spiritual decline. An abstract legal creation can be no more than an instrument and a means of government; it fails when governors or governed no longer wish, or are able, to apply it.

The choice of the name of Christian presupposes the acceptance of the teachings of Christ and the attempt by the individual, in some measure at least, consciously to direct the mode of his behavior and the pattern of his life according to these principles as set down in the Gospels. The man who elects the narrow way of the monastic life lives the Christian life on a more difficult plane, for the monastic life is only the Christian life lived extraordinarily. Christ Himself is the ideal of the monk.

Throughout the long history of the Roman Catholic Church, and in the last one hundred years in the Lutheran,

Calvinist, and Anglican branches of Protestantism,[5] the monastic corporations and the religious orders have all professed one thing — the following of the precepts and counsels of Christ in the gospel according to a carefully defined and "regular" life. They invite men to aim at, to attempt, more than what is expected of the lay Christian. They encourage men to strive for what they believe to be the spiritual perfection of a life of self-denial and the imitation of Christ. Measured against such an awesome standard, it may be easy to criticize the Cistercians for failing to meet the demands of their profession, but it is impossible to judge them.

Still, the example of the Cistercians is instructive. At the present moment in Roman Catholic monasticism a serious dialogue is going on between those who favor a revision of the conventual life to meet the needs and attitudes of the twentieth century and those who favor the preservation of a strict application of the *Rule of St. Benedict* according to the traditions of particular congregations. Those who see the mission of the Church as the identification with and the involvement in the social and moral problems of modern society favor radical changes in the external form of monasticism and in the outward life of the religious. More traditional thinkers believe that the best interests of the monk as an individual and of the Church as a whole are served by the preservation of customary practices and of what they consider an appreciation of the lessons of the past. In a century when many men, especially educated men, are ill-disposed to take *any* religious beliefs seriously, the manner in which this struggle is settled will be extremely portentous for the future of the Church. No institution, certainly no Christian institution, can survive in a world in which it does not bear witness according to terms which that society can understand.

The early Cistercians created a constitutional framework

5 See François Biot, *The Rise of Protestant Monasticism* (Baltimore, 1963), a scholarly work; and Peter F. Anson, *The Call of the Cloister* (London, 1956).

for their lives which looked backward to the time of a more agrarian, fragmented, and particularistic society. Given, therefore, the economic and social conditions of their own world, the realization of their constitutional ideals was, if not totally impossible, certainly very improbable. But ideals, by definition, cannot be attained. Between the interests of monastic and religious corporations and the interests of this world, there will always be tension, conflict. In so far as the Cistercians set forth a new solution to this problem, they aided the cause of ecclesiastical liberty. In so far as the "new model of Cîteaux" set forth a new ideal of the Christian life, it succeeded. For in summoning men to strive for an ideal above themselves, it justified itself.

appendix

CISTERCIAN ABBOTS SERVING AS PAPAL JUDGES-DELEGATE 1170–1210

The following table will give some indication of the activities of Cistercian abbots holding papal commissions as judges-delegate in England at the end of the twelfth century. It does not claim to be exhaustive, not only because we know that many commissions have been lost but because others are continually appearing in a number of places. It should be noted that these abbots most frequently held their commissions together with archdeacons and bishops, that is, with persons of recognized legal knowledge.

Ford

1173	Alexander III requests the Bishop of Chester, the Abbot of Ford (Baldwin), and the Dean of Chichester to settle the disagreement between the abbot and monks of Fountains and the Archbishop of York over possession of the grange of Warstale.[1]
1170–78	Alexander III requests the Bishop of Hereford and the Abbot of Ford (Baldwin) to settle the conflict between certain clerks of the Hereford diocese over the possession of two churches.[2]

[1] Holtzmann, *P.U.*, III, 341–342.
[2] Mansi, *Sacrorum Conciliorum*, XXII, cols. 336–337.

| 1185 | Lucius III requests Bishop Baldwin of Worcester, the Abbot of Westminster (London), and the Prior of Holy Trinity (London) to arbitrate in the property dispute between Herbert, Archdeacon of Canterbury, and the nuns of St. Mary's in Davington and to discover if the archdeacon has been threatening the nuns.[3] |

Rievaulx

| 1170–73 | Alexander III assigns the Dean of Lincoln, the Archdeacon of Lincoln, and the Abbot of Rievaulx (Silvanus) to settle the conflict between the canons of Guisborough and Robert, clerk, over the church of Carthorn.[4] |

| *ca.* 1171–81 | Alexander III requests Bishop Bartholomew of Exeter and Abbot Silvanus of Rievaulx to arbitrate in the dispute between the Bishop of Durham and the monastery of St. Alban's and to forbid the bishop to collect any taxes belonging to the monastery.[5] |

| *ca.* 1174–81 | Alexander III assigns the Dean of Lincoln and the Abbot of Rievaulx to investigate the complaint of P., a clerk, that he had been violently despoiled of the church of Sprotborough, as against the enjoinder of the latter's opponent that P. had voluntarily abjured the said church.[6] |

| *ca.* 1174 | Alexander III requests the Abbot of Rievaulx and the Prior of Bridlington to settle the dispute between the monks of Newhouse and the nuns of Elstow over the church of St. Peter's of Halton.[7] |

---

3 Holtzmann, *P.U.*, III, 461–462.
4 Holtzmann and Kemp, *Papal Decretals*, pp. 6–9. This case had previously been heard before the Dean of York and the Prior of Newburgh, but they had been unable to reach a decision and themselves had appealed the case to Rome. Because the facts as presented did not satisfy him, Alexander III assigned new judges, this time adding a third, "because a three-fold knot is not easily broken."
5 Holtzmann, *P.U.*, III, 445.
6 Holtzmann and Kemp, *Papal Decretals*, pp. 40–41.
7 *Ibid.*, pp. 12–17.

23 May 1177	After one year of litigation, the church of Halton is adjudged to the canons of Newhouse, and Pope Alexander III confirms the decision of the Abbot of Rievaulx and the Prior of Bridlington, and orders the Archbishop of Canterbury to protect the canons of Newhouse against the molestations of the nuns of Elstow.[8]
Vaudey	
1177–81	Alexander III confirms the judgment given by the abbots of Fountains and Vaudey in the dispute between the prior and canons of Drax and Guido, a deacon of Waltham, over possession of the church of Swineshead; the canons of Drax are to maintain possession.[9]
1179	Alexander III requests the Abbot of Vaudey and Master Vacarius to help the clerk O. to regain possession of the church of Cumbe and the interest on that property, of which someone had dispossessed him. The decision of these judges is to be without appeal.[10]
ca. 1170–80	Alexander III requests the Abbot of Vaudey and the Archdeacon of Norwich to render a decision in the conflict over the control of several churches between the monks of Thorney and the canons of Bourne. The judges should examine the suspicious role of the Archdeacon R. in the entire affair.[11]
Bruern and Thame	
1187–91	Clement III requests the Bishop of Lincoln and the abbots of Bruern and Thame to examine the appeal of Master R. of Lewknor who claimed that he had been illegally dispossessed of the church of Walnesford by the bishop of his diocese who had promised one of his clerks the first church to fall vacant. The judges are to

[8] Holtzmann, *P.U.*, I, 4.   [9] *Ibid.*, III, 434–435.   [10] *Ibid.*, I, 440–441.
[11] *Ibid.*, III, 400–401.

enforce the principle that churches ought not to be granted (or promised) to anyone before they are vacant. There is to be no appeal to the judges' decision.[12]

1196   Celestine III requests the Bishop of Lincoln and the abbots of Bruern and Thame to make a decision in the appeal of the priest I. that whereas he was appointed perpetual vicar of the church of Westwell, he had been despoiled of it by G. de Bocland who had tried to force I. to renounce the church publicly. If the facts are as the priest I. presented them, G. de Bocland is to undergo ecclesiastical censure, and without appeal.[13]

Combe and Stoneleigh

1195   Celestine III requests the abbots of Combe and Stoneleigh and Master Alexander of St. Alban's to arbitrate in the terrible struggle between the prior and canons of Lanthony and P., rector of the church of Colesburne, over certain church tithes.[14]

Boxley

1185   Lucius III requests the Abbot of Boxley, the Archdeacon of Rochester, and Master Henry of Northampton to end the dispute between the prior and canons of St. Bartholomew and the Brothers of the Hospital of St. Bartholomew (London) over the ground in which one of the brothers of the Hospital is buried.[15]

Buckfast

1191   Celestine III requests the Abbot of Buckfast, the Archdeacon of Cornwall, and the Prior of St. Nicholas (Exeter) to settle the conflict between the clerks of Batcombe (Somerset) and a clerk, Thomas, over the chapel of Spargrove which it ap-

---

12 Holtzmann and Kemp, *Papal Decretals*, pp. 54–55.
13 *Ibid.*, pp. 58–59.   14 Holtzmann, *P.U.*, I, 619.
15 *Ibid.*, I, 519–520.

pears that the aforesaid Thomas had dispossessed the clerks of.[16]

Kirkstall

1195   Celestine III requests the abbots of Kirkstall and Swainby and the Prior of Malton to settle the complaint of the prior and canons of Guisborough against two clerks of the diocese of York for the latter's illegal seizure of tithes.[17]

Wardon

1192   Celestine III calls on the Abbot of Wardon, the Prior of Chicksands, and the Archdeacon of Huntington to end the struggle between the nuns of Harrold (Bedfordshire) and a clerk, Baldwin, over possession of the church of Stevington.[18]

Fountains

1177   Alexander III requests the Abbot of Fountains and Master Vacarius to determine whether William, Earl of Lincoln, compelled a man, O., to marry and, if this man did marry, whether the marriage was consummated. The judges' decision will determine the validity of O.'s second marriage.[19]

1177–81   Alexander III confirms the judgment given by the abbots of Fountains and Vaudey in the dispute between the prior and canons of Drax and the deacon Guido over possession of the church of Swineshead.[20]

[16] *Ibid.*, III, 527–528.   [17] *Ibid.*, I, 625.   [18] *Ibid.*, III, 587–588.
[19] Holtzmann and Kemp, *Papal Decretals*, pp. 20–21.
[20] Holtzmann, *P.U.*, III, 434–435.

BIBLIOGRAPHY

⛨

PRIMARY SOURCES

Atkinson, J. C., ed., *Cartularium Abbathiae de Rievalle*, Surtees Society, vol. LXXXIII (Durham, 1889).

———, ed., *The Coucher Book of Furness Abbey*, 3 vols., Chetham Society, no. IX (Manchester, 1886–1919).

Bell, Dom Maurice, ed., *The Life of Wulfric of Haselbury*, Somerset Record Society, vol. LXVII (1933).

Bond, E. A., ed., *Chronica Monasterii de Melsa* (Meaux), vol. I (Rolls Series, no. 43, London, 1866).

Bouquet, M., ed., *Recueil des historiens des Gaules et de la France*, vols. XII, XV, XXIII (Paris, 1840–1904).

Brewer, J. S., ed., *Giraldi Cambrensis Opera*, vol. II (Rolls Series, no. 21, London, 1862).

Butler, H. E., ed., *Chronicle of Jocelin of Brakelond* (London, 1951).

Canisius, P., ed., "Exordium Parvum," *Analecta Sacri Ordinis Cisterciensis*, vol. VI (Rome, 1950).

Canivez, Dom J. M., ed., *Statuta Capitulorum Generalium Ordinis Cisterciensis 1116–1220*, vol. I (Louvain, 1933).

d'Achéry, L., and J. Mabillon, eds., *Acta Sanctorum Ordinis S. Benedicti*, 9 vols. (Paris, 1668–1701).

Davis, R. H. C., ed., *The Kalendar of Abbot Samson of Bury St. Edmund's*, Camden Society, Third Series, vol. LXXXIV (1954).

Delisle, Leopold V., ed., *Rouleau mortuaire du B. Vital, abbe de Savigny* (Paris, 1909).

Dimock, J. F., ed., *Giraldi Cambrensis Opera*, vols. IV and VII (Rolls Series, no. 21, London, 1877, 1891).

Douglas, D. C., ed., *English Historical Documents*, vol. II (London, 1953).

Dugdale, W., ed., *Monasticon Anglicanum*, 6 vols., esp. vol. V (new ed., London, 1846).

Earle, J., and C. Plummer, *Two of the Saxon Chronicles Parallel*, vol. I (Oxford, 1892).

Farrer, William, ed., *Early Yorkshire Charters*, vols. I, II, III (Edinburgh, 1914–23).

Forester, T., ed. and trans., *Chronicle of Florence of Worcester* (London, 1854).

———, ed., *Ordericus Vitalis' Ecclesiastical History of England and Normandy*, vol. IV (London, 1856).

Fowler, G. Herbert, ed., *Cartulary of the Cistercian Abbey of Old Wardon, Bedfordshire* (Manchester, 1931).

Gams, P. B., *Series episcoporum Ecclesiae Catholicae* (Ratisbon, 1873).

Giles, J. A., ed., *Lanfranci Opera*, 2 vols. (Oxford, 1844).

———, ed., *William of Malmesbury, Chronicles of the Kings of England* (London, 1847).

Guignard, Ph., ed., *Les Monuments primitifs de la règle cistercienne* (Dijon, 1878).

Hall, H., ed., *The Red Book of the Exchequer*, 3 vols. (Rolls Series, no. 99, London, 1896).

Holtzmann, W., ed., *Papsturkunden in England*, in Abhandler Akademie der Wissenschaften in Göttingen, Philologisch-Historische Klasse, vol. I (1930–31), vol. II (1935), vol. III (1952).

———, and E. Kemp, eds., *Papal Decretals Relating to the Diocese of Lincoln in the Twelfth Century*, Lincoln Record Society, vol. XLVII (1954).

Howlett, R., ed., William of Newburgh, *Historia Rerum Anglicarum*, and Richard of Hexham, *Historia*, in *Chronicles of the Reigns of Stephen, Henry II, and Richard I*, vols. I and III respectively (Rolls Series, no. 82, London, 1884, 1886).

Jaffe, Ph., ed., *Regesta Pontificum Romanorum*, vol. II (2nd ed., Lipsiae, 1888).

Laveille, A., ed., *Histoire de la Congregation de Savigny par Dom Claude Auvry*, 3 vols., Société de l'histoire de Normandie, no. 30 (Rouen and Paris, 1896–99).

Luard, H. R., ed., *Annales Monastici*, vols. I, II, III, IV (Rolls Series, no. 36, London, 1864–69).

McCann, Dom Justin, ed. and trans., *The Rule of St. Benedict* (Westminster, Md., 1952).

McNulty, J., ed., *The Chartulary of the Cistercian Abbey of St.*

Mary of Sallay in Craven, Yorkshire Archeological Society, Record Series, vol. LXXXVII (1933).

Madden, Frederic, ed., *Matthaei Parisiensis Historia Anglorum*, vol. I (Rolls Series, no. 44, London, 1866).

Mansi, J. D., ed., *Sacrorum Conciliorum Nova et Amplissima Collectio*, vol. XXII (Paris, 1778).

Migne, J. P., ed., *Patrologiae Latinae cursus completus*, vols. LXXV, CLXXI, CLXXXI, CLXXXII, CLXXXV, CLXXXVIII, CXCV, CCIV (Paris, 1844–64).

Millor, W. J., and H. E. Butler, eds., *The Letters of John of Salisbury, 1153–1161*, vol. I (London, 1955).

Pipe Roll Society, *Great Roll of the Pipe for the Fifth Year of the Reign of King Henry the Second A.D. 1158–1159* (London, 1884).

Potter, K. R., ed., *Gesta Stephani* (London, 1953).

Powicke, F. M., ed., *The Life of Ailred of Rievaulx by Walter Daniel* (London, 1950).

Robertson, J. C., and J. B. Sheppard, eds., *Materials for the History of Archbishop Thomas Becket*, 7 vols. (Rolls Series, no. 67, London, 1875–85).

Round, J. H., ed., *Calendar of Documents Preserved in France 918–1206*, vol. I (London, 1899).

Salter, H. E., ed., *Cartulary of the Abbey of Eynsham*, Oxford Historical Society, vol. XLIX (Oxford, 1907).

———, ed., *The Thame Cartulary*, Oxfordshire Record Society, vol. I (1947).

Sammarthani, D., ed., *Gallia Christiana*, tome XI (Paris, 1874).

Sauvage, Eugene P., ed., "Vita BB. Vitalis et Gaufridi, primi et secundi abbatum Saviniacensium," *Analecta Bollandiana*, vol. I (Paris, 1882).

Sauvage, Hippolyte, trans., *Etienne de Fougères, Vie de Saint Vital, premier abbé de Savigny* (Mortain, 1896).

Stenton, F. M., ed., *Documents Illustrative of the Social and Economic History of the Danelaw from Various Collections* (London, 1920).

Stubbs, Wm., ed., *Memoriale Fratris Walteri De Coventria*, 2 vols. (Rolls Series, no. 58, London, 1872–73).

———, ed., *Radulfi De Diceto Opera Historica*, vol. I (Rolls Series, no. 68, London, 1876).

———, *Select Charters* (rev. ed., Oxford, 1913).

Victoria County Histories (in progress, London, 1900–). The accounts of religious houses usually appear in the second volume.

Walbran, J. R., ed., *Memorials of the Abbey of St. Mary of Fountains*, vol. I, Surtees Society, vol. XLII (Durham, 1863).

SECONDARY SOURCES

Anson, Peter F., *The Call of the Cloister* (London, 1956).

Aubin, H., "Medieval Agrarian Society in its Prime: The Lands East of the Elbe and German Colonisation Eastwards," in J. H. Clapham and Eileen Power, eds., *The Cambridge Economic History of Europe*, vol. I (Cambridge, 1941).

Barley, M. W., "Cistercian Land Clearances in Nottinghamshire: Three Deserted Villages and Their Moated Successor," *Nottingham Medieval Studies*, vol. I (1957).

Barraclough, G., *Origins of Modern Germany* (Oxford, 1952).

Bennett, H. S., *Life on the English Manor* (rev. ed., Oxford, 1960).

Berlière, Dom Ursmer, "Les origines de Cîteaux et l'ordre bene- dictin du XII siècle," *Revue d'histoire ecclésiastique*, vol. I (1900).

Biot, François, *The Rise of Protestant Monasticism* (Baltimore, 1963).

Bishop, T. A. M., "Monastic Granges in Yorkshire," *English His- torical Review*, vol. LI (1936).

Blum, O. J., *St. Peter Damien: His Teachings on the Spiritual Life* (Washington, D. C., 1947).

Bock, P. Colomban, "Les Cisterciens et l'étude du droit," *Analecta Sacri Ordinis Cisterciensis*, vol. VII (Rome, 1951).

Boehmer, Heinrich, *Kirche und Staat in England und in der Nor- mandie im XI und XII Jahrhundert* (Leipzig, 1899).

Bouscaren, S.J., T. L., and A. C. Ellis, S.J., *Canon Law: A Text and Commentary* (rev. ed., Milwaukee, 1953).

Brooke, C. N. L., "Gregorian Reform in Action: Clerical Marriage in England, 1050–1200," *Cambridge Historical Journal*, vol. XII (1956).

Brooke, Z. N., "The Effect of Becket's Murder on Papal Authority in England," *Cambridge Historical Journal*, vol. II, no. 3 (1928).

———, *The English Church and the Papacy from the Conquest to the Death of John* (Cambridge, 1952).

Buhot, Jacquelin, "L'Abbaye normande de Savigny, chef d'Ordre et fille de Cîteaux," *Le Moyen Age*, vols. XLV–XLVI (1935– 36).

Canivez, Dom J. M., "Cîteaux," in R. Naz, ed., *Dictionnaire de droit canon*, vol. III (Paris, 1935–).

Cantor, N. F., *Church, Kingship and Lay Investiture in England, 1089–1135* (Princeton, 1958).

———, "The Crisis of Western Monasticism," *American Historical Review*, vol. XLVI (1960).

Chadwick, O., ed., *Western Asceticism* (Philadelphia, 1958).

Cheney, C. R., *From Becket to Langton: Studies in English Church Government* (Manchester, 1956).

Cheney, Mary, "Compromise of Avranches and the Spread of Canon Law in England," *English Historical Review*, vol. LVI (1941).

Clapham, Sir John, *A Concise Economic History of Britain*, vol. I (rev. ed., Cambridge, 1963).

Colvin, H. M., *The White Canons in England* (Oxford, 1951).

Commission d'histoire de l'Ordre de Cîteaux (Paris, 1953).

Constable, Giles, *Monastic Tithes from Their Origins to the Twelfth Century* (Cambridge, 1964).

Cooke, A. M., "The Settlement of the Cistercians in England," *English Historical Review*, vol. VIII (1893).

Cronne, H. A., "Ranulf de Gernons, Earl of Chester, 1129–1153," *Transactions of the Royal Historical Society*, 4th Series, vol. XX (1937).

Cross, F. L., *The Oxford Dictionary of the Christian Church* (rev. ed., London, 1958).

Darby, H. C., ed., "The Economic Geography of England, A.D. 1000–1250," in *An Historical Geography of England Before 1800* (Cambridge, 1936).

Davis, H. W. C., "The Anarchy of Stephen's Reign," *English Historical Review*, vol. XVIII (1903).

———, "Some Documents of the Anarchy," in *Essays in History Presented to Reginald Lane Poole* (Oxford, 1927).

Davis, R. H. C., "Geoffrey de Mandeville Reconsidered," *English Historical Review*, vol. LXXIX, (1964).

———, "King Stephen and the Earl of Chester Revised," *English Historical Review*, vol. LXXV (1960).

———, "What Happened in Stephen's Reign," *History*, vol. XLIX (1964).

———, *King Stephen, 1135–1154* (Berkeley, 1967).

Delatte, Dom P., *Commentary on the Holy Rule of St. Benedict*, trans. Dom Justin McCann (London, 1921).

Denholm-Young, N., *Seignorial Administration in England* (Oxford, 1937).

Dickinson, J. C., *Origins of the Austin Canons* (London, 1950).

Donkin, R. A., "Cattle on the Estates of Medieval Cistercian Monasteries in England and Wales," *Economic History Review*, Second Series, vol. XV, no. I (1962).

———, "The Cistercian Settlement and the Royal Forests," *Cîteaux in de Nederlanden*, vols. X–XI (1959–60).

———, "The Disposal of Cistercian Wool in England and Wales During the Twelfth and Thirteenth Centuries," *Cîteaux in de Nederlanden*, vols. VIII–IX (1957–58).

Donnelly, James S., "Changes in the Grange Economy of English and Welsh Cistercian Abbeys, 1300–1500," *Traditio*, vol. X (1954).

——, *The Decline of the Medieval Cistercian Laybrotherhood* (New York, 1949).

DuCange, Charles du Fresne, ed., *Glossarium Mediae et Infimae Latinitatis*, vol. II (Niort, 1883–87).

Duggan, Charles, "The Trinity Collection of Decretals and the Early Worcester Family," *Traditio*, vol. XVII (1961).

——, *Twelfth Century Decretal Collections and Their Importance in English History* (London, 1963).

Evans, Joan, *Monastic Life at Cluny* (London, 1931).

Fletcher, J. S., *The Cistercians in Yorkshire* (London, 1919).

Fletcher, S. W., *Soils* (New York, 1907).

Fliche, A., "L'Influence de Gregoire VII et des Idées grégoriennes sur la pensée de St. Bernard," in *St. Bernard et son temps*, vol. I (Dijon, 1928).

——, *La Réforme grégorienne*, 3 vols. (Louvain, 1924–27).

——, and V. Martin, *Histoire de l'Eglise*, vol. IX, part 1 (Paris, 1944).

Fox, Levi, "The Honour and Earldom of Leicester: Origin and Descent, 1066–1339," *English Historical Review*, vol. LIV (1939).

Galbraith, V. H., "Monastic Foundation Charters of the Eleventh and Twelfth Centuries," *Cambridge Historical Journal*, vol. IV, no. 3 (1934).

Genestal, R., *Rôle des monastères normands comme établissements de crédit* (Paris, 1901).

Ghellinck, S.J., Joseph de, "Magister Vacarius," *Revue d'histoire ecclésiastique*, vol. XLIV (1949).

Graham, Rose, *English Ecclesiastical Studies* (London, 1929).

Graves, C. V., "The Economic Activities of the Cistercians in Medieval England," *Analecta Sacri Ordinis Cisterciensis*, vol. XIII (Rome, 1957).

Guilloreau, L., "Les Fondations anglaises de l'abbaye de Savigny," *Revue Mabillon*, vol. V (1909).

Hallinger, Kassius, *Gorze-Kluny*, 2 vols., Studia Anselmiana, vols. XXII–XXIII (Rome, 1950).

Haskins, C. H., *Norman Institutions* (Cambridge, Mass., 1918).

Hoffman, E., "Die Entwicklung der Wirtschaftsprinzipien im Cisterzensorden während des 12. und 13. Jahrhunderts," *Historisches Jahrbuch*, vol. XXX (1910).

Holdsworth, C. J., "John of Ford and Early Cistercian Writing, 1167–1214," *Transactions of the Royal Historical Society*, 5th Series, vol. II (1961).

Hoyt, R. S., *The Royal Demesne in English Constitutional History* (Ithaca, 1950).

James, Bruno Scott, trans., *The Letters of St. Bernard of Clairvaux* (Chicago, 1953).

King, A., *Cîteaux and Her Elder Daughters* (London, 1954).

Knowles, Dom M. D., "The Case of St. William of York," *Cambridge Historical Journal*, vol. II (1936).

——, *Cistercians and Cluniacs* (London, 1955).

——, *The Episcopal Colleagues of Archbishop Thomas Becket* (Cambridge, 1951).

——, *The Monastic Order in England* (corrected ed., Cambridge, 1950).

——, "The Primitive Cistercian Documents," in *Great Historical Enterprises and Problems in Monastic History* (London, 1963).

——, *The Religious Orders in England*, vol. I (Cambridge, 1956).

——, ed., "The Twelfth and Thirteenth Centuries," in *The English Church and the Continent* (London, 1959).

——, and R. N. Hadcock, *Medieval Religious Houses: England and Wales* (London, 1953).

——, and J. K. S. St. Joseph, *Monastic Sites from the Air* (Cambridge, 1952).

——, *From Pachomius to Ignatius: A Study in the Constitutional History of the Religious Orders* (Oxford, 1966).

Kosminsky, E. A., *Studies in the Agrarian History of England in the Thirteenth Century* (Oxford, 1956).

Kuttner, S., and E. Rathbone, "Anglo-Norman Canonists of the Twelfth Century," *Traditio*, vol. VII (1949–51).

Ladner, G., *The Idea of Reform* (Cambridge, Mass., 1959).

Lavisse, E., *Histoire de France*, tome II, part II (Paris, 1901).

Leclercq, Dom Jean, "Les Meditations d'un moine du XII siècle," *Revue Mabillon*, vol. XXXIV (1944).

——, "Les Paradoxes de l'économie monastique," *Économie et humanisme*, vol. IV (1945).

——, "St. Bernard et la théologie monastique du XII siècle," *Analecta Sacri Ordinis Cisterciensis*, vol. IX (Rome, 1953).

——, "St. Bernard et le XII monastique," in M. Viller, ed., *Dictionnaire de spiritualité*, vol. IV (Paris, 1958).

——, "La Vie économique des monastères au moyen âge," in *Inspiration religieuse et structures temporelles* (Paris, 1948).

——, F. Vandenbroucke, and L. Bouyer, *La Spiritualité du moyen âge* (Paris, 1960).

Lekai, L. J., *The White Monks* (Okauchee, Wisc., 1953).

Lennard, Reginald, *Rural England, 1086–1135* (Oxford, 1958).

Lewis, Archibald R., "The Closing of the Medieval Frontier 1250–1350," *Speculum*, vol. XXXIII (1958).

Lohmann, Hans Eberhard, "Die Collectio Wigorniensis, ein Beitrag zur Quellengeschichte des Kanonischen Rechts im 12 Jahrhundert," *Zeitschrift der Savigny-Stiftung für Rechtsgeschichte*, Band LIII (Weimar, 1933).

Lot, F., and R. Fawtier, *Histoire des institutions françaises au moyen âge*, tome II: *Institutions royales*; tome III: *Institutions ecclésiastiques* (Paris, 1958–62).

MacDonald, A. J., *Lanfranc* (2nd ed., London, 1931).

Mahn, J.-B., *L'Ordre cistercien et son gouvernement* (2nd ed., Paris, 1951).

Maitland, F. W., "Magistri Vacarii Summa de Matrimonio," *Law Quarterly Review*, vol. XIII (1897).

———, ed., *Pleas of the Crown for the County of Gloucester* (London, 1884).

———, *Roman Canon Law in the Church of England* (London, 1898).

Matthew, Donald, *Norman Monasteries and Their English Possessions* (Oxford, 1962).

Megaw, Isabel, "The Ecclesiastical Policy of Stephen, 1135–1139; A Reinterpretation," in H. A. Cronne, T. W. Moody, and D. B. Quinn, eds., *Essays in British and Irish History in Honour of James Eadie Todd* (London, 1949).

Merton, T., *The Silent Life* (New York, 1957).

———, *The Waters of Silence* (London, 1950).

Morey, Dom Adrian, *Bartholomew of Exeter, Bishop and Canonist: A Study in the Twelfth Century* (Cambridge, 1937).

———, and C. N. L. Brooke, *Gilbert Foliot and His Letters* (Cambridge, 1965).

Müller, P. G., *Cîteaux unter dem Abte Alberich* (Berlin, 1909).

Mullin, F. A., *A History of the Work of the Cistercians in Yorkshire, 1131–1300* (Washington, D.C., 1932).

Naz, R., "Dime," in Bernard Loth and Albert Michel, eds., *Dictionnaire de théologie catholique, Tables générales*, vol. IV (Paris, 1955).

O'Callaghan, J. F., "The Affiliation of the Order of Calatrava with the Order of Cîteaux," *Analecta Sacri Ordinis Cisterciensis*, vol. XV (Rome, 1959–60).

Orwin, C. S., *The Open Fields* (London, 1931).

O'Sullivan, J. F. *Cistercian Settlements in Wales and Monmouthshire, 1140–1540* (New York, 1947).

Painter, S., "English Castles in the Early Middle Ages," *Speculum*, vol. X (1955).

————, *Studies in the History of the English Feudal Barony*, Johns Hopkins Studies, Series 61, no. 3 (Baltimore, 1943).

————, *William Marshall* (Baltimore, 1933).

Parker-Mason, W. A., "The Beginnings of the Cistercian Order," *Transactions of the Royal Historical Society*, New Series, vol. XIX (1905).

Pichery, E., ed., *Jean Cassien: Conferences*, vol. I (Paris, 1955).

Pollock, F., and F. W. Maitland, *The History of English Law Before the Time of Edward I*, 2 vols. (2nd ed., Cambridge, 1952).

Poole, A. L., *From Domesday Book to Magna Carta* (Oxford, 1951).

————, *Obligations of Society in the Twelfth and Thirteenth Centuries* (Oxford, 1960).

Poole, R. L., "The Early Lives of Robert Pullen and Nicholas Breakspear," in *Essays in Medieval History Presented to Thomas Frederick Tout* (Manchester, 1925).

Power, Eileen, *The Wool Trade in English Medieval History* (Oxford, 1941).

Powicke, F. M., "The Abbey of Furness," in *Victoria County History*: Lancaster, vol. II.

Prestwich, J. O., "War and Finance in the Anglo-Norman State," *Transactions of the Royal Historical Society*, 5th Series, vol. IV (1954).

Raftis, J. A., "Western Monasticism and Economic Organization," *Comparative Studies in Society and History*, vol. III, no. 4 (1961).

Richardson, H. G., and G. O. Sayles, *The Governance of Medieval England from the Conquest to Magna Carta* (Edinburgh, 1963).

Round, J. H., "The Abbeys of Coggeshall and Stratford Langthorne," *Transactions of the Essex Archeological Society*, New Series, vol. V (1894–95).

————, *Feudal England* (London, 1895).

————, *Geoffrey de Mandeville* (London, 1892).

————, "King Stephen and the Earl of Chester," *English Historical Review*, vol. X (1895).

————, *Studies in Peerage and Family History* (London, 1910).

Russell, J. C., " The Clerical Population of Medieval England," *Traditio*, vols. II–III (1944–45).

Sackur, E., *Die Cluniacenser* (Halle, 1892–94).

Saltman, Avrom, *Theobald, Archbishop of Canterbury* (London, 1956).

Salzman, L. F., "Sussex Domesday Tenants. IV. The Family of Chesney or Cheyney," *Sussex Archaeological Collections*, LXV (1924).

Sanders, I. J., *English Baronies*: *A Study of Their Origin and Descent* (Oxford, 1960).

———, *Feudal Military Service in England, Study of Constitutional and Military Power of the 'Barones' in Medieval England* (London, 1956).

Sayles, G. O., *Medieval Foundations of England* (rev. ed., London, 1958).

Scammell, G. V., *Hugh du Puisset, Bishop of Durham* (Cambridge, 1956).

Schmitz, Dom Philibert, *Histoire de l'ordre de Saint-Benoît*, tome I (rev. ed., Maredsous, Belgium, 1948).

Smith, L. M., *Cluny in the Eleventh and Twelfth Centuries* (Oxford, 1930).

Southern, R. W., *The Making of the Middle Ages* (New Haven, 1953).

———, "The Place of Henry I in English History," *Proceedings of the British Academy*, vol. XLVIII (1963).

———, *Saint Anselm and His Biographer* (Cambridge, 1963).

Stenton, F. M., "Acta Episcoporum," *Cambridge Historical Journal*, vol. III (1929).

———, *The First Century of English Feudalism 1066–1166* (rev. ed., Oxford, 1961).

———, *William the Conqueror* (London, 1908).

Strayer, J. R., "Feudalism in Western Europe," in R. Coulborn, ed., *Feudalism in History* (Princeton, 1956).

Talbot, C. H., "New Documents in the Case of St. William of York," *Cambridge Historical Journal*, vol. X (1950).

Tellenbach, G., *Church, State, and Christian Society at the Time of the Investiture Conflict*, trans. R. F. Bennett (Oxford, 1959).

Thompson, E. M., *The Carthusian Order in England* (London, 1930).

Thompson, J. W., *Economic and Social History of the Middle Ages* (New York, 1928).

Ullmann, W., *The Growth of Papal Government in the Middle Ages* (London, 1953).

Vacandard, E., *Vie de S. Bernard*, 2 vols. (5th ed., Paris, 1927).

Van Zeller, Dom H., *The Benedictine Idea* (Springfield, Ill., 1959).

———, *The Holy Rule* (New York, 1958).

Vignes, Maurice, "Les doctrines économiques et morales de Saint Bernard sur la richesse et le travail," *Revue d'histoire economique & sociale*, vol. XVI (1928).

Vinogradoff, P., *The Growth of the Manor* (London, 1905).

———, *Villeinage in England* (Oxford, 1892).

Volpe, Gioacchino, *Movimenti religiosi e sette ereticali nella so-cieta medievale italiana* (Florence, 1926).

White, G. W., "The Career of Waleran, Count of Meulan and Earl of Worcester," *Transactions of the Royal Historical Society,* 4th Series, vol. XVII (1934).

———, "King Stephen's Earldoms," *Transactions of the Royal His-torical Society,* 4th Series, vol. XIII (1930).

White, Hayden V., "The Gregorian Ideal and St. Bernard of Clairvaux," *Journal of the History of Ideas,* vol. XXI, no. 3 (1960).

———, Review of Dom M. D. Knowles, *Great Historical Enterprises and Problems in Monastic History, Speculum,* vol. XLI, no. I (1966).

Williams, Watkin, *Monastic Studies* (Manchester, 1938).

———, "St. Benedict of Aniane," *The Downside Review,* vol. LIV (1936).

———, *St. Bernard of Clairvaux* (rev. ed., Manchester, 1953).

Wood, Susan, *English Monasteries and Their Patrons in the Thir-teenth Century* (Oxford, 1960).

Workman, H. B., *The Evolution of the Monastic Ideal* (rev. ed., Boston, 1962).

index

✠

Avranches, Ewan de: makes Savigniac settlement at Fulket in Lancashire, 97

Badsley Endsor, town of: supports Garendon, 33
Baldwin, Abbot of Ford, Archbishop of Canterbury: acquainted with Abbot of Buckfast, 141; encourages study of canon law, 146; made Bishop of Worcester, 135; praised by Gerald of Wales, 143; secures appointments for Cistercians, 135–36, 142–43; served as judge-delegate, 133, 135; Totnes, Archdeacon, 133
Baldwin, clerk: involved in dispute over church of Stevington, 141
Balliol, Bernard de: grant to Rievaulx, 71
Baronage: desire for power in Stephen's reign, 23 *et seq.*; endowments to religious orders, 30 *et seq.*; favored founding of Cistercian monasteries, 148–49; usurping royal prerogatives, 16, 26
Bartholomew, Bishop of Exeter: acquainted with Abbot of Buckfast, 141; makes Baldwin, Abbot of Ford, archdeacon of Totnes, 133; praised by Gerald of Wales, 143; served as judge-delegate with Silvanus, Abbot of Rievaulx, 138; served by Baldwin of Ford as clerk, 133
Basingwerk Abbey: founded by Ranulf de Gernons, 35; Savigniac settlement, 98
Basset, Richard: founded monasteries, 30; sheriff under Stephen, 30
Basset family: came to England with Conqueror, 30
Beaumont family: monastic endowments, 34
Bec: administrative experience of Lanfranc, 128
Becket, St. Thomas, Archbishop of Canterbury: conflict with Henry II, 126; burial by Abbot of Boxley, 139; praised by Gerald of Wales, 143; supported by Baldwin, later Abbot of Ford and Bartholomew, Bishop of Exeter, 134
Bedford, Hugh "the Poor," Earl of: holdings by Wardon, 58; receives earldom, 27
Benedict, St.: on clothes, 88; *Rule*, 3
Benedict, St., of Aniane: on acquisition of property, 78; monastic reformer, 3; reliance on Holy Roman Emperor, 4
Benedictine monasticism: modified by eleventh century, 8; monks as English bishops, 125; rights of patronage, 44; St. Albans, 54
Bennett, H. S.: *jus faldae*, 77
Bernard, St., Abbot of Clairvaux: abbot to obey bishop, 12; arrives at Cîteaux, 6; Cluny, 11; death, 13–14; frequently out of his monastery, 87; influence on Cistercians, 6, 29; obtains dispensation for earl of York, 52; personality traits, 129–30; supports Gregorian Reform, 93, 116, 118 *et seq.*; supports union of Savigny and Cîteaux, 101, 104, 150–51
Besacle, Peter de: "rented" land to Kirkstall, 74
Bigod, Hugh: made earl of Norfolk, 27

Damian, Peter: furthers growth of monasticism, 123
David, King of Scotland: sends army south, 98–99; surrenders castles to Stephen, 21
Decretal collections: Fountains, Worcester, and Exeter compared, 139–40
Decretum of Gratian: with study of canon law by Cistercians, 145–46
Delegate jurisdiction: detrimental to monastic spirit, 145; participation by Cistercians, 153; reduced clogging of Curia, 130–31
Derby, Henry Ferrers, Earl of: with grandson William Ferrers, 59
De Sacramento Altaris of Baldwin, Abbot of Ford, 134, 142
Devon, Baldwin de Redvers, Earl of: gains earldom, 27; revolt crushed, 21
Dieulacres Abbey: founded by Combemere, 98
Dijon: center for early Cistercian activity, 82
Diocesan authority: over religious orders, 93
Domesday Book: preconquest sheep in England, 77; Walter Espec, 31
Dompierre Priory: founded by St. Vital and Henry I, 89
Donatio: basic to monastic grant, 43
Donations: complicated by legal disabilities, 51
Doncaster, Hugh de: "rented" land to Kirkstall, 74–75
Dore, Abbot of: removed by visitation, 115
Duggan, Charles: decretal collections, 139–40
Dunstan of Glastonbury: on acquisition of property, 78

Earldoms: increase in, 26–27
East Anglia counties: emphasis on sheep farming, 55
Empire, German: spread of Cistercians, 39
Espec, Walter: arrangements for foundation of Rievaulx, 43; founded Rievaulx and Wardon, 30–31, 139; holdings increased by Henry I, 31
Eugenius III, Pope: appoints Baldwin as tutor to Gratian, 133; confirms union of Savigny and Cîteaux, 105; deposes William Fitzherbert, Archbishop of York, 120; involved with Furness problems, 105–106; present at General Chapter of 1147, 104
Exemption, episcopal: possessed by Cistercian houses causes litigation, 132
Exordium Cistercienses Coenobii, 7
Exordium of Stephen Harding: formulates monastic life, 86
Exordium Parvum: 7; against tithes, 110; for stricter monasticism, 44
Ewan, Abbot of Savigny: succeeded Geoffrey, 101

Family relationships: and monastic endowments, 31
Ferrers, William: and knight service due from Cistercians, 59

Feudal world: rejected by Cistercians, 7–8, 10–11

Filiation: Cistercian, 95 *et seq.*; Cluny, 94 *et seq.*; Savigny, 96–97, 100

Fitzgilbert, Richard: territorial demands refused, 21

Fitzherbert, William, Archbishop of York: opposed and deposed by the Cistercians, 119; patron of Hugh du Puisset, Bishop of Durham, 122

Flanders: manufacturing with wool, 55

Foliot, Gilbert, Bishop of London: secures archdeaconry of Hereford for kinsman Ralph, 121; supported Henry II against Thomas Becket, 126

Ford Abbey: center of learning, 143, 146
— Abbot of Ford: did not attend General Chapter, 115; served as judge-delegate, 136

Forncett: increase in sheep farming, 55

Fougères, Etienne de: biographer of St. Vital, 87

Fountains Abbey, St. Mary's of: donation from William de Stuteville, 67; founded Vaudey and Kirkstall, 140; gifts from gentry, 71; grant from Thurstan, Archbishop of York, 56; grants from gentry requiring recompense, 69, 72–73; knight service, 59, 62
— Abbot of Fountains: helps formulate marriage laws, 142; served as judge-delegate, 136, 139, 142

Fountains, brethren of: complaints of financial burdens of judges-delegate, 144–45

France, Kingdom of: spread of Cistercians, 40

Frankalmoin tenure: burdened with superadditions by gentry, 68, 70 *et seq.*; concerning mill rights, 73 *et seq.*; deprives king of assistance, 63; grants to Cistercians in twelfth century, 56

Frederick Barbarossa, Emperor: strengthening imperial authority, 39

Fribois, Matilda de: gift to Rievaulx, 71

Fulket in Lancashire: settlement of Savigniacs by Ewan d'Avranches, 97

Furness Abbey: corrected by Alexander III, 107; feudal character, 98, 103; founded by Stephen, 102; rejects union with Cistercians, 105; turns away monks of Calder, 99
— Abbot of Furness: claims on Byland, 99; did not attend General Chapter, 115

Furnival family: gift to Kirkstall, 72

Garendon Abbey: abbot removed by visitation, 115; aided by nobility, 35; founded by Robert "le Bossu," 33; on inadequate land, 49; knight service, 58

Gaul: monastic reform movements, 3–4

Gentry: endowed later Cistercian monasteries, 65–66, 149; importance in reign of Henry II, 65; knight service, 65; patronage of monasteries, 63 *et seq.*, 66 *et seq.*

Geoffrey, Abbot of Savigny: real guiding influence on Congregation of Savigny, 90, 97; succeeds St. Vital, 89; visitations and General Chapter, 96

Geoffrey, Archdeacon of Lincoln: becomes bishop of Lincoln, 12

Geoffrey, Archdeacon of York: secures office, 121

Geoffrey de St. Patrick: gift to Kirkstall, 71

Gerald, Abbot of Calder: sought refuge at Furness, 99

Gerald of Wales: lists six most praiseworthy bishops, 143; quotes Alexander III, 120, 134

Gesta Stephani: and Earl of Chester, 24–25

Gilbertines, 42

Glastonbury Abbey: knight service, 61

Gloucester, Robert, Earl of: cooperates with Matilda, 22; submits to Stephen, 20

Gloucester, earldom of: at beginning of Stephen's reign, 32

Godfrey, Abbot of Garendon: presides over commission on Byland, 100

Granges: introduced into Cistercian system, 45

Gratian: formulates marriage laws, 132; furthers work of Gregorian Reform, 130

Gregorian Reform: Cistercian role, 11, 29; nature of movement, 117–18; role of judges-delegate, 146; and St. Vital, 84

Gregory the Great, Pope: nature of monasticism, 2

Gregory VII, Pope: political pretensions not supported by Lanfranc, 128; revolutionary pretensions, 5

Guisborough, prior and canons of: involved in dispute over tithes, 141

Gyrovagues: and St. Vital, 87

Hallinger, Dom Kassius, 9

Harding, Stephen: and *Exordium*, 86; formulates Cistercian program in reaction to feudalism, 78, 93, 97; reform supported by Gregory VII, 116; as third abbot of Cîteaux, 5

Hardred, monk of Furness: reinhabits Calder, 99

Harrold in Bedfordshire, nuns of: in dispute over church of Stevington, 141

Haverholme Abbey: on poor lands in Lincolnshire, 48

Henley, town of: supports Garendon, 33

Henry I, king: advised by Robert, Count of Meulan, 33; death, 16; disputed succession of, 18 *et seq.*; gives earldom to Ranulf, 34; harsh government, 16, 21; relations with Savigny, 84, 88, 89; and de Senlis, 26

Henry II, king: conflict with Thomas Becket, 126; endowment of Roche, 72; presides over Council of London (1175), 127; receives

scutage from monasteries, 58; right to throne, 18; trying to reduce papal authority, 153

Henry V, Holy Roman Emperor: husband of Matilda, 18

Henry, Abbot of Bindon: confessor to King John, 127

Henry, Bishop of Winchester: family relations, 19, 122; papal
legateship conflict with Archbishop Theobald, 138; praised by
Gerald of Wales, 143

Henry, son of Robert de Lovetot: grant to Kirkstead, 72

Henry, son of Swane of Denby: grant to Byland, 66, 70

Herding, Robert de: grant to Fountains, 68

Hertford, earldom of: given to Gilbert de Clare II, 27

Hertfordshire: lands of de Grentmesnil, 32

Holy See: close connection with monasteries against royal power,
38; census paid by protected churches, 95

Hood hermitage: second home for monks of Calder, 99

Hugh, Archbishop of Lyons: papal legate in France, 7

Hugh, Archbishop of Rouen: appointed by Pope to settle Furness
affair, 106

Hugh, Bishop of Lincoln: Carthusian monk as bishop, 125; praised
by Gerald of Wales, 143

Hugh, son of Daniel de Tong: given in grant to Kirkstall, 67

Hugh "the Poor": given earldom of Bedford, 27

Huntingdon, earldom of: restored to Simon de Senlis, 26

Huntingdonshire: contains Sawtry, 34

Ingram, Walter: grant to Rievaulx, 70

Innocent II, Pope: letter from St. Bernard, 120

Instituta, 7

Italy: originating monastic reform, 4

Jerusalem, hospital of: grant from Henry, son of Swane of Denby,
66, 70

John, king: confessors were Cistercians, 127

John, Abbot of Ford: confessor to King John, 127; deplores extra-
monastic activity, 144

John, kinsman of archdeacon of Cleveland: grant to Rievaulx,
69–70

Judges-delegate: Cistercian appointments, 136 *et seq.*

Kent, William of Ypres, Earl of: founded Boxley, 54

Kingswood Abbey: knight service, 59

Kirkstall Abbey: abbot served as judge-delegate, 136, 141; assisted
by William de Roumare, 35; gifts from gentry requiring recompense, 72–73, 74; grants from gentry, 67, 71; knight service, 59;
man granted to abbey, 67

Kirkstead Abbey: built by Adam of Fountains, 51; donations from

Lombard, Peter: formulates marriage laws, 132

London, Council of: St. Vital (1102), 84; attended by Abbot of Boxley (1175), 127

London Synod of 1159: decided claims of papal rivals, 133

Longchamp, William: appointed Cistercian abbots to search for King Richard, 126

Louth Park: lands endowed to Haverholme, 48

Louth Park Abbey: aided by Ranulf de Gernons, 35

Lucius II, Pope: on disorders of Congregation of Savigny, 103; on financial burdens of judges-delegate, 144–45

Maine: center for early Savigny activity, 82

Maitland, F. W.: system of judges-delegate, 130; tenure in free alms, 56–57

Malebisse, Richard: donation to Byland, 66

Malmesbury, William of: on Robert, earl of Gloucester, 37–38

Malton, Prior of: appointed as judge-delegate, 141

Mandeville, Geoffrey de: charters for castles, 23–24

Mans, diocese of: and priory of Dompierre, 89

Manual labor: emphasized by Cistercians, 11, 151

Marriage laws: formulated by Gratian and Peter Lombard, 132

Mary, Blessed Virgin: devotions at Savigny, 89; early Marian piety, 83

Matilda, queen: aided by Robert of Gloucester, 22; area controlled, 22–23; relationship with feudal barons, 18, 37; supported Savigniac Coggeshall, 98

Meaux Abbey: dispute with Merton priory over property, 113; founded by Earl of York, 51–52; gifts from gentry requiring recompense, 72–73; knight service, 59

Melsa, *see* Meaux

Meppershall, Robert de: escheated lands to Earl of Leicester, 51

Merevale Abbey: dispute with Bordesley over property, 113

Merton, Thomas: monastic vocation, 2

Merton Priory: dispute with Meaux over property, 113

Meulan, comte of: inherited by Robert de Beaumont, 33

Midlands: Cistercian monasteries in, 36

Mills: profit forbidden to Cistercians, 73

Molesmes Abbey in Burgundy: wealth, 5

Monasticism: acquisition of property, 78; basic principle, 1; feudalism, 38; God as objective, 10; growth during chaos, 28; independence from secular control, 5; reform movements, 4–5, 147–48; western, 2–3

Mortain, Guillaume, Count of: gives grant to Congregation of Savigny, 84–85

Mortain, Robert, Count of: foundations, 86, 89; patron of St. Vital, 83

Premonstratensian canons: connection with feudalism, 29
Puisset, Hugh du: supported by king, 122

Quarr Abbey: abbot does not attend General Chapter, 114; knight service, 59; Savigniac settlement, 98

Ralph, Archdeacon of Hereford: office obtained through nepotism, 121
Ralph, son of Nicholas: gift to Fountains, 71
Ralph, son of Swane de Waltershelf: grant to Kirkstead, 70
Raoul I, Lord of Fougeres: gives land to begin Congregation of Savigny, 84
Reading Abbey: and Henry I, 16
Redvers, Baldwin de: made earl of Devon, 27
Reginald, Archdeacon of Salisbury: becomes bishop of Bath, 121
Rent: reality of "frankalmoin tenure," 74
Revesby Abbey: founded by William de Roumare, 35; knight service, 59; supported by Ranulf de Gernons, 35
Richard, Archbishop of Canterbury: reform measures, 127
Richard, Archdeacon of Ely: receives office through nepotism, 121
Richard, king: found by two Cistercian abbots, 126
Richard, son of Essolfus de Tong: grants a man to Kirkstall, 67
Rievaulx Abbey: competitor of Fountains for prestige, 140; founded by Walter Espec, 30; founded Wardon, 138–39; grants from gentry, 67, 68, 71, 76; grants from gentry requiring recompense, 72–73; knight service, 59, 62
— Abbot of Rievaulx: did not attend General Chapter, 114–115; served as judge delegate, 136, 141
Robert, Abbot of Molesmes: leads monks to Cîteaux, 5; reform supported by Gregory VII, 116; trained in monastic environment, 86
Robert, Archdeacon of Huntington: appointed as judge-delegate, 141
Robert, Archdeacon of Oxford: becomes bishop of Hereford, 121
Robertsbridge, Abbot of: appointed to search for King Richard, 120
Roche Abbey: gifts from gentry, 72
Rochester, see of: monk bishop of, 125
Roger, Abbot of Byland: rejects claims of Calder, 99
Roger, Bishop of Salisbury: secures Archdeaconry for nephew Alexander, 121
Roger, Bishop of Worcester: mentioned by Gerald of Wales, 143; praised by Alexander III, 134
Roger de Pont de l'Éveque, Archbishop of York: secures archdeaconry for nephew, 121; served by Vacarius, 138; and William de Accum's gift to Cistercians, 69

184